C000124661

THE MEN WHO FLEW THE
HALIFAX

THE MEN WHO FLEW THE
HALIFAX

MARTIN W. BOWMAN

Pen & Sword
AVIATION

First published in Great Britain in 2020 by
PEN AND SWORD AVIATION
an imprint of
Pen & Sword Books Limited
Yorkshire – Philadelphia

Copyright © Martin W. Bowman, 2020

ISBN 978 1 52670 568 6

The right of Martin W. Bowman to be identified
as the author of this work has been asserted by him in accordance
with the Copyright, Designs and Patents Act 1988.

A CIP record for this book is available from the British Library
All rights reserved. No part of this book may be reproduced or
transmitted in any form or by any means, electronic or
mechanical including photocopying, recording or
by any information storage and retrieval system, without
permission from the Publisher in writing.

Typeset in Times New Roman 11/13.5 by
Aura Technology and Software Services, India.

Printed and bound in the UK by TJ International.

Pen & Sword Books Ltd incorporates the imprints of Pen & Sword
Archaeology, Atlas, Aviation, Battleground, Discovery,
Family History, History, Maritime, Military, Naval, Politics, Railways,
Select, Social History, Transport, True Crime, Claymore Press,
Frontline Books, Leo Cooper, Praetorian Press, Remember When,
Seaforth Publishing and Wharncliffe.

For a complete list of Pen and Sword titles please contact
PEN & SWORD BOOKS LTD
47 Church Street, Barnsley, South Yorkshire, S70 2AS, England
E-mail: enquiries@pen-and-sword.co.uk
Website: www.pen-and-sword.co.uk

Or

PEN & SWORD BOOKS
1950 Lawrence Rd, Havertown, PA 19083, USA
E-mail: Uspen-and-sword@casematepublishers.com
Website: www.penandswordbooks.com

Contents

Inability to Identify Aircraft.

Chapter 1

Stop the *Scharnhorst*!

In March 1941 German the battle-cruisers Scharnhorst *and* Gneisenau *sailed into Brest on the Atlantic coast of France to refit and the first attack by the RAF on them there was made on the night of 30/31 March. The raid was ineffectual and the two battle-cruisers were joined at the beginning of June 1941 by the cruiser* Prinz Eugen, *which had fled to Brest to escape the* Bismarck's *fate. On 22 March the* Scharnhorst *and* Gneisenau *sailed into the port of Brest. They had been at sea for sixty days – a record for German capital ships. During those sixty days they had sunk 22 merchant ships and had been a constant problem for the Royal Navy. Over the next few weeks Brest was attacked many times by RAF bombers. The* Gneisenau *was badly damaged on three occasions. The* Scharnhorst, *known throughout the German Navy as a 'lucky ship' (in England the two capital ships were known as Salmon & Gluckstein, a British tobacconist founded in London in 1873 by Samuel Gluckstein and Barnett Salmon), lived up to its reputation by always escaping damage. From the end of March 1941 four thousand tons of the heaviest armour-piercing bombs were dropped on Brest. On the night of 1/2 July, a force of fifty-two Wellingtons attacked the dry dock in which the* Prinz Eugen *was then lying. Later there were several reports that the* Prinz Eugen *was hit by two bombs and damaged by a third which fell close to the hull of the ship. One bomb was said to have fallen down her funnel and to have done serious internal damage. There were also reports of more hits on the* Prinz Eugen *during attacks made in October and November 1941. It cannot be known for certain how much damage she sustained, but the* Prinz Eugen *was unable to move until 12 February 1942, from a most dangerous harbour. On 22 July 1941 the* Scharnhorst *left Brest to make a trial run, southwards along the coast of France. On 23 July an RAF Spitfire reconnaissance aircraft found her moored to a breakwater in the harbour of La Pallice, the harbour to La Rochelle, about 250 miles south of Brest. Alarm bells began ringing in the Admiralty. On the other side of the Atlantic a convoy with 30,000 Canadian troops was preparing to sail. The* Scharnhorst *could wreak havoc in that convoy. She had to be stopped.*

After the fall of France in 1940, the Germans occupied the naval dockyards at Brest. The French officer in charge, Captain Jean Le Normand, to prevent the transportation of his skilled French work force to Germany as forced labour, became a reluctant collaborator. One of the men Captain Le Normand had chosen to serve with him was Lieutenant Armand Jean Marc Philippon, usually called Jean. This young officer, born 1 November 1909 in Bordeaux, had little love for the British after the attack by the Royal Navy on the French Fleet at Oran when nearly 1,300 Frenchmen were killed.[1] However, working in occupied dockyards he had even less reason to love the Germans and towards the end of 1940 he joined the Resistance. The Resistance group in Brest arranged for him to become an agent for British Naval Intelligence and he was given the code name 'Hilarion'. His information was transmitted by a wireless operator named Bernard Anquetil, an ex-Naval Quartermaster, born 20 December 1916 at Bernières-d'Ailly in Calvados. This brave man lived 250 miles away at Saumur. The dangerous task of conveying information to the wireless operator was undertaken by Paul Mauger, code-named 'Mimi'.

Soon after the arrival in the port of Brest by the great capital ships on 22 March 1941, Philippon had reported to London that a pile of burnt-out boiler tubes from the *Scharnhorst* was on the quayside. From this the Admiralty was able to deduce that the ship would be out of service for some time. Early in July Philippon discovered that a large order for provisions had been placed for delivery to the *Scharnhorst* with 20 July as the deadline. As this could only mean the imminent sailing of the surface raider, he reported the fact to London via his Resistance network. 'Sunrise', a major daylight operation against the German warships at Brest, had been under preparation for some time. The original plan was to send approximately 150 aircraft but this had to be changed at the last minute because of the departure

---

1 The attack on Mers-el-Kébir, part of Operation 'Catapult', also known as the Battle of Mers-el-Kébir, was a British naval bombardment of the French Navy ('Marine nationale' informally 'La Royale') at its base at Mers-el-Kébir on the coast of what was then French Algeria on 3 July 1940 as a response to the Franco-German armistice of 22 June which had seen Britain's sole continental ally replaced by a collaborationist, pro-Nazi government administrated from Vichy. The raid resulted in the deaths of 1,297 French servicemen, the sinking of a battleship and the damaging of five other ships.

of the *Scharnhorst* for La Pallice. A daylight bombing raid on 24 July on Brest by three Fortresses, eighteen Hampdens escorted by three squadrons of Spitfires with long-range fuel tanks and 79 Wellingtons was decided upon but with the *Scharnhorst* now more than 600 miles away, fighter cover over La Pallice was out of the question. As the then new Halifax bombers were considered able to defend themselves without fighter support, the task was given to them. At that time the Halifax had only been in service for four months and only two squadrons were in existence; 35 Squadron at Linton-on-Ouse and 76 Squadron at Middleton St. George.

On the afternoon of 23 July six crews on 76 Squadron and nine on 35 Squadron were summoned to their briefing rooms, where, to their surprise, they were told they would be 'bombed up' and take off that evening for Stanton Harcourt in Berkshire where they were to land with a full bomb load and full fuel tanks. Two members of the ground crew were to accompany each Halifax to ready the aircraft for take-off the next day.

At Linton-on-Ouse, 25-year-old Squadron Leader Terence Patrick Armstrong 'Braddles' Bradley DFC sent for Pilot Officer Richard Charles Rivaz, his 34-year-old tail gunner. 'Braddles' had been on 76 Squadron in Yorkshire as 'A' Flight commander before being posted to 35 Squadron. Rivaz had volunteered for the RAF one evening in August 1940 and had found that he was too old for pilot training. Born in Assam, India, on 15 March 1908, his father was a colonial officer in the Imperial Civil Service. On his return to England he studied painting at the Royal College of Art. During the 1930s he became an accomplished artist with a studio in Chelsea and exhibited at the Royal Academy of Arts in Piccadilly. Unable to make a good living from painting he decided to go into teaching and at Collyer's School in Horsham he taught art and physical training. Rivaz volunteered for the RAF soon after the outbreak of the Second World War. He was bitterly disappointed when he learned that, at 32, he was too old to become a pilot. Instead he was trained as an air-gunner. In the summer of 1940 he joined 102 Squadron based at Driffield flying Whitleys.

'I've some news for you Riv,' 'Braddles' said. 'We're on a daylight raid tomorrow and you're flying with me [on Halifax L9524-V].'

'Good show!' Rivaz replied. 'D'you know where we're going?'

'No, not definitely, but we're after the *Scharnhorst*. She's left Brest and gone south, but I've not been told where yet. We load up here and go down to Stanton Harcourt sometime this evening and set off from there tomorrow.

I don't know any details yet. We'll air-test as soon as I've made out the crew lists: I'm leaving all the gunnery side in your hands. There are nine of us going from here and we're leading.'

One of these crews was skippered by Bradford-born Flight Sergeant 'Stan' Greaves on L9512 'U-Uncle'. His 2nd pilot was Sergeant Noel 'Gibby' Gibson, Sergeant Wilfred 'Sammy' Walters was the navigator and Sergeant Gordon 'Oggie' Ogden was flight engineer. Sergeants Albert 'Bert' Henery and Ernie 'Connie' Constable were WOp/AGs and Sergeant Alan 'Gilly' Gillbanks was rear gunner. Having raided Hanover on the night of the 19th/20th and Mannheim on the night of the 21st/22nd they had expected a couple of days rest. To the relief of the aircrews and even greater relief of the ground crews, all the Halifaxes landed safely with their bomb loads and full petrol tanks. Greaves was last in and, although by then it was dusk, he made a perfect landing. The Group Captain was so impressed with it that he took him aside to congratulate him on his skill.

'There was plenty to do that morning and afternoon of 23 July,' continues Richard Rivaz on 35 Squadron.[2] 'In fact, until we moved at about 2100 hours guns had to be harmonized, ammunition checked, turrets and guns tested; all the usual routine jobs before an operational trip; only even more so. As this was to be a day raid and not a routine night trip, we had a picked crew. Douglas Rowley-Blake the 21-year-old second pilot had attended High Storrs Grammar School in Sheffield from 1932 to1937.[3] He had been in one or two night raids, but, like the rest of us, this was his first day raid and he was very thrilled at the prospect of going. Pilot Officer 'Nick' Nixon had recently been commissioned, was 20 years of age and one of the best navigators we had. He was very keen, really knew his job and he had done over forty trips. Sergeant 'Jerry' [Peter George] Bolton, 1st wireless operator, was another very experienced man and about the same age as Nick. He too was very keen and seemed to take a real pleasure in everything he did. Wheeler the engineer and I chose a Canadian – [Wallace Llewellyn] Berry [25, of Virden, Manitoba] – as front gunner because of his keenness to fly. He had not done an operational trip as yet, but I felt confident that I could rely on him. He had been with us for about a month and was waiting to be crewed-up. I think he was very disappointed at not being put on crew sooner. His one ambition was to fly operationally and I felt quite happy about having him in the nose of our aeroplane.

---

2 *Tail Gunner* by Flight Lieutenant R.C. Rivaz DFC (Jarrold Publishers).
3 Rivaz described him as 'a Somersetshire man'.

'We arrived at Stanton Harcourt just as it was getting dusk and had several miles to drive to the Mess, where they had supper ready for us. I saw several people there whom I knew and had not seen for some time but I did not stay up talking long, as we had to be up early next morning and had to be fresh. There was not room for us all to sleep in the Mess, so there were beds put ready for us in the Roman Catholic chapel as it was apparently the only available space they had. We did not know until the following morning that we had been sleeping in a chapel and I hope we did not desecrate it. Had we known I don't know whether we would have been more subdued, as we were in high spirits and there was considerable horseplay and ragging.'

Ernie Constable recalled that 24 July 'dawned bright and clear after an uncomfortable night sleeping on the floor of a hangar', but when Richard Rivaz was awakened at five o'clock there was a thick white mist which completely obscured objects thirty yards away and it considerably damped his spirits. 'Everyone said it was heat mist and would clear when the sun got stronger but it looked pretty hopeless at the moment and I thought it might hang about for hours.

'Briefing was at seven o'clock and we were due to take off at ten-thirty. Briefing was less formal than usual, as we were in a makeshift hut, so unlike our own briefing-room with its walls hung with maps and charts and photographs. "The Colonel", our intelligence officer, had been up all night collecting the latest information and weather reports and working with the CO [32-year-old Wing Commander W.R.P. 'Ray' Collings AFC, a pre-war test pilot and English bobsleigh champion who competed in the late 1940s; at the 1948 Winter Olympics in St. Moritz he finished fifth in the two-man and seventh in the four-man events] and Navigation Officer on our route. We were shown photographs of the harbour, which was easily recognizable as there was an island quite close to it. The *Scharnhorst* was lying alongside what looked like a sea wall or large breakwater running some way out to sea. We had to drop our bombs from 15,000 feet, to allow them to have their full power of penetration. The *Scharnhorst* had vast thicknesses of armour-plating on her decks and an ordinary bomb would have little or no effect: certainly it would not sink it, although it might do a certain amount of superficial damage. It is necessary for an armour-piercing bomb to be dropped from a great height to reach its terminal velocity and so have the necessary power behind it to pierce the thickness of armour before exploding. There are only two ways of sinking a ship as heavily armoured as the *Scharnhorst* – either torpedoes or heavy armour-piercing bombs. She would be very difficult to hit lying as she was by herself and would appear very small at 15,000 feet: actually she would look about the size of the small lead ships that children have. Her importance to the Germans was pointed out to us by the colonel, particularly in blockading our supplies crossing the Atlantic. It was essential that she should be kept out of commission or sunk. She was a very difficult target and we had to make every effort to hit her: the raid was timed to coincide with plans made for another attack that same day on the *Gneisenau,* which was still lying at Brest. The colonel told us all he could about the organization of both raids.'

This 'peerless summer day' would be etched in Sergeant-Observer 'Monty' Dawson's memory forever. He had only recently served on 78 Squadron, an Armstrong Whitworth Whitley two-engine bomber squadron, before a posting to 76 Squadron. Montagu Ellis Hawkins Dawson was born at Langley, Buckinghamshire, on 9 September 1919. His father was killed in a road accident when he was 6. His mother, faced with bringing up five children in straitened circumstances, placed him in the care of the Royal Orphanage of Wolverhampton. In the late 1930s Monty worked for John Lines, a wallpaper firm, but escaped the tedium of office life in the RAF Volunteer Reserve. Although he was rejected for pilot training, he qualified as an observer and had joined Sergeant Henry Howard Drummond's crew. Monty had less than 22 hours night-flying experience when he took part in bombing raids over northern Europe in 1941.

The captain of L9517, Pilot Officer Joseph Francis Patrick John McKenna, born on 3 May 1917, came from a large family also. He was one of five brothers, who attended Belvedere College, Dublin. In 1933, when he was still only in third year, 'Joffre', as he was known, was a plucky enough rugby player to work his way onto the Senior Third XV. He left Belvedere after his fourth year in 1934 and went to England. In England he worked for Pye Radio until the war broke out in 1939. As he was already in the RAF reserve, he was immediately called up and soon became a Pilot Officer. He apparently showed as a pilot the same characteristics he had shown on the rugby pitches of Dublin. He married; he and his wife Dorothy had one child.

The six crews on 76 Squadron went out to their aircraft.

'The mist was clearing as we came out after briefing,' continues Richard Rivaz, 'and we could see the sky a soft blue but it was turning into a glorious morning as we moved out to our aeroplanes. As I stood by our Halifax I was excited at the prospect of a new experience but that numb feeling at the bottom of my chest and the dryness in my throat came back as I started to get into my flying kit. I looked at the others and wondered if they were feeling the same. 'Braddles' was talking to Wing Commander Collings and the colonel – who was prodding him in the chest with the stem of his pipe and grinning his cherubic grin. 'Nick' and 'Jerry' were smoking cigarettes and joking. Rowley-Blake was being helped into his Mae West by one of the ground crew. Wheeler was looking up at one of the engines as though he was talking to it and Berry was standing beside me already fully clothed. They all looked perfectly normal and I suppose I looked the same. I remember having exactly the same feeling while standing outside the headmaster's study at school waiting for a probable beating. I was not frightened, unless you can call 'stage fright' being frightened. I was more apprehensive. If anyone had come to me and said 'may I go instead of you?' I would have said 'No!' without hesitation, even if I had been in the position to say otherwise.

'By the time I was fully clothed I was wet through to my tunic with perspiration and was beginning to think I was a bit of a fool to wear so many clothes but I consoled myself with the thought that I would probably be glad of them at 15,000 feet!

"Braddles' climbed into the aeroplane, followed by Wheeler and Rowley-Blake. Wing Commander Collings and the colonel, after wishing us luck, had moved off to say goodbye to the other crews. I intended to wait until the last moment before getting in, as it was cooler outside than in the aeroplane. I heard one of the ground crew call up to 'Braddles', who was in his pilot's seat; "Contact port outer." Almost immediately the airscrew blades of the port outer engine began to turn slowly and then burst into life. It was followed by the port inner engine then the starboard outer and finally the starboard inner engine. I stood behind the engines to get the draught from their slipstream; I turned my face towards them with my head lifted and felt the cool air fanning my skin and I stood there for several seconds taking deep breaths. 'Jerry' Bolton scrambled in, as excited as a schoolboy at an outing. Nick followed him, with his satchel full of maps and he was closely followed by Berry. I followed suit. The heat in my turret was stifling and the sweat was soon pouring off me.

'As 'Braddles' ran up the engines, clouds of dust were thrown up by the slipstream, completely obscuring my vision, When the engines were running normally, I signalled to an armourer who was standing near to dust the outside of my perspex for me. As he was finishing rubbing it over we started to move. He walked a few steps with us still polishing and then gave a cheery wave of his hand and a grin and rejoined his pals.

'When we moved onto the runway preparatory to take-off, I saw the usual group of people standing watching us set out. The group was larger than usual. I recognized the CO and the colonel; but there were several whom I did not know. The tail shook and vibrated as the engines roared and I could feel the aircraft straining ready to leap forward. The runway raced beneath me faster and faster and appeared to drop away lower and lower and its place was taken by fields below me; I looked back and saw the next aircraft already in position and that too started to move down the runway. I was feeling perfectly normal now and quite impersonal and seemed to be working from outside myself. I was not an individual any longer, but part of a team.'

Wing Commander Geoffrey Twyford Jarman DFC, born in New Zealand on 20 February 1906, would lead the first wave of three 76 Squadron Halifaxes and the whole of the 35 Squadron contingent to the target. Squadron Leader Walter Williams would lead 76 Squadron's second wave of aircraft. After leaving Stanton Harcourt the fifteen Halifaxes would fly out via Lizard Point and then across to a position fifty miles west of Ushant, while maintaining a height of 1,000 feet or less to avoid detection by enemy radar. From there they would fly direct to the target, intending to bomb from 19,000 feet, but as events turned out it was carried out from 15,000 feet.

Ernie Constable recalls: 'At 1030 the roar of 36 Merlin engines filled the air and at 1035 the nine aircraft of 35 Squadron took off at one minute intervals and joined up in vic formation of three, these sections of three forming again into vic formation. Soon the six aircraft of 76 Squadron joined the formation and the raid was underway.'

Mechanical failure caused a delay of twelve minutes before Squadron Leader Walter Rice Williams was able to lead 76 Squadron's second wave of aircraft into the air. Over the radio Jarman and Williams agreed to rendezvous over Swindon, but in the event the formations missed each other and were compelled to make for the target independently.

"Braddles' set course straight away,' continues Rivaz, 'and we climbed gently. He called through to me and asked if I could see any of the others and I told him that numbers two and three were airborne and that I could just see number four on the runway. I spent the next half-hour of the trip reporting to 'Braddles' on the movements of the formation.

'Number two was the first to come into position on our right.[4] The pilot's name was 'Johnny' and I could see him sitting with one hand on the control column and the other on the throttles. Johnny was one of those large, quiet and absolutely unshakable men. His tail gunner told me that he was always the same and completely calm, no matter what happened. On one occasion when a shell burst particularly close behind the tail and tore a large chunk out of the tailplane, the gunner reported it through to Johnny who said in a casual way: "Has it burst yet?" The gunner replied that it had whereupon Johnny said: "You're not dead yet, are you?"

"No."

"Well, what are you worrying about, then?"

'But he said it in such a way as to make the gunner feel quite confident and happy. Most gunners get attached to their pilots and I know this one worshipped Johnny. Incidentally, Johnny thought the world of his gunner.

'The other aircraft came into position one by one. We flew in three separate formations of three aircraft each with our own aeroplane leading and one on either side of us and slightly behind. As I looked at the aircraft behind me I thought they seemed like some impersonal monsters and it was strange to think that they each contained seven men; seven individuals, each with his own life. We were all bent on the same object: all out to destroy a ship that was a menace to civilization. We would do all in our power to prevent that ship from doing the job for which it was intended. While I watched the other aeroplanes I wondered how those people would be feeling and of what they would be thinking. The pilots and navigators, I knew, would be too busy to let their thoughts wander, but the other people would not have much to do yet. The gunners would be sitting in their turrets and probably talking occasionally to their pilots or other members of their crews and they would be chewing gum or sucking barley sugar. Some, I believe, knew they would not return. One gunner I was told about afterwards had given full instructions for he wanted done with his body. He had his head blown off by a cannon shell! I was talking to him a few minutes before we went to our aeroplanes; he was cheerful and appeared quite unconcerned.

---

4 Probably Halifax L9500/H flown by Flight Lieutenant Peter James who took off two minutes behind 'Braddles' Halifax with his crew of Sergeants Scott and Kenneth Randolph Sewell (KIA 15.8.41); Flight Sergeant John Johnston Rogers (KIA 15.8.41); Sergeants John Alfred Arthur Cox (KIA 14.8.41); Sergeant M.A. 'Tony' Sachs; and Edward Torrens McQuigg (KIA 15.8.41). The other aircraft in the leading vic was probably Halifax L9501/Y skippered by Flying Officer Owen with his crew of Sergeants Hayward, Gibb, Hogg, Mullally, Higgins and Hays.

9

'The sun was beating down on to my turret and the sweat was running freely out of me: my face was wet and my clothes were sticking to my body. The sky was absolutely cloudless; the mist had cleared and I could see for miles. I could see every detail of the ground below. We were over country I knew very well having motored over it many times and I was thrilled when we passed over landmarks I recognized. Most of these landmarks brought back memories of holidays; of people I was with, or of people I was going to see. I began thinking of those people and I realized with a shock how many I had lost touch with since the war began. Some, no doubt, were continuing as they always had done, with the routine of their lives altered very little by the war; some like myself would be fighting and others I knew had been killed. Some people who were fighting were rather revelling in it and probably having a jolly sight better time than they did in peace-time; some would be fighting because they had to and others because they felt they ought to.

'We were over the hilly and more broken country of the west counties and some of the higher hills were only a few hundred feet below us. The rivers, looking invitingly cool, were sparkling in the bright sunlight as they wound about the valleys, sometimes hidden by the woods and trees. I had fished some of these rivers and I tried to see if I could recognize any of the stretches I had actually visited. We crossed over Dartmoor with its great expanse of heath and rock and bog. The surface of the hills made them look less ferocious than they really are. I could see the sheep and ponies grazing peacefully in the sunshine, quite oblivious to our scrutiny. I felt I wanted to get out and walk for miles as far as I could see. Those moorland hills seemed to be calling out to me to join them.

'The tors looked almost neatly placed on the highest tops of the moors, instead of being great rugged hunks of granite. The streams were like pale blue threads trickling through the valleys and down the slopes: the grey stone cottages seemed if anything even more isolated and lonely than they actually are, as I could see the miles of empty moorland surrounding them. I had seen Dartmoor in all her variety of moods and changes but this was the first time that I had seen her from above. Her beauty from here was quite new to me: she seemed more gentle and more easy to know and I felt I ought to be reintroduced. I had camped on Dartmoor just over a year before and it looked as though we were going to pass close to our camp site now. I was getting excited as I recognized parts of the moor that I knew very well. I forgot all about the mission we were on; it was like meeting an old friend one had not seen for a long time. Yes there was the actual spot where our tent had been pitched! There was the stream where we had got our water, the old dead tree we had used for firewood, the stone wall over which we had to climb to reach our tent and countless other little familiar things. A lot had happened to me since then – far more than I had ever thought would happen and I would not have missed any of it. I used to read with envy about the adventures of other people and wonder if I would ever see any real excitement.

'We left Tavistock on our right and could just see some ruins in Plymouth on our left. Although the tail gunner sits with his back to the direction of travel, if he sees something on his left-hand side, he refers to it as being on the right or starboard. This prevents confusion. The sky is divided into areas around the aeroplane, each area occupying an angle of forty-five degrees, referred to in naval terms. Thus 'starboard bow' would be somewhere ahead but on the right; 'port quarter' would be somewhere behind but on the left and port or starboard beam would be on the left- or right-hand side.

'We crossed the coast and flew almost parallel with it for some distance. The sea was a lovely blue and calm. Near the shore it was extraordinarily clear and I could see light patches below the water where there was sand and dark patches where there were rocks and seaweed. There were many people bathing and they might have been watching us. When they read about the raid next day, or heard about it on the wireless, they would probably remember us and tell their friends that they had seen a formation of bombers going over. If they guessed we were on a raid when we passed over, perhaps they would wish us luck.

'As we moved further away from the coast I could no longer see any people. I missed them, though they were all strangers and probably I should never see them again. They were part of England. I felt slightly homesick as the coastline got thinner and less distinct.

'I called through to 'Braddles' and told him I was going to test my guns and he told me to carry on. I pointed the guns downward and pressed the firing button. There was slight vibration as they fired. I felt comforted at this power in front of me. If I should have to use it I would have to be cool and think quickly, but I had the necessary power – the rest was up to me. I heard Berry ask if he should test his guns and shortly afterwards I heard him say. "My guns are OK Captain!"

To avoid enemy radar the bombers flew below 1,000 feet to Lizard Point and then to a point fifty miles west of La Pallice. From the turning point they climbed steadily. The intended bombing height was 19,000 feet. There was a cloudless sky with brilliant sunshine and perfect visibility.

'Our shadows sped across the sea below,' continues Rivaz, 'keeping us company all the way. We were flying south – I called through to Berry and told him to keep a careful lookout and to beware of attacks from out of the sun. A fighter will often attack from the glare of the sun if he can and it is very necessary to keep a close watch in that direction. When we reached the Bay of Biscay there were many small fishing boats about. Some looked like steam trawlers while others had sails, some of which were brightly coloured. They were a lovely sight in the bright sunshine, with their colours standing out vividly against the blue background of the sea. I wondered if they were French or German. They were probably wondering far more who we were and where we were going! I hoped none were carrying wireless transmission sets.

'Just as we entered the Bay we saw an open boat crammed with men; obviously a shipwrecked crew. They waved frantically to us as we passed above them, but there was nothing we could do except note their position; on no account could we use our wireless and risk giving our own position away. My heart went out to those men, as I had some idea what they must be suffering. They must have been overjoyed when they saw us approaching and felt sure they would get some help, but their dismay must have been awful when they saw us pass by without apparently noticing them. I wondered how long they had been in that boat and how much water they had left. I have often thought about them since and wondered if they were ever picked up. They were about fifty miles from the coast and there was no sign of any other shipping near them at the time. I had no idea of their nationality, but I imagined them to be British.

'As we climbed, the French coast could just be seen away out on our port side. Occasionally it would disappear as the coastline withdrew into bays. I thought how different that stretch of coast must be to what it had been a few years before. It was no longer the playground of the rich and the holiday-makers but the hiding place of fighters which might come at us at any moment!

'We had to be very alert now as we were well within the range of enemy fighters. I could no longer afford to let my mind wander. My job was to defend our aeroplane: I was its ears and, if necessary, its sting! My job was just beginning.

'I could sense the tension in the whole crew. No longer was there any idle chatter, but a silence to be broken only by a remark vital to the job in hand. Each man was looking, searching intently in the direction most convenient to his position in the aeroplane.'

As the formation neared the Île d'Yeu, about a hundred miles from the target, the formation was reduced to fourteen aircraft as Flight Lieutenant Walter Stanley Hillary DFM in the last section on 76 Squadron had been forced to turn back with engine trouble. Hillary, born in Lambeth in 1917, had served on 10 Squadron in the early months of the war. On 23 March he and Sergeant Clarence Godwin had been piloting a Halifax on an air firing exercise over Filey Bay and on landing at Linton on Ouse the tail wheel collapsed slightly damaging the aircraft. He had already survived a number of flying accidents in Yorkshire. This time he landed safely at Linton.[5]

'Although a height of only 14,500 feet had been achieved on approaching La Pallice it was decided to attack from that height. Suddenly the silence on 'Braddles" Halifax was broken by 'Nick' Nixon exclaiming, "I can see a ship ahead. She looks like a cruiser!" This sighting of the bomber force was unfortunate. 'Braddles' swore. It would mean that as soon as they were spotted, their position, course and height would be signalled all along the coast, if it had not been done already by one of the trawlers over which they had passed.

'Within a few minutes the ship opened fire on us and I saw puffs of smoke appear in amongst the formation as if from nowhere. I called through to 'Braddles' but before I had finished speaking there was a salvo right underneath! We could hear the shells bursting very near and the aeroplane would lurch as it was buffeted by the blast. They had got our range and height accurately straight away and for the next few minutes we had to fly through the barrage around us.

'The sky was getting thick with the smoke from bursting shells and several times I could smell the burnt explosives as we flew through them. More shells were bursting all the time and I could see their yellow flashes followed instantly by grey puffs. Sometimes they would burst just beside or underneath the aeroplane, which would heel over or jump up several feet; sometimes there would be a string of grey puffs just beside us, dark at first, but getting lighter, which would rush by and be broken up as Johnny or some other aeroplane flew through them; or sometimes they would continue rushing past just above or below the aeroplanes and be joined by more of the devilish little clouds. Occasionally I actually saw the shell on its upward flight, like a silver streak soaring upwards; it would suddenly stop and turn into a grey puff. They were never alone; they were always

---

5 While in the rank of acting squadron leader he was awarded the DFC for service on 76 Squadron, gazetted on 30 January 1942.

surrounded and followed by others. Those near us could be heard: the sound was rather like the noise a brick might make as it hit the water when dropped down a deep well.

'Nobody spoke. We were too intent on controlling our emotions. I sat perfectly still in my turret, watching with fascination this fury about me and wishing it would stop! It only needed for a shell to burst a few feet nearer and we would be blown from the sky.

'How small the ship looked – like a toy – to be sending up so many shells! It seemed strange to think that there were men – our enemies – working furiously in the hot sunshine to fire and reload the guns. And the ship was taking no chances: she thought she might be our target too and was zigzagging all about. She was safe however: we were after bigger fry!

'When we got out of range of her guns the barrage ceased and we continued on our way as before. No one had been shot down or seriously damaged as far as I could see. We were still in formation and were flying as though nothing had happened. The sky was absolutely clear except for a grey haze behind us where the smoke from the shells still lingered. The ship had finished her snaking and had settled down to a straight course, as I could see from the wake she left behind her.

"Another fifteen minutes'll see us there," said Nick down the intercom.

"Keep a very careful look-out, everybody!" said 'Braddles'.

'We were nearer the French coast now and I could just distinguish the fields and woods. I would have liked to look longer at the coast, as this was the first time I had flown near France in the daytime, but I had to search the sky above, below and all around me. My eyes ached, staring and straining into the dazzling blue of the sky.

'Berry suddenly said one word – "Fighters!" down the intercom. The word sounded distinctly dramatic coming through the intercom in his Canadian accent. It was followed a few seconds later by, "They're away out on our port beam!"

'They were too far round for me to see them but in a few seconds I saw three more, flying in formation several miles away and well above us. They were not closing in, but were flying from the port quarter round to the starboard quarter and I gave their position and range to 'Braddles'.

"There is some more climbing up," Berry said.

'Evidently they did not intend to attack until they were up in full force: they seemed to be sizing us up and wondering how formidable a target we would be. Well they were soon to find out! More fighters were still climbing to join those already up. I could see three formations of three, which were shortly joined by six more. They were all about three miles away and showed no signs of coming in yet. Berry said he could see about twelve more from the nose which were flying across our track and all several miles away. Still they did not come in to attack. Evidently they did not consider themselves strong enough yet. Johnny had closed right in to us, with his wing tip only a few feet from our tail, as had number three. They did this for mutual support, as the nearer they flew to us the better we would be able to protect ourselves by the combined fire from our turrets. 'Braddles' was flying well and the others were able to formate perfectly. Any hope we had of carrying out a surprise attack had gone, probably thanks to the cruiser we had flown over a quarter of an hour before.

'We were within a few minutes of the target and Nick said he could see it clearly. The rest of the formation got into position ready to drop their bombs. I sat keyed up, waiting for what should come. Sitting waiting to be attacked was a great strain. When were they going to come at us?'

Thirty-one Bf 109s were counted circling the area. Despite the formidable opposition the formation carried on in echelon to attack as planned. The fighters closed in and attacked as the bombers neared the *Scharnhorst*. The giant ship was protected by fifty-one guns as well as those of its destroyer escort. With the addition of shore batteries a flak box was put up through which the formation had to fly to press home the attack. The enemy fighters, paying little heed to the flak, made repeated attacks. The gunners in the Halifaxes fought back fiercely as the fighters came in. L9529 on 76 Squadron flown by Flight Lieutenant Austin Ellerker Lewin was attacked by a pair of Bf 109s and was shot down near L'Aiguillon-sur-Mer. Lewin, his flight engineer, 23-year-old Flight Sergeant William Henry James Gourley RAAF; 30-year-old observer, Flight Sergeant Charles Henry Horner and the WOp/AG, Sergeant Percy James Vickery were killed. Sergeants B. Phillips and W.A. Finlayson and Flying Officer N.W. McLeod were taken prisoner. One of 35 Squadron's Halifaxes was shot down.

'Harry' Drummond's Halifax approached the target at only 100 feet above the sea. Then, as Drummond climbed to 15,000 feet, 'Monty' Dawson left his observer's seat for the bomb aimer's forward belly position. In that moment the Halifax encountered heavy fire from both the *Scharnhorst* and anti-aircraft batteries on the shore; meanwhile, Bf 109s dived on the tight bomber formation. To starboard of Drummond's aircraft, a Halifax was shot down leaving his aircraft further exposed to enemy fire as Dawson lined up his skipper on the target and released his bombs. 'Our bombs landed alongside the *Scharnhorst*,' recalled 'Monty' Dawson. 'One may have hit but the stick was a little short. There was a great deal of flak and constant fighter attacks. As we flew over the battleship there was a yellowish explosion – whether from our bombs or not, I just don't know.'

But when a 109 cannon shell hit the rear gunner, Dawson crawled to the rear of the aircraft and dragged him to the midsection where he injected him with painkillers. Now under attack from twenty-one enemy fighters, George Fraser, one of the gunners, claimed two shot down, before the pilot's windscreen, instrument panel and port inner engine were shot out.

'We were extensively damaged, with the windscreen and some of the instruments shot away,' wrote 'Monty' Dawson. The ailing bomber struggled home on three engines. Approaching the coast, the port outer engine also failed and the Halifax reached Stanton Harcourt with only the two starboard engines working; the aircraft was a write-off. 'Harry Drummond's flying was magnificent and he was awarded the DFM afterwards; as I was,' concluded Dawson. So too was George Fraser.'[6]

Finding themselves alone in the sky Squadron Leader Williams and Pilot Officer Joe McKenna faced the full force of the ground defences. Both pilots made their bomb run but when Williams' bomb aimer shouted over the intercom that he could identify the target clearly, Williams made the courageous decision to go round again, followed by McKenna. As the pair held steady for their second run over the target, McKenna's aircraft was badly damaged by flak and plunged almost immediately into the sea off La Rochelle. The bodies of only four of the seven men on board were recovered after the tides had washed them ashore. Williams' Halifax was now the only British aircraft in the area and it came under attack from all sides. One of its starboard engines was hit by flak and began to leak glycol and, as the bomber battled its way out to sea, a Bf 109 put the remaining starboard engine out of action. Williams eventually ditched about eight miles off the French coast. All the crew were able to get out before the aircraft sank and they were picked up from their dinghy by a French fishing

---

6 'Harry' Drummond was commissioned three days after his DFM was awarded and was later awarded the AFC, gazetted on 1 January 1944, and rose to the rank of wing commander by the end of the war. He remained in the RAF in the post-war period and relinquished his commission in July 1952. 'Monty' Dawson completed a tour on 76 Squadron, was commissioned in November 1941 and was awarded the DFM for this tour (gazetted on 30 January 1942). He was given an instructing role but later returned to operational flying with 196 Squadron and awarded the DFC (gazetted on 11 February 1944) and a posting to 7 Squadron PFF. He was awarded the Bar to DFC (gazetted on 6 November 1945) and completed a third tour. By the end of the war Dawson had completed 74 operations.

boat almost immediately. Upon their return to port they were handed over to the Germans.

'Suddenly the tell-tale puffs of smoke appeared,' continues Rivaz. 'I looked around for fighters watching those I could see and searching the sky for fresh ones. The sky behind us was getting thick with the fumes and smoke of shell bursts. They were firing all they had got at us and as hard as they could. The thirty guns from the *Scharnhorst* were blazing away, supported by many more from the shore. Many times I was blown against the side of my turret or off the seat. The sky was getting thick with smoke and it was difficult to see.

'Jerry Bolton and Rowley-Blake had gone back into the fuselage to man the beam guns, which were situated two on either side and about half way along the fuselage. They were standing there looking out and waiting for attacks. Suddenly the fighters were amongst us, diving, climbing and twisting. For a time our aeroplane was left alone while those behind us got the brunt of the attacks. The fighters were in amongst the flak bursts, which died down considerably when they started their attacks. I saw one burst into flames, roll over on its back and dive down towards the sea, leaving a trail of black smoke behind it. Almost at the same time I saw one of our own aeroplanes diving with smoke pouring from two of its engines and with three fighters on its tail. I could not tell which one it was or who was in it and I did not dare to watch it for long as I was too busy turning my turret first one way and then the other and peering through the clouds. All the time Johnny was near us, following our every move, I saw two fighters diving on his tail from above. One of them continued on its dive past his tail with smoke belching from it.

'Through all the medley and the noise of shell bursts I heard Nick giving direction to 'Braddles' in his bombing run-up; he sounded oblivious to the mayhem around him and only conscious of the target below him. As I heard 'left', 'right', 'steady', I could feel the aeroplane turn and check as 'Braddles' made the corrections. 'Bombs gone!' he finally said and then, almost immediately, I got a wizard sight.

'All the time I was waiting and wondering why we were not being attacked: I almost wished we were, as I could do something then. As it was, all I could do was to sit and watch and wait for our turn and watch our aeroplanes being shot at. Under normal conditions I should have been absorbed and scared by the flak bursting so frequently and so near us. Several times I felt the jar and thud as splinters hit us and tore through the fuselage and tail, yet only part of my mind registered. I could do nothing about it anyway. I could only sit and watch and hope that we got no fatal hits. My mind was absorbed with the fighters, wondering when they were going to attack. I could do something about them; that was what I was there for.

'Almost as soon as Nick had said "Bombs Gone" I saw a fighter diving down on us. I immediately called through to 'Braddles': "Fighter diving down port quarter up!"

'I started giving him directions for turning and at the same time I elevated my guns to meet the attack. As we turned, the fighter passed over the top of us and disappeared from my range of vision.

'As soon as I lost sight of this one, I saw another one climbing up at us and again I called through to 'Braddles':

"Fighter starboard quarter down!"

'The fighter started firing at us almost as soon as I spotted it and I saw the flashes from his guns and the tracers streaking past us. He was using cannon and was really out of range of my machine guns. But I opened fire, hoping to put him off, as I had plenty of ammunition and could afford to use it. He came steadily in, firing in bursts and I replied with my guns. He still came in getting nearer and still I fired back. I could hear and feel his shells and bullets striking the fuselage just behind me and still he came in, ever nearer. I felt no antagonism, but was calm and determined to shoot him down. 'Why hasn't he gone down?' I kept thinking, 'surely I must be hitting him?' but he was still able to hit back and his tracers still kept streaming past me!' And why haven't I been hit?' I thought. Now were twisting about the sky and he was following us, shooting all the time.

'I had no feeling of fear, only that neither of us had been shot down, as we seemed to have been shooting at each other for so long.

'Out of the corner of my eye I saw part of our tail plane ripped away by a cannon shell and almost at the same time the fighter rolled over on his back and went into a spin! I felt a surge of relief as I called through to 'Braddles' and said, "I've got him!"

'The combat seemed to have gone on for a very long time, although really it could have lasted only for a few seconds. I began to feel scared. I was too intent while we were being attacked to feel frightened but now there was a lull, I felt my heart pounding and mouth felt dry. Outwardly I was perfectly calm though and ready for further attacks.

'I heard Rowley-Blake calling: "Jerry's been hit, sir."

"Is he bad?" 'Braddles' asked.

"Yes sir, I think so. I'm doing all I can."

'The air was even blacker now with smoke like great dark clouds. Bombers and fighters were flying and twisting among it. I saw another Halifax diving down with smoke pouring from it and two more fighters diving to their doom, one in flames and the other obviously out of control. I could see another Halifax with three fighters close behind its tail.

'My turret was thick with cordite fumes, which were making me cough.

"I think he's dead, sir," Rowley-Blake said.

'Fighters were all around now, but none were actually attacking us. We were getting away from the flak and the air was becoming clearer. Two fighters were chasing us from behind but were not yet within range.

"Where's he hit?" 'Braddles' asked.

"In the chest," Rowley-Blake answered. "I can't see any other marks."

'Jerry was standing by his guns watching out for fighters when he was hit. He was jumping up and down in his excitement, as he had just seen a fighter crash into the sea in flames. Suddenly he turned round and looked at Rowley-Blake with a surprised expression on his face and slowly sank down and rolled over ... dead.

'The fighters who were chasing us gave up and I saw them turn away; they had probably had enough for one day and did not want to get taken too far from their base. Two of my guns had jammed and were out of action, but I still had two guns working and I felt confident of them in an emergency.

'Now that there were no fighters within about half a mile, I had a look at the stopped guns. One I was able to put right quite easily and I fired a short burst to make sure it was working, but the other one I would have to dismantle when we were well clear of the target.

'Johnny was fairly close behind us and on our starboard, with another Halifax slightly behind him – they were all I could see at the moment. The second one I noticed had white smoke coming from behind one of his engines which meant that one of his radiators had gone and that soon that engine would stop. However, he could carry on with three engines quite well.'

After successfully bombing the *Scharnhorst*, 'U-Uncle' was encircled by seven Me 109s who took it in turns to attack the bomber. When the cockpit exploded 'Stan' Greaves had perspex embedded in his face. Only 'Sammy' Walters and 'Bert' Henery were unscathed. Sergeants 'Oggie' Ogden and 'Connie' Constable, who were manning the beam guns, both received leg wounds. The second pilot, Sergeant 'Gibby' Gibson, was wounded in the ankle. During this battle, Sergeant 'Gilly' Gillbanks, the rear gunner, claimed two of the enemy fighters destroyed before he was seriously wounded in the face. By this time three engines were on fire and the fuselage looked like a colander. It was a miracle that anyone survived the onslaught. With one engine functioning Stan Greaves fought desperately to keep the aircraft on an even keel as the enemy fighters kept up their attacks. With the fires spreading he gave the order to bail out. Despite their injuries all the crew managed to leave the stricken bomber. Greaves had only just cleared the aircraft when it exploded – a sad sight to the crew strung out across the sky in their parachutes. On reaching the ground or in some cases the sea, the crew were taken prisoner. Those needing medical treatment were taken to hospital to be patched up before being sent to PoW camps, where they were to spend the next three years and nine months. Thanks to the skill of the German surgeons, the sight of Sergeant Gillbanks was saved.

Flying Officer Peter Stanley James (24) kept 'H-Harry' (L9500) in close formation throughout, with 'Y-Yoke' captained by Flying Officer Owen. James lived with his family at Wollaston, Northamptonshire, and attended Wellingborough School from 1928 to 1933 before joining Nicholson Sons and Daniel Ltd, a tannery based in Little Irchester in late 1933. Between 27 October 1940 and 11 February 1941 Flying Officer James had flown fifteen operations on Whitleys with 78 Squadron, including trips to Hamm and Duisburg, Lorient, Wilhelmshaven and Bremen, when, on the return leg after eleven hours flying and with the loop aerial and port exactor unserviceable, he ordered his crew to bail out. All landed safely in South Molton, Devon. On 5 March 1941 James was posted to 35 Squadron. During his time with the squadron, he took part in sixteen trips, including the first three Halifax operations of the war, the bombing of the Leuna oil plant south of Merseburg. He returned safely from La Pallice and landed at Weston Zoyland at 1740. Two minutes later they were joined by Owen's Halifax. Sergeant M.A. 'Tony' Sachs, the tail gunner on 'Harry', not only successfully defended his aircraft, but succeeded in shooting down one 'confirmed' and two 'probable' enemy aircraft and damaging several others. Tony Sachs was awarded the DFM and James the DFC.[7]

Intense and accurate flak from both ground defences and the *Scharnhorst* and blast from bursting shells blew Owen's Halifax off target and holed it in many places, but it suffered no worse damage. Enemy fighters delivered in all ten attacks on this aircraft, one being claimed as shot down. Great coolness was shown by Sergeant Higgins, the tail gunner, while fighting back and successfully defending his aircraft. On seeing an apparently

---

7 Wing Commander Peter Stanley James DFC AE RAFVR died on 11 January 1999.

disabled Halifax being attacked by two Bf 109s he directed Owen to the scene of the combat and succeeded in drawing off one of the attackers.

Bombs dropped by 'W-William' skippered by Pilot Officer Johnston were seen to fall short to the north of the jetty, no doubt due to the captain having to take evasive action just at the time of release. The aircraft was then attacked by enemy fighters. The 20-year-old tail gunner, Sergeant Joseph Sankey, a native of Blackpool, proved his ability, not only successfully defending his aircraft against seven encounters, but shooting down one of the enemy and probably another. The aircraft returned safely to England landing at Stanton Harcourt at 1740.[8]

'M-Mother', captained by 24-year-old Flight Sergeant Clarence Arthur Godwin of Milton, Weston-super-Mare, seriously damaged by flak, was attacked by three Bf 109s over the town of Angles, about fifteen kilometres WSW of Luçon. An explosion rattled through the nose of the aircraft making it lurch and the front turret filled with smoke. In the meantime Sergeant Eric O.T. Balcombe, the air bomber, had been firing at a Bf 109 when the turret became u/s and the guns stopped firing. The flak burst had broken some of the perspex in the turret and Eric's sunglasses, bought for sixpence in Woolworths, were destroyed. One engine started to smoke and with three fighters attacking them it's a wonder the aircraft did not blow up. Godwin and the 19-year-old second pilot, Sergeant Greville Gascoyne Esnouf, were suffering from severe wounds as was Sergeant Conrad Howard Newstead the 24-year-old flight engineer who was manning the side Vickers gun. All Balcombe could see was the bloody mask of a face somehow held together by the side straps of his helmet. Somehow he managed to stay on his feet although mortally wounded. Both pilots were fighting with the controls but the aircraft was going into a spin. Sergeant Reginald Thomas Rudlin, the 27-year-old WOp/AG, was slumped over his set, and the rear gunner, Flight Sergeant Sidney Harry James Shirley (32), over the controls of his gun. The navigator, Pilot Officer Arthur G. Eperon, was also wounded and Balcombe helped carry him to the front hatch as the doomed bomber began a slow spiral downwards with smoke coming from one or two of its engines. As Balcombe left the aircraft his chute was seen to open. A French lady, in 1985, remembered that Eric Balcombe, who had parachuted from a stricken 78 Squadron Whitley near Doncaster a few months before, coming down in his chute and a Bf 109 continuing to fire around him. The aircraft crashed below him at Angles near a farm known as *Terrier du Fout* and he

---

8 Flight Sergeant Joseph Sankey DFM was shot down on Cologne on the night of 14/15 February 1943. He evaded and returned to England on 24 July.

felt the heat from the explosion. Balcombe was soon picked up and taken by a German staff car to see the wreck. Godwin, Esnouf, Rudlin, Shirley and Newstead died in the aircraft. At the funeral of the five members of his crew, three French people followed the coffins to the graveside. The next day the graves were covered with flowers which the Germans quickly removed. A plank of wood adorned with the British flag and an inscription *Your memory is with us everywhere we go. France cries out with hope and in praise of you* was placed on the site.[9]

'D-Dog' captained by Pilot Officer Holden came under accurate and heavy AA fire immediately upon entering the target area and the port wheel was burst and the aircraft holed in many places. Although preparation was made to deliver attack, the bombs hung up. The aircraft was then attacked by enemy fighters, the first attack with cannon fire killing the tail gunner Pilot Officer Harold Walter Stone DFM and raking up through the fuselage and wounding both beam gunners, Sergeants Smith and Perriment slightly. Holden held steady both his aircraft and his section in the formation. Perriment, although in acute pain, kept his post and continued in the defence of the aircraft and Smith in a state of semi-coma and barely able to see persisted in remaining by the second operator supervising the operation of the set and so the aircraft returned safely to England, landing at St. Eval at 1645. On entering the target area 'X-X-ray' skippered by Flight Lieutenant Elliot encountered accurate heavy flak and its starboard outer engine was damaged. Attack was delivered however, although under great difficulties and the Halifax returned safely, landing at 1705. 'J-Johnny' skippered by Pilot Officer Miller was hit by flak immediately upon entering target area, the port wheel being burst and port inner engine damaged. Miller continued on to deliver his attack from 13,000 feet although unable to take correct sight as his height bar was shot away. Bombs were seen to burst in the dock area. During the attack the aircraft was engaged in five encounters with enemy fighters, the first attack wounding the tail gunner, Sergeant Walker, in the leg and rendering his turret unserviceable. He remained in his turret however and continued giving directions to his captain until a further attack with cannon fire wrecked the intercom. The remaining guns were made full use of and the aircraft otherwise successfully defended through the engagement. This Halifax landed safely at St. Eval at 1708.

There was one more Halifax on 35 Squadron that made it back to England safely. Leaving the scene of the battle Richard Rivaz looked back to see the

---

9 See *We Act With One Accord, the history of 35 Pathfinder Squadron* by Alan Cooper (1998).

area 'thick with what looked like dark ugly clouds consisting of smoke fumes hanging like a pall over the target where twenty minutes before there had been bright blue sky. It seemed to be hanging there in mourning for the dead.'

'As I watched this dark and dreary mass behind us I saw two more Halifaxes appear; we were making for sea level or rather about a thousand feet above it and they were doing the same.

"How many Halifaxes can you see from the tail?" 'Braddles' asked.

"I can see three altogether: our number two and two others some way behind," I replied.

"Let me know if you see any more."

We were still within sight of the French coast and I kept a lookout chiefly in that direction.

"How are you feeling, front gunner?" I asked.

"I'm feeling fine sir. How about you?"

"I'm OK," I replied.

"I'm going to fly well clear of the coast navigator," I heard 'Braddles' say to Nick.

'I looked round at the tail plane that had been hit: there was a large ragged hole there and the fabric where it had been ripped away was flapping behind like streamers. I saw that the hole was in the starboard elevator and that the whole structure was badly damaged.

'I called through to 'Braddles' to tell him about it and he sent Wheeler back to have a look. Wheeler reported that it was OK. He also said that the fuselage round by the tail was full of holes. I knew it must be so, as I had heard and felt the bullets and cannon shells hitting it. 'Braddles' asked him how the engines were and he replied that one was running very hot and that it would probably pack up pretty soon. He also said that one of the tanks must be badly damaged, as it was neatly empty. We had a good two hours' flying before reaching our own coast, so our position did not look too good. What further damage had been done we could not tell, but we were still flying, which was the main thing anyway.

'I felt depressed. All the excitement I had felt while I was in combat had died down and the reaction had set in. Jerry was lying dead just behind me and I was thinking of him all the time: I remembered how cheerful and happy and how much alive he had always seemed and how he had always been smiling and laughing. Less than half an hour ago he had been alive not thinking of himself – only that our trip should be a success – and now he was dead; killed by a fighter he never even saw. I had shot down the fighter that killed Jerry, but not before Jerry had been killed.

'I turned and looked through the glass panel behind my back and saw him lying on the floor with his helmet still on and his oxygen mask over his face. Rowley-Blake had folded his hands across his chest. I remembered how I had seen him before, how he had sprung into the aeroplane laughing and I felt miserable as I saw him lying there dead and still. I thought of his mother and how she would feel; it is those who are left behind who have to suffer.

'Rowley-Blake was sitting beside Jerry with his head between his hands and he looked about all in, poor chap. I suggested to 'Braddles' that he might go forward now, as we were well away from the target, so he called him. Rowley-Blake said he thought he had something in his eye. Actually there was a tiny shell splinter embedded there. We discovered later that he had three other wounds as well: two bullet wounds in his left thigh and calf and a shell splinter in his shoulder, but he said he knew nothing about them and did not even know he had been hit until after he had got out of the aeroplane. He said his leg felt a bit stiff![10]

'We were silent for some time. I think we all felt rather miserable. The silence was broken by Berry's Canadian accent: 'Say, Captain; is there a lavatory aboard this ship?' The tension was broken for me then and I was able to laugh, particularly when 'Braddles' said he had not heard and asked him to repeat it.

'We had lost sight of the French coast and were flying about a thousand feet above the sea calm and blue, a great contrast to the grimness we had left behind. The sun was beating into my turret and again I was conscious of the heat.

'I felt suffocated in my turret, which still stank with the burnt cordite fumes and I would have given anything to be able to stand in a cool breeze. I felt cramped too and would have loved to get out and stretch. However, I would have to stay where I was; it was not safe to leave my turret even for a minute: at any moment more fighters might come at us from the shore, just beyond the horizon on our starboard. Reports would have been sent all along the coast that we were returning and even now fighters were probably looking for us. We would not be safe until we reached the shelter of our own shore, still about an hour and a half away.

'There were not so many ships and boats about now, as we were considerably further out to sea than we had been on our outward journey. Those we did see seemed to have lost the beauty they had before.

---

10 Sergeant Douglas Rowley-Blake recovered from his wounds. He was killed on
    58 Squadron on 8 November 1941 on Berlin when Whitley V Z6972 is believed to have
    come down in the sea. The five-man crew all died.

"D'you know where we are navigator?" 'Braddles' asked Nick.

"Not exactly, sir, but I think we're all right. I can't be certain though, without the wireless."

"How are we off for petrol Wheeler?"

"About another hour and a half sir."

"We'll make for the Cornish coast," 'Braddles' decided. "I'll land at St. Eval!"

'This bucked me up quite a lot, as it was near my home and with any luck I should be able to get there that night.

'Johnny was flying in close formation to us again: he had all his four engines running and I could not see any sign of damage to his machine. Once he flew right over the top of us and I imagine he was having a close look to see how much damage we had sustained. The other aircraft had dropped back, about a mile behind. I told 'Braddles' this and he asked me to let him know if it dropped back any farther. Johnny was evidently worrying about him too, as he turned around and flew alongside. I reported this to 'Braddles', who said we would continue as we were. Johnny seemed to be OK and we would have only just enough petrol to get back as it was and he could not afford to lose any distance by turning round. Johnny and the other aeroplane were flying together and there was nothing we could do by flying with them.

'I watched our shadow on the water, now all alone. I missed seeing Johnny just behind us: he had seemed so secure and steady. I could still see him and the other aircraft behind us, but they were gradually disappearing into the distance.

'We were running into some low, misty cloud, which in a way was an advantage as it would shield us from possible fighter attacks. It looked like a sea mist and seemed to go right down on the water. When we ran into it I lost sight of the aeroplanes behind us. The mist was in patches and we kept flying through it and into bright sunshine again alternately. When we came out of it I could see a film of moisture on the tailplane and on the perspex around my turret. It was quite a relief flying through this mist, as the sun for a short time ceased to blaze down on me and I felt cool. This misty cloud did not last for long and once again we flew into clear, cloudless sky. The sun beating down onto the sea below and behind us sent up a dazzling, shimmering brightness which burnt my eyes. I looked at my watch and saw that we had about another forty-five minutes to go before reaching our coast.

Nick gave 'Braddles' a change of course which meant that we must have been somewhere west of Brest and were making a turn to starboard to bring us to the Cornish coast. After we turned, the sun was no longer right behind us but slightly to our starboard, which I found a relief.

'There was no sign of shipping or land, only a vast expanse of sea below us, calm and clear and blue, disappearing into a misty horizon. It would be the same sea beating against the shores of Cornwall, a coast I knew well and loved.

'Uncomfortable thoughts began passing through my mind. I imagined what would happen if Nick was wrong in his navigation, if the course he had given 'Braddles' did not take us to the Cornish coast but past Land's End and up the Irish Sea. We might go right past the west coast and run out of petrol without ever seeing land! Or Wheeler might be wrong in his calculations of our petrol supply and we might run out just as land came in sight. The petrol gauges might be wrong and even at this moment the tanks might be nearly dry and the engines sucking their last few gallons.

'As I was trying to drive these thoughts from my mind, 'Braddles' asked, "How is the petrol, Wheeler?"

"About another forty-five minutes sir," Wheeler told him.

"What is our ETA at the coast, navigator?" 'Braddles' asked again.

"Another thirty minutes should see us there," Nick answered.

"As soon as we hit the coast, give me a course for St. Eval," 'Braddles' said.

The aircraft was flying quite steadily, but the engine that Wheeler had his doubts about was losing power.

"I think I can see some land," I heard Berry say from the nose some time later.[11]

"Pray God he's right!" I thought and began to feel more cheerful.

'With land in sight we should soon be back and an unpleasant day would be just another memory.

'There was no sign of the other aircraft: I had not seen anything of them since we got into the misty clouds. I hoped they were all right. They had probably changed course before we had; one of them was sure to have wireless, in which case they would know exactly where they were.

'I peered on either side of me, looking for the land, but I could not see far enough forward. It must have been quite close, as I heard 'Braddles' say to Nick: "Can you get a pin-point yet, navigator?"

'We must have been a bit too far west, for in a moment I heard Nick give a course bringing us further east.

---

11   Sergeant Wallace Llewellyn Berry, son of Lewis David and Philipena Lavina Berry of Virden, Manitoba, was killed on 14/15 August 1941 on the operation on Magdeburg when he was flying as tail gunner on Pilot Officer Ronald Lisle's crew. All were killed.

'At last, by leaning forward I was just able to see the coast some miles away on my right. What a glorious sight it was! I had never been so pleased to see the shore. It was even better than when returning home at night, as I was able to see it clearly in the sunlight – at night usually all one can see is a thin, pale streak.

'Our journey was nearly over and I was beginning to realize how tired I was. The past few hours had been a great strain owing to the constant concentration and also the uncertainty of wondering if we would make it.

'As we crossed the coast and I was able to look down onto the rocks and wonderfully clear sea below, a wave of happiness and relief surged over me. This was home and looking at its best, alive, clear and clean. We passed over the short green turf and scrubby trees above the cliffs. Cattle and sheep were grazing as I had seen them six hours earlier. We crossed the valleys with their rocky streams, the hills criss-crossed with their stone walls, over the woods and the little villages, all so peaceful and unhurried. This was home and England, a sight one has to be away from to fully appreciate and enjoy.

'The ambulance came alongside after we landed and I stayed in my turret until Jerry had been lifted from the aeroplane. I had seen him jump in so cheerfully and I could hardly bear to see him carried out dead.

'There was a group of people round our plane as we got out and one of them said to me: "Who was he; the tail gunner?"

"No," I replied. "I'm the tail gunner."

'We were not the only Halifax to land there; there were four of us altogether. We had parked next to one and I saw that the tail turret had been nearly blown away. Medical orderlies were still trying to extricate the gunner.

'I felt weak and sat down on the grass. Someone offered me a cigarette. I said I would smoke my pipe.

'After we had been interrogated and had a meal and some drinks, I hired a car and drove home, taking Nick with me.'

One Halifax on 35 Squadron landed safely but was Damaged Beyond Repair (DBR). Five more were damaged to the extent that they required approximately three weeks to repair, while two others were damaged to a lesser degree. The remaining two suffered only superficial damage.

All crews, except one whose bombs had hung up, had succeeded in delivering an attack – but only 'U-Uncle' piloted by Stan Greaves claimed a direct hit. Five direct hits had actually been scored, but three were by armour-piercing bombs that passed right through the *Scharnhorst*, each leaving only a small hole; the remaining two exploded but caused only minor damage. The *Scharnhorst* had, however, been damaged, shipping 3,000 tons of water.

On 29 December 1947, Stan Greaves received the DFM for his 'Marked display of determination and coolness in pressing home a successful attack on the *Scharnhorst* in the face of considerable anti-aircraft and fighter opposition.' This was one of the last decorations of the war. In the eyes of his crew there was no worthier recipient of that award. Two of the crew were also mentioned in dispatches.

The Germans decided that *Scharnhorst* should return at once for the better repair facilities and flak cover at Brest and she sailed that night with much water aboard (reports vary between 3,000 and 7,000 tons). This operation was, therefore, a major success in that it ensured that this powerful warship was forced to stay in harbour for a further prolonged period, four months being required for repairs. Six hits were claimed on the *Gneisenau* but could not be confirmed. The German fighter opposition was stronger and more prolonged than expected and ten Wellingtons and two Hampdens were lost to fighter attack or flak.

When the *Scharnhorst* limped back into Brest, Lieutenant Jean Philippon sent a message to that effect to his wireless operator for transmission to London. German detector vans had been trying to pinpoint Bernard Anquetil's location for some time and during this transmission on 30 July, just after the message about the *Scharnhorst*, Anquetil was arrested and transferred to Fresnes Prison. Sentenced to death on 15 October, he refused to reveal the origin and content of the transmitted messages, despite the promise of court support for clemency and despite torture by the Gestapo. As a result Philippon continued his activities until the end of the war. Bernard Anquetil was executed at Fort Mont Valerien on 24 October. Jean Philippon later became commander in chief of the French Mediterranean Fleet.

In early 1942, after repeated British bombing raids, the *Scharnhorst* and *Gneisenau* made a daylight dash up the English Channel from occupied France to Germany. In early 1943 *Scharnhorst* joined the Bismarck-class battleship *Tirpitz* in Norway to interdict Allied convoys to the Soviet Union. *Scharnhorst* and several destroyers sortied from Norway to attack a convoy; the Germans were instead intercepted by British naval patrols. During the Battle of the North Cape, the Royal Navy battleship HMS *Duke of York* and her escorts sank *Scharnhorst*. Only 36 men were pulled from the icy seas, out of a crew of 1,968.

Wing Commander Terence Patrick Armstrong 'Braddles' Bradley DSO DFC commanding 27 Squadron was killed on 10 April 1945 in the Chiringa region of Burma, flying a rocket-firing Beaufighter which crashed killing the pilot and navigator Pilot Officer G.C. Holmes as they hit a vulture when coming in to land. 27 Squadron was part of 907 anti-shipping/jungle rescue strike Wing SEAC and Bradley had been on the squadron for only a few weeks. 'Riv' Rivaz completed his tour of operations in December 1941. He was then posted to Canada to train as a pilot. On his return to England he toured the country with the Ministry of Aircraft Production and ferried aircraft with the Air Transport Auxiliary. On 13 October 1945 the B-24 Liberator in which Richard Rivaz was a passenger caught fire on take-off from Brussels, killing all on board.

Chapter 2

Sink the *Tirpitz*!

Grand Admiral Erich Johann Albert Raeder, the 65-year-old commander of the Kriegsmarine, proposed on 13 November 1941 that the 52,000 ton German battleship Tirpitz be deployed to Norway so that it could attack convoys bound for the Soviet Union and deter an Allied invasion of Norway. The capital ship was taken into dock for modifications for the deployment and Kapitän zur See (KzS – Captain at Sea) Karl Topp pronounced the ship ready for combat operations on 10 January 1942. The following day, Tirpitz *left for Wilhelmshaven and then left at 2300 on 14 January for Trondheim. On 16 January British aerial reconnaissance located the ship in Trondheim.* Tirpitz *then moved 15 miles north to Fættenfjord. Three quarters of a mile wide with steep cliffs on three sides, it protected the ship from air attacks from the south-west. The ship's crew cut down trees and placed them aboard* Tirpitz *to camouflage her. Additional anti-aircraft batteries were installed around the fjord, as were anti-torpedo nets and heavy booms in the entrance to the anchorage.*

The British Prime Minister, Winston Churchill, wrote on 25 January, 'The destruction or even crippling of this ship is the greatest event at sea at the present time. No other target is comparable to it.' He decided that the Tirpitz *should be attacked immediately 'both by carrier-borne torpedo aircraft and with heavy bombers by daylight or at dawn.'*

Late in January two detachments from 10 and 76 Squadrons and seven Stirlings on 15 and 149 Squadrons were secretly sent north to Lossiemouth on the Moray Firth Operation 'Oiled' on 29/30 January. As the closest point possible, it was still over 600 nautical miles to the target and at the extreme limit of the Halifax's loaded range and there were almost no navigational aids available for the mainly featureless journey. The Stirlings took off just after midnight, the four Halifaxes on 10 Squadron and five on 76 Squadron taking off at 0204 hours. Starting at an altitude of 2,000 feet the Halifaxes had to descend during a timed run to reach the dropping point at a height of 200 feet, were to fly straight at the great

30

battleship beamwards and drop their modified Royal Navy Type 19N 1,000 lb spherical mines on the side of the mountain. At 31 inches diameter they did not quite fit into the bomb bay, with the result that the bomb bay doors did not fully close when the Halifaxes were flying. The ground crews said they looked like 'pregnant mayflies'. The mines would then roll down the slope and lodge between the land and the Tirpitz fifty feet from the shore and explode. Fitted with hydrostatic fuses, this should ensure a 'beautifully restricted explosion' which would blow in the steel panels of the ship's relatively vulnerable lower hull!

Weather conditions were not good, with cloud from sea level to 20,000 feet. One of the Stirlings reported having seen the mast tops of Tirpitz but was unable to gain sufficient height to drop its bomb load. All the Stirlings returned to base. All four Halifaxes on 10 Squadron had to return to base before reaching the target due to lack of fuel. The five Halifaxes on 76 Squadron reached the target area, but weather conditions meant that they failed to locate the target. All aircraft returned to base with the exception of L9581/Q which lost a port engine during the return flight and even after jettisoning the mines the pilot was forced to ditch three miles off Aberdeen, the crew fortunately being rescued by the Aberdeen lifeboat. 149 Squadron lost one of its Stirlings which, returning to its base, skidded on the ice, hit a trench and collapsed the undercarriage.

Early on 9 March an air attack was launched on the Tirpitz at sea by twelve Fairey Albacore torpedo bombers from Royal Navy carriers, but the great ship successfully evaded the torpedoes and anti-aircraft gunners shot down two of the British aircraft. Tirpitz then made for Vestfjord and from there to Trondheim, arriving on the evening of 13 March. Having moved north to Scotland, 34 Halifaxes on 10, 35 and 76 Squadrons carried out another attack on the Tirpitz in Åsenfjord on the night of 30/31 March. The bombers crossed to Norway at 1,000 feet to avoid detection by German radar and they were able to identify the islands of Smöla, Hitra and Fröya as they flew over them en route for Trondheim fjord. However, they then encountered low 10/10ths cloud, were unable to see the ground below and were unable to locate the target. The Halifaxes remained in the target area as long as their fuel reserves would allow but they were eventually forced to abort. Most jettisoned their four 1,000 lb mines in the fjord at 2258 hours; three dropped theirs on the local flak and searchlight batteries, which promptly ceased to operate. Six of the Halifaxes failed to return. There is little doubt that fuel starvation accounted for most, if not all, of the missing Halifaxes.

On Thursday 23 April 1942, Halifax crews on Nos. 10, 35 and 76 Squadrons, six Lancasters on 44 Squadron and six on 97 Squadron, arrived at their advanced bases in the north-east of Scotland for another attack on the *Tirpitz*. The crews were briefed on 25 April but were prevented from taking off on the 25th and 26th due to 'haar', as the coastal sea fog is known in that part of the world. It was not until 1650 hours on Monday the 27th, when a Mosquito landed at Lossiemouth on the Moray Firth with photos of the exact position of the *Tirpitz*, together with a close-up of the latest camouflage, that the crews were told 'Ops on'. These photos had been taken by a Norwegian patriot at the risk of his life and rushed to Sweden where a Mosquito was standing by to fly to Northern Scotland. The weather report was good, with slight sea fog at the target, so the waiting crews were briefed, bombed up and fed.

One of the pilots on 76 Squadron, Squadron Leader Michael William Renaut DFC, who was one of two pilots to drop an 8,000 lb bomb on Germany during a raid over Essen on the night of 10/11 April 1942 and whose party trick was to write the Lord's Prayer on the back of a postage stamp, had completed his Whitley course at Kinloss before joining 78 Squadron. As for the plan to bomb the *Tirpitz* he wrote that 'he had never heard such rubbish' and imagined 'some young statistician at Bomber Command sitting down and working out this insane plan'.[12] Nonetheless, the plan, which went ahead on the night of 27/28 April, was for Halifaxes on 10 and 35 Squadrons to attack at mast height with modified naval mines and 76 Squadron to drop 4,000 lb bombs to put off the gunners and the shore batteries at Fættenfjord. As with the attack in March, this operation was to be carried out in two phases. The Halifaxes on 76 Squadron and the dozen Lancasters who would each carry a 4,000 lb bomb to be dropped from 6,000 feet would open the attack. They would also carry 500 lb bombs to use against flak and searchlight positions. 'The Halifax,' continued Renaut, 'was not the ideal aircraft to carry a 4,000 lb bomb because it was about the size of a pillar box and the bomb doors wouldn't quite close. This meant that there was a good deal of air resistance which slowed down the aeroplane. With a 4,000 lb bomb on board we couldn't take a full petrol load either. Consequently the operation to Trondheim was stretching our endurance to something like twenty minutes flying in hand.'

The second phase would see the mine-carriers on Nos. 10 and 35 Squadrons fly over the *Tirpitz* at an incredible 150 feet to each drop

---

12   *Terror by Night* (published posthumously in 1982).

their four mines along the length of the ship between the ship and the shore. In the event that *Tirpitz* could not be located, the alternative targets were the *Prinz Eugen, Admiral Hipper* and *Admiral Scheer*, which were lying in Lofjord two miles to the north of Fættenfjord.

Wing Commander Donald Clifford Tyndall Bennett, who had commanded 77 Squadron at Leeming flying Whitleys in 4 Group from the beginning of December 1941 until mid-April 1942 when he was transferred to command 10 Squadron, recalled: 'The Halifax had a considerably greater payload than the Whitley and with better performance. We were carrying five mines though the bomb doors would not close properly, which was of no great importance.' The Australian aviation pioneer and bomber pilot, born in Toowoomba 'deep in the rich mud of the Darling Downs' of Queensland on 14 September 1910, where he lived for twenty years, was the youngest of four brothers, all of whom were raised on the family cattle station at Condomine before the family moved to Brisbane. As a small boy, Don saw the Wright Brothers demonstrating their flying machine on the racecourse at Toowoomba and he never forgot the experience. By the time of the *Tirpitz* operation Bennett had a 'strange idea that he knew a little about the bombing game,' but as he said, 'I was soon to have a small object lesson to bring me back to earth – literally.'[13]

At 2001 hours double British summer time on 27 April the first of the forty-three bombers commenced take off in failing light from their temporary Scottish bases. Two Halifaxes and one Lancaster returned early due to technical problems. The remaining forty aircraft set course for Norway, which meant about four hours flying across the North Sea. The night was brightly lit by the moon and there were no clouds. Continues Renaut: 'We saw with relief about four destroyers 25, 50, 75 and 100 miles from base in a line to Norway and realised they were there for our benefit on return, in case anyone ran short of petrol. While the North Sea crossing was tedious, at least we had no flak or fighters and all one needed to dwell on was the forthcoming reception at Trondheim! We crossed the Norwegian coast and the scenery looked marvellous from the air since it was never really dark. We then saw the most colossal barrage ahead from the *Tirpitz* and it seemed as if every gun in Norway had been moved to Åsenfjord. We were at 4,000 feet and at this height there was a slight risk that we might be hit by our own bomb fragments or at any rate we could feel the blast.'

---

13 *Pathfinder* (Frederick Muller Ltd, 1958).

Phase one of the attack commenced with the leading Lancaster on 44 Squadron flying over *Tirpitz* and dropping its 4,000 lb bomb at 0006 hours. At this time the target was clearly visible, but within minutes smoke barrels and smoke ships that were strategically placed around the fjords began to emit a thick blanket of smoke which soon covered the fjord and shipping making it extremely difficult for the aircraft to locate the *Tirpitz* or other ships.

Renaut started his bombing run and could see clearly 10 Squadron going in at mast height. He saw a Halifax [W1037 ZA-U on 10 Squadron flown by Flight Lieutenant G.E. 'Dusty' Miller RAAF] clearly below start its run in and drop its load. As the Halifax flew away from *Tirpitz* and into the next fjord to start making for home it was hit by gun fire from some of the German ships. Initially the crew were unaware that any damage had been done to the aircraft and continued to fly on. However, the tail gunner, Sergeant B. Curran, alerted the pilot that one of the wings was on fire and that they were trailing 300 feet of flames. Miller knew that with the wing on fire he didn't have much time to get the aircraft down and told the crew that he was going to ditch the Halifax on the Åsenfjord, three miles from the shore at Røkke in Skatval, which was fortunately flat calm at the time. During the landing the wing exploded. Miller, Sergeant Jake Ryder the wireless operator-gunner and the observer, Pilot Officer Peter John Jagoe Roberts RAFVR, were rescued from the freezing water by a Kriegsmarine patrol vessel which was guarding the U-boat nets at the entrance of Åsenfjord and then were taken onboard the *Prince Eugen* where they spent the rest of the night before being taken ashore and marched off into captivity. Sergeant Herbert Harry Stott, the 22-year-old second wireless operator from Selby in Yorkshire and Sergeant Eric Annable, the flight engineer from York, died either during the crash landing or from being hit by flak. Curran and the 2nd pilot, Sergeant Gregory RNZAF, managed to climb into the aircraft's life raft and through the rest of the night paddled and drifted until they came ashore near Malvik. They were discovered as day broke and taken prisoner too.

Continues Michael Renaut: 'We could see the *Tirpitz* faintly in the light from the blaze and Tim Collins asked me to hold a steady course. It was not fear that prevented me, it was the sheer intensity of the flak – I just couldn't hold the Halifax steady and listened to the flak punching holes in us. The first bombing run was hopeless because the Hun had laid a smokescreen – the *Tirpitz* had now disappeared. But we knew near enough where she lay and I attempted to hold the Halifax steady for a moment, imploring Tim to drop the bomb. Tim's temper was raised and he said, 'I haven't come all this bloody way to drop the bomb haphazard – you hold a steady course and I'll let it go.'

'Round I went for a third bombing run, frightened to death and not anxious to be shot down over the snow-covered mountain. Tim said 'Hold her steady,' but the flak was murderous and I could hear chunks of it hitting the Halifax again. Just then I saw another low level Halifax hit and burn and crash in the valley below – a flaming torch disintegrating as it ploughed its way on its belly.'

The second phase commenced with the 35 Squadron Halifaxes followed by 10 Squadron flying low up the fjord. *Tirpitz* was totally obscured by the smokescreen and the crews had to use an outcrop of rock above *Tirpitz* as an aiming point.

In total, four Halifaxes and a Lancaster were lost.[14] On 35 Squadron, 'K for King' flown by Pilot Officer Michael Reginald Mark Pools and crew crashed into a hillside about seven miles from *Tirpitz* at Borås with the loss of everyone on board.[15] Halifax II W1048 was damaged by flak; its pilot, Pilot Officer Donald P. McIntyre, a 24-year-old Canadian, crash-landed it on the frozen surface of Lake Hoklingen where it sank gently twelve hours later. McIntyre and the observer, Pilot Officer Ian Hewitt, the 1st wireless operator, Sergeant Dave Perry, the second wireless operator and mid-upper gunner Sergeant Pierre Blanchett and tail gunner Sergeant R.H.D. 'Ron' Wilson evaded capture. Vic Stevens the flight engineer, who had broken his ankle in the landing, was helped over the 150 yards of ice to the shore by the others was later taken prisoner and hospitalised by the Germans before being taken into captivity.[16]

On 97 Squadron, Lancaster 'L for Leather' flown by 28-year-old Canadian Flight Lieutenant John Goodsir MacKid DFC was hit by AA fire and caught fire plunging to the ground near Ausetvatnet (Auset Lake) with the loss of all the crew.

Little did Michael Renaut know then that the second low-level Halifax he had seen crash in the valley below was 'B for Baker' flown

---

14   A PRU aircraft flew over *Tirpitz* on 28 April and photographs taken showed no damage despite the twenty 4,000 lb bombs and 44 mines that the aircraft had dropped overnight. At midday the crews were told they were to fly again that night to the same target. On 28/29 April a repeat raid on the *Tirpitz* was made, again with no damage to the battleship. Of 23 Halifaxes and 11 Lancasters dispatched, 2 Halifaxes, both on 35 Squadron, were lost. The squadron had dispatched 9 aircraft following the loss of 2 the previous night, so had lost a third of its strength in two night raids.

15   Sergeant Hubert Allan Booth; Pilot Officer Gerard John Peter Henry; Sergeant Donald Edgar Rarity; Sergeant Allan Wilstrop and Pilot Officer Frank William Gosnell Hill.

16   In 1973, W1048 was salvaged from the bed of the lake and after restoration by airmen at RAF Wyton was placed on public display in the RAF Museum at Hendon. McIntyre was killed in the crash of a Halifax VII on 13 February 1947.

by Wing Commander Don Bennett. Bennett's Halifax hit the coast at an angle; ran up to the chosen island immediately north-west of Trondheim and then turned towards the target. In 1958 Bennett described the raid in his book, *Pathfinder*: 'We had chosen a track which, according to our Intelligence, was free from defences and should give us a good run in across the island. All was peace and quiet before we arrived, but as we crossed the coast everything opened up on us and we were hit many times. The tail gunner was wounded and things were far from peaceful. The procedure laid down was nevertheless carried out strictly according to plan and the tail gunner, Flight Lieutenant H.G. How, kept completely quiet in spite of the pain he was in during the whole of the performance.

'We ran across our datum point at exactly 2,000 feet and started our stop watch, descending at the prescribed rate exactly on course and at the right air speed. As we got near the *Tirpitz* herself, all the other units of the fleet to our left picked on us and by this time the starboard wing was burning fiercely. This attracted more attention and we certainly had the pleasure of a complete welcoming committee. We were down to the required two hundred feet exactly at the time (as called over the intercom, from the stop watch) at which we should have released. To my horror, the bomb aimer could not see the ship and with good reason. Below us there was a white haze. I was 'mistified' – literally. The mist was not due to Nature, but was a man-made camouflage of which our Intelligence had reported nothing, even although I subsequently discovered that it had been known several months earlier. A split second later the ship's superstructure passed beneath us, but it was too late to let go and I vaguely hoped that I would be able to hold the aircraft in the air long enough to turn back for a second run. I completed the turn and headed towards the ship, but the flames on the starboard side were now mounting, the starboard undercarriage had come down and the starboard flap had begun to trail. I pointed towards the ship's position and released the mines. I often wonder where they went! I then turned east towards neutral Sweden and tried hard to climb, but things were obviously bad and I therefore gave the order "prepare to abandon aircraft".

'I regret to say that one member of the crew became a little melodramatic. He said, "Cheerio, chaps; this is it, we've had it." I told him very peremptorily to shut up and not to be a fool; that we were perfectly all right but that we would have to parachute. Soon it became obvious that I could not possibly clear the mountains which rose steeply to about 3,000 feet just beyond the target and I was therefore forced to turn back west and to give the order "abandon aircraft; jump, jump". I then told the flight engineer [Flight Sergeant John Colgan] to assist the tail gunner [Flight Lieutenant George How]. The parachute drill went perfectly. I realised, however, after I had given the order and sat there alone, holding the wheel hard over to port with all my strength and with the port outer engine slightly throttled back to keep the aircraft on an even keel with full port rudder, that I was not wearing my parachute! It was a nasty thought. Just after this rather uncomfortable fact dawned on me, I was surprised and relieved when the flight engineer came back to me, found my parachute down in the fuselage, brought it up and clipped it on the hooks on my chest so that I had a chance of escape. He risked his own life in doing this. He then disappeared again and in due course he went the full length of the fuselage and helped the tail gunner to parachute to safety. I stayed as long as I could; things were getting fairly hot in the cockpit and the flames were very extensive and fierce in the starboard wing. We were losing height rapidly and I was heading away from the mountains back towards the east and towards trouble. The ground was getting very close. Finally, as I was holding the wheel hard over to port, I eased myself out of my seat preparatory to jumping and just at that moment the starboard wing folded up. I jumped through the hatch below me like a shot and pulled the ripcord the moment I was clear. It was only just in time; my parachute opened just as I was striking the snow and all was well. My reaction, I suppose, should have been one of deep gratitude, but instead the only thing I thought of was the shock it would be to my wife Ly. I said out loud a few words addressed to her and suddenly realised that I should be getting on with the job of trying to get back to her.'

The observer/navigator, Sergeant T.H.A. 'Phil' Eyles, had been the first to leave the aircraft, followed by the second pilot, Sergeant Harry Walmsley. The two wireless operators, Sergeants C.R.S. Forbes and J.D. Murray, went next. Flight Lieutenant George How was helped from his turret by Colgan and they also left the aircraft. Eyles landed safely on the ground and at first started to climb up a large hill. He was somewhat worried to find paw prints in the snow, which he took to be those of a wolf. Fearing an encounter with these wild animals and after discovering yet more of their tracks in the snow, he followed a stream back down the hill until he came to some houses. He knocked on the door of one of the houses and was taken inside where an elderly couple gave him some food and then fetched someone from the nearby log clearing station to help. Having explained using sign language and drawings that he wanted to rest before continuing to Sweden he settled down for the night. Unfortunately, someone had informed the Germans of his presence and before he awoke to continue his journey, the Germans had arrived and he was taken prisoner. After being held in Trondheim for several days he was taken by train to Oslo and from there by air to Germany where he spent the remainder of the war in PoW camps.

George How landed in a fir tree with broken ribs as a result of his parachute straps pulling tight when he left the aircraft. He had also lost his boots as they had been ripped off by the slipstream as he left the aircraft. It is thought that How landed about four miles south of the crashed aircraft, to the west of Lake Øystre Sonvatnet. The only way How could get down from the tree was to unfasten the quick release on his parachute and drop down some ten feet onto the snow below. This he did, slightly injuring his knee and forehead as he did so. It was a cold but very brightly lit moonlight night and after recovering himself from his drop he hid his parachute as best he could under some trees and prepared to set off on foot. At this point Murray, who must have landed nearby, joined him. They were pleased to see one another and set off together walking until the sun came up. With the sun in the sky warming the day the two men stopped and examined the contents of their escape kits. They found some Horlicks tablets and a silk map of the area and a compass. Unfortunately the compass didn't work, so they headed off in what they thought was the general direction for Sweden, unsure if they were going the right way or not. Although the sun provided some warmth during the day, it also melted the snow making walking difficult, particularly for How with no boots. The two airmen found themselves wading through snow that was sometimes waist deep. By nightfall it got freezing cold again and How and Murray were exhausted. They arrived at a plateau where they found quantities of dead wood, which they gathered and made a fire with using matches from their escape kits. The next day they continued on their journey, walking all day through the deep snow until nightfall when they came across a small log cabin. Inside they found blankets and a bed but no food. They were very hungry and thirsty by now. Early the next morning, they were woken up by someone knocking on the door. A middle aged Norwegian man entered the cabin. He had with him a map and compass and he indicated to the two men where they were and where the Swedish border was. When he left he took the map but left the compass behind. An old pair of leather ski boots found in the cabin provided How with some much-needed if none-too-comfortable footwear.

Again the two set off to make their way to the Swedish border. The compass left for them by the Norwegian didn't work and after trudging through the snow for twelve hours they were devastated to find themselves back at the log cabin from where they had set off that morning! There was nothing left for them to do. Too exhausted to continue, they made use of the beds in the cabin once more and went to sleep. While they slept some Norwegians who had been sent by the Germans arrived at the cabin with a horse pulling a stretcher to collect them. How was put on the stretcher and he and Murray were taken to the village of Østkil where they were well looked after by the Norwegians. Within hours, the German police arrived and took them to a railway station where they were taken by train to Oslo. There they met up with Sergeant Vic Stevens. All three prisoners were flown to Germany where they spent the rest of the war in PoW camps.

Walmsley and Colgan landed just to the west of Sonvatn. Colgan had seen Walmsley come down a short distance ahead of him and had sought him out. They examined their escape kits and decided to head east to try to reach Sweden. They came across a small isolated farm in the forest and as they were both very hungry, not having eaten for many hours, they decided to chance knocking on the door. The family at the farm took them in and gave them food, but they felt that by staying any length of time they might risk capture. They left the farm and continued on their way, at first heading north, in case anyone had found out that they had been at the farm and went looking for them. Their direction of travel was taking them towards Sona. Just after sunrise they arrived at a farm at Brobakk, where a man was out chopping wood. Although surprised to see the airmen, the man willingly took them in to his home where they were fed and shown the direction to take to Sweden on their map. As darkness fell he took the airmen to another house in Sona where they were given more details about the route they should follow and advice on how to avoid the Germans. They were advised to travel only at night and to follow the railway line. They were also told where they could expect to find German sentry posts. After about 22 miles, they approached another farm, Havgen, near Meråker, for food and assistance. Once again, despite the risk to themselves and the shortage of food, the Norwegians generously helped the airmen. They were shown the next stage of their route on the silk escape map and set off through the woods to continue their journey to Sweden. The airmen followed the route which had been drawn onto their map; it took them north-east from Meråker into the hills and past Lake Fjergen to Lake Hallsjøen, the eastern shore of which was on the border of Sweden. During this part of the journey they had to contend with a severe blizzard which soaked their clothes again. Having crossed the frozen Lake Fjergen, they met a young couple on skis who were staying at a little fishing hut on the shore of the lake. They took Walmsley and Colgan into the hut, fed them, allowed them to have a long sleep and dried the airmen's soaking clothes and boots. After sleeping for about twelve hours and with dry clothes to wear, the airmen were ready for the next part of their journey. The young Norwegian couple set off ahead of them on skis to make tracks they could follow, making for Lake Hallsjøen. Before parting company, the airmen gave the Norwegian couple the remainder of their survival money.

Having been assured by the Norwegians that there were no Germans in the area, Walmsley and Colgan proceeded to cross the frozen lake. Before they reached the other side they were met by a Swedish army patrol who took them to their mountain hut and gave them plenty to eat and drink. After being taken to the Swedish military authorities at Storlien for questioning, they were put on a train taking them to a Swedish internment camp at Falun. On the train they found themselves sharing a carriage with Donald McIntyre's French Canadian mid-upper gunner Pierre Blanchett and the tail gunner on W1048 TL-S, Sergeant Ron Wilson! McIntyre and his 1st wireless operator, Ian Hewitt, were repatriated after a few weeks: the second wireless operator Sergeant Dave Perry and Blanchett and Wilson after about a year. Wilson even rented a flat and worked in Sweden for a while![17]

On their arrival at the internment camp Walmsley and Colgan were delighted to be reunited with Wing Commander Bennett and wireless operator Sergeant Forbes. Four weeks after the attack against *Tirpitz*, Walmsley was returned to the UK. Colgan was returned to the UK over a year after being shot down.

Bennett and Forbes landed somewhere in Flornesvollen. Bennett's parachute had time to only partially open during his jump as he was only 200 feet or so from the ground when he left the aircraft. However, it was enough to slow his descent and combined with landing in deep snow he

---

17   Wilson was a London 'cabbie' in later life. McIntyre eventually returned to service. He and Pilot Officer Hewitt later received the DFC. Hewitt became a squadron leader navigator with the Path Finder Force. A chartered accountant, he died in June 2015 aged 94.

survived. He shortly met up with Sergeant Forbes who had landed nearby and they set off, heading east. Concerned that the Germans might be using tracker dogs to find them, they waded across a stream. They came to a railway station at Guda and just to the east of the station they could see a bridge over the river. They also spotted a German sentry post, possibly two, which ruled out their chances of crossing the river at this point. Continuing on they found a house on a hill not too far from the station and, being very tired by now, they entered a shed beside the house to rest. Unable to sleep due to the cold they decided to continue their journey and set off uphill towards the mountains in the direction of Sweden.

A little sunshine the following day failed to warm the air much at that altitude and they carried on walking until the evening when they came upon a farm, Bjørnås in Torsbjørkdalen. Exhausted and hungry the airmen knocked on the door of the farmhouse. Once it was established that the airmen were genuine and not Germans trying to trick the Norwegians, they were invited in and given food and somewhere to sleep for the night.

The next morning they were escorted by a Norwegian to the highest farm up the valley, Mannsæterbakken, arriving in the evening. The family from Bjørnås had sent word asking the people there to assist the airmen to Sweden. They were given food and beds for the night. Very early the next morning the Norwegian farmer set off on his skis with the airmen on foot heading for the Swedish border. They travelled towards Vattendalen and then to Litlefjell, Gilsåfjellet, towards Hårradålen and the south side of Storeklukken. From here the Swedish border could be seen and after giving Bennett and Forbes a piece of paper that he had drawn the route to the border on he left them and returned to his farm.

Bennett and Forbes walked over the border into Sweden and carried on for a further five miles until they came to Storvallen where they gave themselves up to the Swedish Army. The next day they were taken to the village of Storlien and handed over to an Air Force officer who escorted them on the train to the Falun internment camp.

Two weeks later, Bennett was on his way back to the UK. Forbes was returned to the UK over a year later.[18] The Australian wing commander's tenure on 10 Squadron was to come to an abrupt end. The squadron was ordered to the Middle East to assist in the bombing of the Italian Fleet, which was considered to be a great strategic danger to the North African campaign. Bennett bade his wife and family goodbye and with

---

18 Thanks are due to Linzee Druce.

the squadron moved down to Hurn ready for the take-off. The Halifaxes were refuelled and prepared for departure. About an hour and a half before take-off the signal arrived that Bennett was to hand over the command to Squadron Leader George Phillip Seymour-Price one of his flight commanders and to report to the C-in-C Sir Arthur Harris at Headquarters Bomber Command, where he found, to his great delight, that the Path Finder Force was to be created. On 5 July 1942 Bennett, now a group captain, was given command of the new force, a position he held with distinction. In turn he was promoted Air Commodore and later Air Vice-Marshal with the CB CBE and DSO, but despite the unquestioned achievements of 8 Group, at the end of the war Bennett was the only bomber group commander not to be knighted.

Chapter 3

'Shiny Ten'

I was told I would have got the Victoria Cross if I had died.
Sergeant Norman Francis Williams CGM DFM* RAAF

At 10 OTU Abingdon, Sergeant Nelson Cobb's crew had trained on Whitleys and flew on the 1,000-Bomber Raid on 24 June 1942 before beginning a tour of operations on 10 Squadron, nicknamed 'Shiny Ten', at RAF Leeming.

The Skipper was a 20-year-old Canadian from Tillsonburg, Ontario, a handsome young man, a dedicated and serious-minded person, very keen to get on with the training and looking forward to getting to grips with the enemy and hitting them hard where it hurt. He was usually addressed by his nickname 'Ty', after the famous baseball player Ty Cobb.

The navigator, David Archibald Codd, was born at Elstree, Hertfordshire, just after the end of the First World War. A few weeks before the outbreak of the Second World War, as a serving Territorial he received a call-up for Active Service in the Royal Engineers. He served in France and Belgium from January 1940 as a driver and Bren gunner, escaping from Dunkirk in a destroyer after all the small rescue boats had left. A year later he was accepted for transfer to the RAF for aircrew training. At 5 AOS Jurby on the Isle Of Man Codd qualified in navigation, bombing and gunnery. He had the gift of being able to play most of the popular songs by ear with most of the correct chords, which was an advantage.

The wireless operator was Pilot Officer Ronnie Fell from Derbyshire. Sergeant Walter Trask from Yarmouth, Nova Scotia, was the bomb aimer, who answered to the name of 'Wally'. At times that nickname was appropriate on account of his occasional eccentricity. He had failed a course as a wireless operator but proved to be an excellent bomb aimer. Sergeant Desmond Smith, the air gunner from Ulleskelf, Yorkshire, was otherwise known as 'Smithy'.

The flight engineer, Sergeant Ron Baldwin, who was 29 years old when he joined our crew at Abingdon, was from Lincoln and referred to as 'Baldy'.

He was married and had worked as a garage mechanic in civilian life – good grounding for a flight engineer. He was somewhat taciturn by nature and preferred having a few drinks in the Sergeants Mess bar rather than going out on the town. On the few occasions that he joined the others for a drink he could drink us all under the table. As a flight engineer he was the tops and quite unflappable whatever the situation. Ronnie Fell was another quiet type, a light drinker who, like 'Baldy', did not mix very much with the others. He was very efficient at his job and when we were all flying together we made a great team.

On arrival at Leeming on 10 July the new crew found the place in chaos as David Codd recalled: 'All 10 Squadron aircrews had been posted to North Africa at very short notice to carry out bombing operations against Rommel's army and their supply lines. The German forces were threatening to overrun Libya and Egypt. The detachment was intended to be a temporary one since the crews' belongings and spare kit had been left behind at Leeming. However, the posting to North Africa became permanent and the kit and belongings had to be flown out to the crews. They would certainly have a longer life expectancy flying the so-called 'Milk Run' to Tobruk and Benghazi rather than to the heavily defended industrial targets of Western Germany. A few days after their departure several crews, including ours, arrived at Leeming to start the formation of the new 10 Squadron. The Halifax bomber had both a rear and a mid-upper turret so we needed to recruit a second gunner. An intake of newly trained gunners arrived within a few days and our skipper made a wonderful choice when he invited Norman Francis Williams, an Australian, to join our crew.'

Williams was born in Narrandera, New South Wales, the eldest child of Elsie Mary Gibbs and William Francis Williams. He was home-schooled by his mother on the family farm until a government subsidy allowed the building of a tin-shed schoolhouse on a neighbouring property. When the family moved to Leeton, New South Wales, where his father ran a garage, he attended St. Joseph's Convent School and then the Catholic College run by the Marist Brothers in Sale, Victoria. Leaving school at 16 he worked at odd jobs in Leeton, where his garage-proprietor father had died from cancer and William almost followed with double pneumonia. He attributed his survival to his uncle George, who set up bottles of oxygen by his bedside. 'Norm' was working for the New South Wales Water Conservation and Irrigation Commission at the outbreak of the Second World War. Joining the Australian Army he transferred to the Royal Australian Air Force in May 1941, becoming the top student in his air gunnery course. In March

1942 'Norm' left for England on the troopship SS *Strathallan*. Posted to Yorkshire, he met 'Des' Smith, whose skipper was looking for a rear gunner. The pair became crewmates and lifelong friends.

'Norm' was a handsome fair-haired blue-eyed specimen,' wrote David Codd, 'a few years older than the rest of us with the exception of 'Baldy' Baldwin the flight engineer. 'Norm' could certainly attract the fair sex, but his main attribute for our crew was that he was a crack shot with any type of gun and was absolutely fearless in any situation. He had been brought up with guns in his native Australia and had spent a lot of time shooting the wild ducks which abounded in the area where he lived. These ducks were a menace to the rice crops grown in that locality. At Leeming there were facilities for clay-pigeon shooting and it was a pleasure to watch him in action – he just never missed!

'With the agreement of 'Des' Smith, who had occupied the rear turret in the Whitley, 'Norm' was to be our rear gunner and Smithy would take the mid-upper position. Smithy and 'Norm' became firm friends and spent a lot of their spare time together. 'Norm' was always welcome at Smithy's home at Ulleskelf in Yorkshire during leave periods. The other members of the crew had got to know one another well in the month we had been flying together at Abingdon. Both Walter Trask and the skipper were visitors to my parents' house during two periods of leave.'[19]

After several frustrating 'stop-go' decisions, Sergeant Nelson Cobb's crew finally flew their first operation on 12 August, to Le Havre, which happened to have been David Codd's port of arrival for his army unit's disastrous campaign in 1940. A few days later 10 Squadron moved to the newly constructed station at Melbourne, south of the main road from York to Hull. The move was made because Leeming was selected as one of several bases earmarked for the newly-formed all-Canadian 6 Group. Melbourne was to become a satellite station of RAF Pocklington. Cobb's crew came through their next two operations to Saarbrücken on 28 August and Karlsruhe on 2 September, but they had a close call two days later, as Codd recalls: 'We took off from Pocklington at 2355 hours, a time when most people would expect to be going to bed, for an attack on the docks of Bremen. We carried mostly incendiaries plus a 1,000 lb GP bomb. This turned out to be an eventful trip. On our route across Northern Holland there was much activity with plenty of flak being sent up. We reached the target without too much trouble and dropped our bomb load, securing what

---

19 *Blue Job - Brown Job* by David Codd DFC.

turned out to be an excellent photograph of the target area. On the way back we were getting close to the Dutch Coast when 'Norm' reported a German Ju 88 night-fighter closing in on us.

"Keep weaving Skipper," he said on the intercom. A few seconds later he said, "The bastard's underneath us. Do a vertical dive Skipper; then pull the nose up quickly so I can get a sight of him."

'Immediately we went into a steep dive with a dramatic increase in speed. Then the Skipper pulled hard back on the stick in a steep climb. As the tail of our aircraft dropped, the Ju 88 was suddenly right in 'Norm''s sights, close enough for him to see the pilot in his cockpit. 'Norm' pressed the firing button and bullets from his four Brownings ripped into the Junkers which immediately burst into flames and dropped out of the sky. 'Norm' watched it go down and saw a flash as it appeared to hit the ground. I recorded the times of the action in my log and it transpired the following day that another crew had seen and noted the 'kill', thus confirming the destruction of one enemy aircraft. We did not return directly to Pocklington because we received a coded message to divert to Oakington in Cambridgeshire because airfields further north, including Pocklington, were experiencing heavy fog conditions.

'We were debriefed at Oakington and gave the intelligence officer full details of our encounter with the Ju 88 and our claimed kill. Later that morning we took off for return to Pocklington and on landing we were met at our dispersal point by the station commander and squadron commander in the staff car. The news of the downing of the Ju 88 had been received overnight – hence the unusual reception on the tarmac and the congratulations on our success. The happy outcome was that 'Norm' was given an immediate award of the Distinguished Flying Medal, the first 'gong' to be awarded to the new 10 Squadron.

'The action and the award were widely reported in the newspapers, which were allowed to publish victories but not disasters. Our tactics in tackling the Ju 88 were fully reported in RAF publications since they might profitably be used again. It was not known at the time that the Luftwaffe were experimenting with guns that fired vertically upwards so that their aircraft could get below a bomber and shoot at its vulnerable underbelly. This could have been the objective of our Ju 88 attacker – we shall never know. At all events it had been a lucky escape for our crew, thanks to the rear gunner's sharp eyesight and some brilliant airmanship by the Skipper.'

By Christmas 1942 Cobb's crew had carried out a further fifteen ops to enemy targets plus a 1,000-bomber trip from Abingdon and were halfway towards the thirty trips which constituted a full operational tour. 'Bearing in mind that six or seven trips were about the average for Bomber Command crews to survive, we had been lucky this far,' recalled David Codd. 'This was due in no small part to the vigilance and skill of our skipper and our rear gunner, Norman Williams. 'Norm' had already been to Buckingham Palace to receive his DFM from King George VI for shooting down the Ju 88. At the investiture he had the temerity to invite the King, an expert in field sports and a renowned shot, to go duck shooting with him in Australia. The King smiled and said he would be delighted to take him up on his offer after the war was won!

'Norman Williams was invited to spend Christmas with Smithy and family at Ulleskelf in Yorkshire. The Canadians and I had a wonderful time at Bournemouth. Mum's friendly butcher did us proud. Rationing for him was a dirty word. (Later in the war he served a jail sentence for black marketing!) Mum's grocer also did not bother too much about rationing, so there was plenty for all. She was an exceptionally fine cook, always baking her own bread and cakes and keeping a large stock of home-made preserves and home-brewed wines. Pre-war our family had lived like fighting cocks.'

The crew's trip to Nurnberg on 8/9 March 1943 proved to be their 27th and final one on 'Shiny 10', as David Cobb recalled: 'Wing Commander (later Group Captain) Hamish Mahaddie DSO DFC AFC had arrived at Melbourne on a 'fishing expedition' to recruit crews for the expanding Pathfinder Force (PFF) and he wanted only the best. Squadron Commanders did not want to lose their best crews but the redoubtable Hamish could be very persuasive in convincing them that a crack Pathfinder Force would help to shorten the War. In fact, some of the crews that started Pathfinder training failed to make the grade and were returned to their main force squadrons. The skipper and I were both keen to transfer to Pathfinders and we consulted the rest of the crew for their opinions. Only Ronnie Fell decided he had had enough for the time being; the others wanted to continue operational flying. Bill Allen's crew did not wish to volunteer for Pathfinders; however, his wireless operator Flight Sergeant Charles 'Doc' Bulloch (soon to be commissioned to pilot officer) heard that we were volunteering and asked to join our crew in place of Ronnie Fell. 'Doc' Bulloch was a first-class wireless operator and we were delighted to have him on board. A young Canadian from Lachine, Quebec, his arrival increased our Canadian contingent to three.

'The upshot was that we volunteered as a full Halifax crew to transfer to 35 Squadron, the original Halifax Pathfinder Squadron and one of the four squadrons that formed the Pathfinder Force at the outset in August

1942. Our squadron commander Wing Commander Edmonds was quite happy to lose us since our tour on 10 was nearly finished anyway. He called us into his office and thanked us for all the sterling work we had put in and wished us all the best for our future with the Pathfinders. He added that he was recommending us all for 'gongs' - DFCS for the officers and DFMS for the NCOs. Norman Williams, already a DFM holder, after shooting down that Ju 88 would get a bar to the DFM. Finally the Wing Commander awarded us a week's leave before our transfer to 35 Squadron would take effect.

'In due course we reported with the rest of the crew to RAF Station Graveley, Cambridgeshire, where 35 Squadron was based in a pleasant rural area. Like Melbourne it was a wartime airfield and most of the accommodation was in Nissen-type huts. 35 Squadron, like 10, was formerly a Main Force Squadron in 4 Group stationed at Linton-on-Ouse in Yorkshire and was similarly equipped with Halifax bombers. When the Pathfinder Force was started in August 1942 under the Command of Air Vice-Marshal Don Bennett (formerly the squadron commander of 10 Squadron) with a squadron from each of the four main Bomber Groups, the chosen selection from 4 Group was 35 Squadron. They were moved lock, stock and barrel from their well-equipped base at Linton to Graveley, about ten miles south of PFF 8 Group HQ at RAF Wyton, near Huntingdon.

'Undoubtedly the so-called 'Battle of the Ruhr' was hotting up. [In June 1943 the Himmelbett Nachtjagd claimed a record 223 victories]. The Germans, realising that Bomber Command was aiming at the complete destruction of the Ruhr industrial powerhouses, had set up a ring of night fighter bases across Holland and eastern Belgium manned by Ju 88 and Me 110 night fighter squadrons ground-controlled using the latest radar equipment. Our bombers had to run the gauntlet en route to Ruhr targets and again on the return flight. At the target area they had to fly through a barrage of predicted heavy flak backed up by radar-controlled searchlights. Add to those the ever-present possibility of collisions with 700 bombers arriving and leaving the target area in the space of forty minutes or so, it was not surprising that aircraft losses were continuing to mount.

'At Graveley on 11 June at 1135 we took off on a one-and-a-half hour training exercise to Birmingham and surrounding towns. On return we were informed that we were required for ops that night. At the early evening briefing we learned that it was a very big operation on Düsseldorf, the administrative centre of the Ruhr, using a force of 860 heavies [including for the first time, more than 200 Halifaxes].[20] Having virtually completed our H2S training we were at last given the role of one of the primary markers immediately behind the Mosquitoes using 'Oboe'. We took off at 2333 – it was a very bright moonlight night – again in HR798 and it turned out to be a disastrous trip for us.[21]

'Twenty miles from the target we were attacked by two Me 110 night fighters in quick succession. In the opening burst from the first one a cannon shell went through the mid-upper turret and out the other side catching 'Des' Smith a glancing blow at the back of his skull on the way. The impact damaged his optic nerve and he was temporarily blinded. In a way he was lucky because he was bending down to pick up something when the shell hit his head. Had his head been in the normal position the shell would probably have killed him outright. The second fighter came in for the kill and its first burst of fire severely damaged the rear turret, badly wounding Norman Williams in the legs and abdomen. Despite this he continued to give the skipper directions to evade further attack.

'The first fighter came in for the second time, its burst of fire hitting our aircraft in several places and causing the starboard wing to catch fire. As it turned away, 'Norm' opened fire with his four Brownings and scored a direct hit from close range, the fighter going down in flames. By then we were less than ten miles from the target with the wing still on fire. The skipper gave the order to jettison the bomb load and then he put the aircraft into a steep dive at speed and succeeded in putting out the fire. As we turned for home the second fighter attacked once more, with Norman still giving evasion instructions. Finally, as it came in, Norman got it in his gunsight and pressed the firing button. The outcome was that the fighter blew up, so close that our aircraft was rocked by the blast. Norman yelled out, "Got the bastard, Skipper." Only when we had passed the Dutch Coast would Norman allow anyone to help him. Wally Trask and I made our way to the rear of the aircraft and we found that the damage to the turret doors was so bad that we had to use the aircraft axe to chop them open and get Norman out. We carried him carefully to the 'Rest Position' in the centre of the fuselage and

---

20 Another 76 aircraft consisting entirely of experienced Pathfinder Crews using the Mk. II H$_2$S set out for Münster. The raid, which lasted less than ten minutes, was accurate and much damage was caused to railway installations and residential areas of the city. Five aircraft were lost.

21 A curious haze made visibility difficult at Düsseldorf and an 'Oboe' Mosquito that inadvertently released a load of TIs fourteen miles north-east of the city caused part of the Main Force to drop its bombs in open country.

laid him down. By then, although still conscious, he was getting weaker and was beginning to feel the pain. With the Skipper's approval I went to the first aid box, got out the hypodermic of morphine and gave 'Norm' a shot in his rump. Coincidentally, just a week or so earlier we had been briefed on the contents of the First Aid box and how to use them in an emergency. The morphine soon took effect and 'Norm' was virtually comatose for the rest of the trip. We were not yet out of the wood however, because in the light of our heavy landing from the Wuppertal trip the engineer made an inspection of the landing gear through the floor hatch which revealed that the port undercarriage was damaged and the port tyre had burst. We were faced with a similar landing problem, but this time we were aware of the damage before touchdown.

'We had radioed ahead to notify base of the severe injuries to both gunners and an ambulance was standing by to rush them to hospital, but first the skipper had to get the aircraft safely to the ground. He did this by touching down on the starboard wheel and holding the aircraft to that side until its speed had been reduced sufficiently for its weight to be distributed to the port wheel as well. Once again the aircraft slewed away to port and came to rest on the grass. It was a superb feat of airmanship on the part of the skipper. The ambulance arrived in a matter of seconds and both gunners were speedily on their way to the RAF Hospital at Ely, Cambridgeshire, where he was to remain for two months.

'At our debriefing the skipper and I gave a full account of the night's happenings. The next day we were sent for by the squadron commander, Wing Commander 'Dixie' Dean. He was highly complementary to the whole crew in the actions we had taken in the face of adversity and informed us that he was recommending Norman Williams for a CGM (Conspicuous Gallantry Medal), the highest award for a non-commissioned officer other than the VC, for his tremendous bravery, devotion to duty and consideration for the rest of the crew.'

The archetypal Australian war hero, the anti-authority larrikin Williams' laconic comment when they told him of his CGM was that 'any one of the other chaps should have received it'. The medal made him Australia's most decorated flying NCO. The crew gave him the bomber's turret door, which contained thirty-seven bullet holes. 'I was told I would have got the Victoria Cross if I had died,' he said in 1992.

In David Codd's humble opinion his skipper's part in the action should have been rewarded with a Bar to his DFC at least, 'but perhaps we were too modest in our account of the operation to impress to that extent!'

'Two other crews of 35 Squadron were not so lucky. Flight Lieutenant Stanley George Howe DFC's crew and Pilot Officer George Racine Herbert DFM's were both shot down by night fighters over Holland on the trip to Münster. Howe and Herbert both lost their lives but the rest of Howe's crew and two of Herbert's crew survived to become PoWs. One of the latter, Pilot Officer Archibald Wallace, made a daring run for freedom but was captured trying to get across the Pyrenees into Spain.'

Thirty-eight aircraft – twelve of them Halifaxes – failed to return.[22] At Düsseldorf 130 acres were claimed destroyed. It was estimated that over 1,200 people were killed, 140,000 were bombed out and scores of other buildings and 42 war industries were destroyed or seriously damaged. At Snaith three Halifax IIs on 51 Squadron were missing. 'Y-Yorker' flown by Flight Sergeant J.H. Collins was hit by anti-aircraft fire from a British convoy in the North Sea while homebound and was ditched in the water about ten miles off Sheringham on the Norfolk coast. The local lifeboat went out but the six survivors were rescued by another vessel. Flight Sergeant 'Jimmy' Anderson's crew were all killed when their Halifax crashed in Holland. The crew on 'D-Donald', which was shot down by flak, had better luck. Flight Sergeant K.J.S. Harvey the pilot, his American flight engineer Flying Officer D.S. Roberts USAAF and the rest of the crew survived but were taken into captivity. Three Wellington X crews on 429 'Bison' Squadron RCAF and nine other 'Wimpys' failed to return. A Canadian Wellington on 431 'Iroquois' Squadron RCAF, which landed safely at Oulton airfield in Norfolk, collided with a Halifax on 427 'Lion' Squadron RCAF while taxiing which took the 'Iroquois' Squadron's total losses to three.

In view of their 'hair-raising experience and the loss of two gunners', Cobb's crew were granted four days' Special Leave. 'In RAF parlance,' continues David Codd, 'this was known as a 'Shaky-do' leave, this being a narrow escape from the 'chop', which hardly needs explaining! At least all our crew had survived. I enjoyed four days at Bournemouth as usual with some swimming and a few games of snooker with my Dad. I also managed a dinner date at the up-market Swiss restaurant with my special friend Margaret, who a few years later would become my wife. The company was good but the food not very special. After all, what could one expect when a

---

22 Five of the fourteen Lancasters lost were from 12 Squadron at Wickenby, which reported the worst loss rate suffered by the squadron in a single night for the whole of 1943. Only 3 men survived from the 35 missing air crew.

restaurant could not legally charge more than the maximum controlled price of five shillings per head?

'Returning to Graveley on 15 June my first priority was to enquire how our two injured gunners were faring. The news was reassuring. For the first twenty four hours Norman Williams had been fighting for his life and at one point a priest was called in to administer the last rites. They hadn't reckoned on 'Norm''s fighting spirit. Though weak, he was beginning to respond and the prognosis became good. In time he was expected to make a full recovery, hopefully to return eventually to flying duties. 'Smithy' was getting over his ordeal but there was a major problem with his eyesight from the damage to the optic nerve – he was not yet able to see anything. In due course he would be transferred to a special unit at St. Hugh's, Oxford, for an operation which would restore his sight but leave an impaired visual field. It would be more than six weeks before he could leave hospital and though allowed to remain in the RAF he would be barred from operational flying. After training he became an 'Oboe' controller and was commissioned.

'The following day, 16 June, we were in action as a complete crew, Flight Lieutenant M.A. 'Tony' Sachs DFM and Flight Sergeant J.E.S. Matthews having joined us as rear gunner and mid-upper gunner respectively. Sachs, who it will be remembered took part in the raid on the *Scharnhorst* on 24 July 1941, had flown his first operational tour on Whitleys followed by a spell as an instructor at Gunnery School and he had even flown a daylight operation to Brest in a B-17 Flying Fortress.

'At 2250 hours we were airborne on yet another op, to Cologne carrying 6 x 500 lb HE bombs plus containers of sky markers and flares. 'Ty' Cobb had been promoted from pilot officer to flight lieutenant and appointed Deputy Flight Commander of 'A' Flight. It was unusual for an officer to jump two ranks in one swoop but the heavy losses of 35 Squadron crews in recent weeks had resulted in a shortage of really experienced pilots. 'Ty' had all the right credentials for the job – an exceptional and fearless pilot with organisational ability and survivor of forty operations in one year. There could be no better choice. The trip, as expected, involved plenty of corkscrewing to dodge the night fighters and heavy flak. When we reached the target we found it obscured by 10/10ths cloud, as forecast – hence the sky markers. Bursts of heavy flak came uncomfortably close on the final straight and level run-in to the target. The first clutch of sky markers was clearly visible and we had no difficulty in dropping our bomb load on them, at the same time releasing our own sky markers. As we turned away onto our course to the Dutch Coast the fuselage received a hit below the mid-upper's position. Fortunately no-one was injured but when we eventually landed back at Graveley we found a gaping hole in the lower fuselage on the starboard side. We were fortunate to escape so lightly. Sixteen aircraft were lost on this operation – it would have been more if the skies had been clear. For once in a while all the 35 Squadron aircraft returned safely. Both our spare gunners acquitted themselves well.'

On the night of 28/29 June 'Ty' Cobb and his crew, flying Halifax HR850 'A-Able', returned to Cologne. Flying Officer Len Whitley accompanied them as 'second dickie'. 'A-Able' unfortunately was one of 25 aircraft – ten Halifaxes, eight Lancasters, five Stirlings and two Wellingtons – that failed to return; shot down by flak fourteen miles from the target. It was David Codd's 42nd trip. A German officer who spoke reasonably good English informed the seven surviving crew after capture that Nelson Cobb, who three months earlier had celebrated his 21st birthday, had been killed; he showed them some slightly burnt identification photographs. 'We were all thunderstruck at the sad news,' recalled David Codd, 'particularly since 'Baldy' Baldwin the engineer assured us that the skipper had apparently been ready to bail out. One possibility was that the aircraft blew up just as he was leaving it. The bombs had been fused by the bomb aimer before we received the direct hit and the TIs were fitted with a barometric fuse which ignited them at about 3,000 feet above the ground and they then dropped slowly to the ground on a small parachute to become markers for the Main Force. It is possible that our aircraft had dropped to 3,000 feet and blew up just as the skipper was about to leave. Another possibility is that he had bailed out successfully but was hit by bits of the aircraft as it hit the ground and exploded. Skipper's parents, the Reverend Herbert and Mrs Cobb, came over from Canada after the war and saw the priest and the lady who had found the remains.'

David Codd spent the rest of the war in PoW camps where his piano and organ playing were much in demand.

Norman Williams returned to Australia in April 1944 and was posted as a tutor at the air gunnery school in Cressy, Victoria. He refused to go, requesting an active posting instead. He became a belly gunner on an RAAF B-24 Liberator bomber on 23 Squadron RAAF in the Northern Territory and on Morotai. He joined the headquarters of 81 Wing RAAF in Japan after the war ended as part of the occupying forces. By then a flight lieutenant, he was demobilised in May 1948. He returned to Australia, taking a soldier's settlement block near Wakool, New South Wales, on the Murray River, developing a rice farm which doubled as a nature reserve. In 1951 he had married Maisie Lamont. Their farms resembled a cross between a rice farm and a nature reserve. Their main concern was always to protect the habitat of hundreds of bird and marsupial species. 'Norm' returned to the RAAF in 1952 with a short-service commission, serving as an air traffic controller during the Malayan Emergency and Korean War. He finally returned to Australia in April 1954, resigned his commission as an acting squadron leader in September that year and lived quietly on his Murray Valley soldier's settlement farm block. There he remained tight-lipped about his military feats and experiences, but his fighting spirit and anti-bureaucracy tendencies bubbled over from time to time, particularly when the NSW government tried in the 1950s to permanently drain Christies Creek, which ran through his beloved rice farm-cum-wildlife sanctuary. Bitterly opposing the plan because of the effect it would have on local wildlife, he successfully staged what today would be called a sit-in. In his later years he derived great pleasure from building a runway long enough to land a Boeing 747 and then flying with his son Bill in ultralight aircraft.

'Norm' was able to visit the village where their Halifax crashed and he located a woman who had found the remains of the skipper's body and the village priest who had organised a local burial. The main part of our bomber had crashed onto a road quite close to the village and bits of it were scattered over a wide area. Just about every window in the village was blown out by the explosion. Norman was able to fill a kitbag with pieces of metal from the bomber and had them melted down and made into a model of the Halifax.[23]

---

23 'Norm' Williams died peacefully at Barham, New South Wales, on 30 June 2007 aged 92. He was survived by his wife and their three children, Denise, Bill and Catherine and their families.

Chapter 4

Final Flight

Squadron Leader Francis John Hartnell-Beavis

John Hartnell-Beavis was born in Hong Kong on 8 June 1913, where his father was practising as a solicitor, educated at Uppingham School, and later spent nine months at Grenoble University and nine months at Freiburg University in the Black Forest, living with a German family. After training and qualifying as an architect at the Architectural Association in Bedford Square, he worked for two years for Sir Herbert Baker & Scott in London, until war was declared. He flew Blenheims on 82 Squadron, suffering appalling injuries in a crash landing in R3759 on Hendon aerodrome on 9 June 1940 after the aircraft was struck by lightning. His navigator Sergeant Phipps lost both his legs. After a long recovery Hartnell-Beavis flew Halifaxes on 76 Squadron at Linton-on-Ouse from mid-February to 4 May 1943 before joining 10 Squadron at Melbourne, twelve miles south-east of York. By July 1943 he was at the end of his second tour, having flown 25 ops, 5 more than the required 20 for a second tour. On 24/25 July 'Bomber' Harris, AOC Bomber Command, launched the first of four raids, code-named 'Gomorrah', on the port of Hamburg. Led by H_2S PFF aircraft, 740 out of 791 bombers rained down 2,284 tons of high explosive and incendiary bombs in two and a half hours on the suburb of Barmbeck, on both banks of the Alster, on the suburbs of Hoheluft, Eirnsbüttel and Altona and on the inner city. The advantages enjoyed by Kammhuber's 'Himmelbett' system, dependent as it was on radar, had been removed at a stroke by the use of 'Window'. The German fighter pilots and their Bordfunkers were blind. Twelve bombers were lost in the action: four Halifaxes, four Lancasters, a Wellington and three Stirlings. When dawn came on 25 July, a heavy cloud of dust and smoke hung over Hamburg and remained above it throughout the hot summer day which followed, obscuring the sun and seeming to the wretched inhabitants of the city to portend yet more devastation. That night, 25/26 July, when bad weather over north Germany prevented all but a handful of Mosquitoes bombing Hamburg, 'Window' was still effective and so 705 heavies – 294 Lancasters, 221 Halifaxes, 104 Stirlings, 67 Wellingtons and

19 Mosquitoes, were dispatched to Essen. Because of the rivalry with the 'Timber' crew, Hartnell-Beavis hoped to get one ahead of them since they were not scheduled to fly the operation. His crew on 25/26 July comprised 31-year-old Pilot Officer Cecil Earl 'High' Hightower RCAF, born at Clover Bar, Alberta, flight engineer; Pilot Officer Wilton 'Jonah' Jones the 34-year-old navigator; Pilot Officer Douglas Baldwin Ackerley, the 22-year-old bomb aimer; Sergeant Raymond A. Smith, radio operator; Sergeant William 'Al' Collins the 21-year-old mid-upper gunner and Flying Officer George Downey the 36-year-old tail gunner.

About mid-February 1943 I was posted to A Flight at 76 Squadron at Linton, not far from York. My CO was Leonard Cheshire, who later received the VC and became quite famous having completed about four tours of operations and survived unscathed. He used to drive around the aerodrome most mornings and sometimes took me in his car, to talk to all the ground crews out at dispersal points. He seemed to know all their names, very often christian names as well and something about their families and as I believe there were about 800 personnel on this Station this was no mean feat. I asked him how he remembered all this information and he said that he had no difficulty at all as he happened to have a photographic memory.

Linton was a pre-war station and I was billeted with one or two others in very comfortable married quarters, solid brick houses and a welcome change from the wooden huts I had been used to.

My crew and I flew to Nuremberg on our first operation, a nine hour round trip, then to Cologne two nights later and then to St. Nazaire the following night, which was well known as a cushy trip. On our way to St. Nazaire, with about fifty miles to go, we could see the flak exploding like glittering fireworks at about our level and my new engineer who had been standing behind my seat started to get extremely agitated and shouted down the intercom, 'We can't go in there Skipper, it's absolute murder.' I told him to shut up but he carried on shouting down the intercom, getting more and more excited and begging me to turn back and was obviously upsetting the rest of the crew. I called up the navigator and mid-upper gunner to get hold of him and keep him quiet, which they did by taking off his oxygen mask and intercom mike and we carried on to line up for our bombing run.

High level flak from a distance on a clear night always looked fairly alarming and dense and always at one's exact height. However, as you flew into it, it always seemed to me to thin out and only very occasionally did one feel the bumps of a near burst and even more occasionally the rattle of flak on the fuselage itself.

During the bombing run one had to fly as straight and level as possible, while the bomb aimer watched the target below creeping along the parallel wires of his bomb sight and gave instructions to the pilot by saying 'Left, left' rather quickly or 'Ri-i-i-ight,' rather slowly and 'Steady, steady' and then 'Bombs gone'. You had to continue to fly straight and level for another twenty seconds or so to enable your camera in the fuselage pointing downwards to take a photograph of your bomb bursts, the illumination for the camera being provided by the photoflash which was dropped at the time of bombing.

On the return from St. Nazaire my crew were unusually silent; normally after a bomb run and turning away from the target area, everybody started jabbering down the intercom and one's nerves became more relaxed. We were all a bit shattered by my engineer's loss of control and after we landed I took him aside and said, 'Although I ought to report you for losing your nerve over the target area, I will give you one more chance, but if you upset the crew on our next trip as you did on the last one, I will have to report you to the CO, who will take you off flying duties.' Though obviously still very shaken, he was grateful and promised that it would never happen again.

Three days later we were sent to Hamburg, together with about 800 other aircraft, on a very heavy raid. The flak over Hamburg was always particularly dense and I had instructed the rest of the crew to take extreme measures to control the engineer should he go to pieces again. In the event, even though the flak was as thick as ever, he behaved perfectly and kept very quiet, not even joining in the usual babble of conversation on leaving the target area.

He told me later that he was absolutely terrified on the first few raids and it took him about six trips to get used to seeing the flak and fireworks. I felt very sorry for him, but glad that I did not have to report him for 'Lack of Moral Fibre' – LMF as they call it – as this was usually a court martial offence. The Air Ministry took the view that if they spent thousands of pounds on training an air crew up to operational standard, it was money wasted if the they failed them.

On 27 March we flew to bomb Berlin, the flight lasting seven hours fifteen minutes. Two days later we were sent to bomb it again, even though the weather was appalling. I never did find out why it was so important to repeat the attack. On the second trip we were climbing through thunderstorms and the turbulence was particularly violent, especially in cloud which was solid up to about 16,000 feet, when we appeared to get flipped over onto our back; all the instruments went haywire and I instinctively hauled back on the stick, half looped out and lost about 8,000 feet before regaining control. I didn't know what damage had been done to the aircraft as many of the instruments were on the blink, so turned back to base, jettisoning the bombs probably over the North Sea, I don't remember. I often think of the strength of the Halifax which could do a half loop with a full bomb load and possibly a ton of ice on the wings without breaking up!

I found that night bombing trips really suited my temperament, particularly on clear nights, flying at about 20,000 feet well above the clouds, the tops of which were illuminated by the moon, trimming the aircraft to fly dead straight and level and setting the Sperry gyro so as to fly hands and feet off. We would drone on for hour after hour, listening to Ivy Benson and her all-girls band which was one of our favourite orchestras at the time, which 'Smithy' my wireless operator would tune in to and connect to the intercom. Vera Lynn was another of our favourites. You could carefully adjust the throttle controls so that the engines were all perfectly synchronized and with the aircraft as steady as a rock you could well have been sitting in an armchair on the ground.

One always flew operations at the maximum height possible; most Halifaxes could get up to about 20,000 feet with a full bomb load, although they varied considerably. I always did a shallow dive over the target area, to build up speed and minimize the time spent amidst the flak and on the return trip would trim the engines for maximum economy by turning the props to full coarse pitch and giving fairly high boost so as to be able to close the throttles as much as possible while still maintaining adequate cruising speed. It would also help if you could get the aircraft 'on the step', as it was called, which meant building up speed in a shallow dive to say 17,000 feet and very slowly levelling off while slowly closing the throttles. We usually had a competition running as to who could return with the most fuel in their tanks.

While we usually bombed from about 20,000 feet, the Lancasters were always above us. The poor old Stirlings could only reach about 14,000 feet and we could see them silhouetted against the target fires below us as we rained down our bombs through them. I never heard how many Stirling casualties there were arising out of this practice.

Halifax taking off on a night operation to Germany.

Halifax 'G-George' on 428 'Ghost' Squadron RCAF in October 1941.

A Halifax Mk.II crew on 76 Squadron pose with a loaded bomb trolley at Middleton St. George in October 1941.

Halifax crew on 76 Squadron boarding B.II Series I MP-B at Middleton St. George.

Flying Officer (later Wing Commander)
Peter Stanley James DFC.

After a number of inconclusive night raids on the harbour at Brest, Operation Veracity, the major daylight operation against the *Scharnhorst* and *Gneisenau* (in dock to the left of the picture while behind the second Halifax the *Prinz Eugen* lies along the quay), went ahead with forty-seven Halifaxes, Stirlings and Manchesters on 18 December 1941. Daylight was considered essential to ensure a reasonable chance of hitting these pin-point targets. Bombing from 16,000 feet, some hits were claimed on the sterns of both vessels, but six bombers were shot down, mostly by fighters. On 30 December, in the last raid of the year, sixteen Halifaxes tried again to cripple the warships during a second daylight operation, but the results could not be accurately assessed. This time the defences claimed three of the attackers.

Wing Commander James talks to employees at a Rotol airscrew factory in the Midlands following the raid on the *Scharnhorst*.

Halifax Mk.II Series I W1170/U on 462 Squadron RAAF taxiing out at Fayid, Egypt, for a night raid on Axis positions in North Africa shortly after the formation of the squadron when Nos. 10/227 and 76/462 combined squadrons were merged at Fayid on 7 September 1942.

B.Mk.II Series Is on 35 Squadron at Linton-on-Ouse preparing for a night sortie. The Series I (Special), an interim design which featured a streamlined Tollerton fairing (named after Tollerton Aircraft Services, which manufactured it) in place of the front turret – one of a number of stop-gap modifications introduced in late 1942 to make the aircraft more aerodynamic.

Mk.II Series Is ZA-F AND ZA-S on 10 Squadron at Melbourne gain height in the failing evening light for a raid on Turin.

A weary crewmember on 405 'Vancouver' Squadron RCAF sips a cup of hot tea after returning from a raid, July-August 1942.

Ground crew and mechanics on 77 Squadron get a well-earned 'cuppa' from the NAAFI wagon after a long day of repairs and maintenance at RAF Elvington in 1942.

American aircraft production representatives during a tour of the English Electric factory at Preston in the autumn of 1942. Halifax II DT567 MH-F and Pilot Officer Alan Lionel Holmes crew were lost on a mine-laying sortie while operating on 51 Squadron at Snaith on 7/8 March 1943.

Wing Commander Gerry Warner and crew on 78 Squadron at Linton-on-Ouse in March 1943.

Sergeant Norman Francis Williams CGM DFM*
RAAF.

The Battle of the Ruhr was well underway when this photograph was taken of B.II Series I W7805/MP-M on 76 Squadron, being bombed-up at Linton-on-Ouse on 3 April 1943. That night, Bomber Command launched its third raid in a month against Essen, inflicting considerable and widespread damage, at a cost of twenty-one of the 348 bombers dispatched. Twelve Halifaxes, including this one, failed to return and three more crashed over Britain.

On 27 May 1943 a special presentation was made to 427 Squadron at Leeming when the Canadian unit was adopted by Metro-Goldwyn-Mayer Studios in Hollywood, California. Mr Samuel Eckman Jr., Managing Director of MGM in England, attended and the 427 commanding officer, Wing Commander Dudley Burnside, accepted MGM's kind offer to adopt the 'Lion' Squadron. Halifax B.Mk.V DK186 ZL-L was painted with nose art featuring the MGM lion flying while holding a bomb between its paws and was named *London's Revenge*. After the adoption, squadron artist Sergeant E.A. Johnson chalk-marked the name *Lana Turner* ('L for Lana'). *Lana* flew the first operation on 29/30 May 1943, when sixty-three aircraft attacked Wuppertal. On this operation the Halifax was flown by Dudley Burnside. The Halifax completed twenty-six operations, the last on 25/26 November 1943 when seventy-three aircraft attacked Frankfurt. Transferred to No. 1664 and then 1667 Heavy Conversion Units, DK186 was damaged when it taxied into a ditch on 22 April 1944 and was later scrapped.

Halifax B.Mk.II Series I BB324 ZA-X with nose art *Haigs For Victory* on 10 Squadron at Leeming which was lost with Sergeant Robert Mitchell Pinkerton's replacement crew off the Dutch coast on 23 June 1943 while returning from a raid on Mulheim. Sergeant Frank Holmes, the flight engineer, was found and buried. A month later Sergeant Fred T. Nuttall and Sergeant John Conway were washed ashore on the same Zandvoort beach.

Over Cologne on 28/29 June 1943 B.Mk.II HR837 NP-'F for Freddie' on 158 Squadron had a bomb pass right through the fuselage without exploding. Flight Sergeant D. Cameron and his crew made it safely back to Lissett with a hole in the fuselage measuring 5 feet by 4 feet. HR837 was repaired and flew a further eleven operations on the squadron before going to 1656 Heavy Conversion Unit. It was SOC on 11 January 1945.

At 0426 hours on 26 July 1943 Flight Lieutenant Colin McTaggart 'Mick' Shannon DFC RAAF on 76 Squadron crash-landed Halifax V Series I (Special) DK148/MP-G at Holme-on-Spalding-Moor. On approach to Essen the port inner engine appeared to have been damaged by shrapnel as vibration set in. Shortly after bombing, at 17,000 feet, the propeller on the port inner became uncontrollable, eventually separating from the engine and slashing into the aircraft's nose. The impact caused a loss of control and when Shannon brought *Johnnie the Wolf* back to level flight it was discovered that Sergeant G.W. Waterman, the mid-upper gunner, had bailed out. The broken wooden propeller blades lessened engine damage but in this case the damage sustained in flight, plus that of the crash-landing, rendered the Halifax a write-off. Two weeks later, on the night of 9/10 August, Shannon and crew failed to return from the raid on Mannheim. All were killed.

Above and right: On 27 September 1943 a Halifax on 58 Squadron flown from RAF Holmsley South by Flying Officer Eric Leeming Hartley was shot down during a U-boat patrol in the Bay of Biscay when he attacked U-221 in the Atlantic 400 miles south-west of Ireland. Hartley, who was on his 28th anti-submarine patrol, dropped eight depth charges that sank the submarine with the loss of all hands, including Kapitänleutnant Hans-Hartwig Trojer, *Ritterkreuz*, [picture 21a] who was known as 'Count Dracula' because he was born in Transylvania. Hartley and five crew were able to scramble into the inflatable life-raft, which had inflated on impact.

Following their briefing, Halifax crews on 76 Squadron board their transports at Holme-on-Spalding-Moor, Yorkshire, to be driven to their dispersals in preparation for a raid on Kassel on 22/23 October 1943. It was to prove the most devastating delivered on a German city since the 'firestorm' raid on Hamburg the previous July.

Halifaxes on 76 Squadron taxing out for the raid on Kassel on 22/23 October 1943.

Above: Work being carried out on the port engines of a Halifax B.II.

Right: Cleaning the front guns on a Halifax B.II.

Halifax crews
before an
operation.

Flying Officer R. 'Jimmy' Wakeman DFC's crew on Halifax B.Mk.III NP931 on 640 Squadron at RAF Leconfield in December 1944.

B.Mk.VII *Ferdinand II* on 432 'Leaside' Squadron RCAF at East Moor with eighty ops signified on the bomb log.

A Halifax is silhouetted against the evening sky as it waits to take off for a raid on Hamburg.

Canadian ground crew sitting on the nose of *The A Train* on 424 'Tiger' Squadron RCAF at Skipton-on-Swale.

On 4 April we flew from Linton to Kiel, our eleventh operation and while flying over the target area at about 19,000 feet we were hit by a bomb from above, obviously from a Lancaster. It dropped through the nose of our aircraft and amputated my bomb aimer's left leg below the knee while he was lying at the bombsight giving instructions on the run-up to the target. We gathered later that this was a small incendiary bomb.

The large hole in the nose left a hurricane blowing through the aircraft and we used up nearly all our fuel on the return trip to get back as quickly as possible. He was obviously in pain and moaned down the intercom. I got my navigator and wireless operator to carry him back to the bed in the rear of the aircraft and give him a shot of morphia. We always carried a first aid kit, which had about a dozen ampoules of morphia. You would stick the needle into the patient's arm and leave it there. I was in touch with my wireless operator through the intercom, who said that the first shot did not seem to help him much, so I told him to give another. He was losing a lot of blood although his thick flying suit did help staunch the flow. The wireless operator told me he was still in a lot of pain, so remembering my time in Colindale Hospital in the early days of continual pain, when morphia was such a relief, I told them to give him a third shot even though this could have been dangerous – but we thought he would probably die in any case before we got home.

I called up the tower and told them to have the ambulance waiting and managed to pull off a very smooth landing. They took him off and operated straight away, amputating his leg just above the knee and within six weeks he was out and about on crutches and used to come and see us off on future operations. The doc ticked me off for giving him a near lethal dose, but added that it might well have saved his life, as he did not wake up until after the operation and had been saved a lot of pain.

We flew one night to Le Creusot to bomb the Schneider Works, a fairly easy target and we were not expecting too much flak over the target area. On the run-in our 2,000 lb bomb hung up and in spite of making eight further runs over the target, amid curses from my crew and in spite of jinking up and down, I could not get rid of the damn thing and had to return to base with the bomb still aboard. I was extremely nervous about the landing, as I had heard of bombs dropping off and exploding while landing the aircraft and killing all the crew. All went well however, apart from a severe ticking off to the ground crew, whom I blamed for the hang up.

I had become quite friendly with one of the WAAF intelligence officers who used to take debriefing on returning from an operation and had arranged a date with her in York for the following weekend when I was posted to 10 Squadron at Melbourne. Postings always seemed to happen very suddenly and I had certainly had my share, namely thirty-one different moves up to this date on 4 May 1943. I had been posted to take over 'A' Flight.

On 76 Squadron we had flown a different Halifax on each trip, although generally speaking I had managed to fly 'A for Alfred', on the nose of which had been painted a picture of King Alfred burning the cakes. Every time an aircraft completed an operation, the ground crew would paint a bomb on the port side of its nose. On 10 Squadron they always kept their own aircraft and the 'B' Flight commander had his family crest painted on his aircraft and it had already achieved about eight bombs. Not to be outdone I had the ground crew paint my family crest on my new aircraft, which is appropriately an inverted arrowhead rather like a bomb hitting the ground.

Two nights after bombing Duisburg, we went back to the Ruhr to bomb Bochum and on this trip we were coned by searchlights for six minutes and came back with a number of holes in the fuselage.

When we weren't operating or on call we often went round to the local to spend the evening drinking pints of beer and as each member of the crew had to get his pint round in we never drank less than seven pints and occasionally I got in a second round; however the beer at that stage of the war was so watered down that it had remarkably little effect. We would meet some of the operational crews' wives in the local sometimes, although they were not really supposed to live near the Station; I think it was felt that their presence would have an adverse effect on crews' morale. It was always a distressing experience for the Flight Commander to have to visit them the day after an operation to tell them that their husband had not returned.

On one occasion we were returning from an operation either in the south of France or northern Italy and on the way back I remember asking 'Jonah', my navigator, where we were and he replied, 'South of Paris'. The next thing I remember was being violently shaken and woken up by George, my rear gunner, who had crawled up from the rear turret. I looked at the altimeter and saw we were down to 6,000 feet; furthermore the balloon squeakers were going full blast and we realized we were flying through the London balloon barrage, well below balloon level!

Our balloons were fitted with a device which caused a squeaking noise on the intercom and I think they normally flew at about 8,000 feet over London. Although we carried balloon wire cutters on the leading edges of the wings, which in theory would cut the balloon cable if you flew into it and it was thrown off by the props, I never really trusted these gadgets. It was obviously no use trying to climb out of the barrage, so we just had to press on and keep our fingers crossed until we were out of the barrage area. After the squeakers died away, we jabbered away on the intercom and realized that we had all been fast asleep for about an hour or so, the plane flying on autopilot and slowly losing height; the Sperry gyros were not so efficient in those days as autopilots are nowadays. This was the only time I ever fell asleep while flying and it was odd that all the rest of the crew did the same; we must have had a bit of a party the night before.

There was a general feeling amongst the flying crews that after about twelve operations you should be lucky enough to survive the rest of the tour, as you learnt to take the right sort of evasive action to avoid night fighters and gained experience in escaping from being coned by searchlights. Although I have a reasonable imagination, I learnt to control it and not think too much about flak and night fighters. One also had to curb one's imagination about the devastating destruction that we were inflicting on the target below and it was only later when I was down below on the receiving end of a heavy bomber raid that I realized what the inhabitants of the Ruhr used to have to go through nearly every night.

One of the less pleasant jobs of being a flight commander was that you had to deal with people who had been put on a charge. They would be marched into your office the next morning by the warrant officer, who would report that they had been picked up the previous night drunk and disorderly or whatever and then he would wait for you to give sentence. I would always give the minimum sentence which was 'Admonished' or 'Severely Admonished' and they would march out again. I often wondered how they managed to get so drunk on the weak beer.

We did one or two trips over to the Baltic and Stettin and used to fly low level over Denmark which is very flat and one could fly quite safely at about 500 feet provided that there was a full moon – it was important to be able to see the other aircraft near you as we were often quite closely bunched together. The idea was to fly beneath the German radar warning system. I remember distinctly seeing lights going on in the houses and people coming out to see what was happening; you could see them standing in lighted doorways waving. The noise of a hundred or so four-engined bombers flying over at low level must have been quite shattering.

There were many near miss collisions particularly over the target area and one did sometimes see real collisions when both aircraft would collide and explode. While flying straight and level on the bomb run, the aircraft would be continually juddering as it flew through other people's slipstreams. Nowadays they make a great fuss if two aircraft fly within a few hundred yards of each other and I often wonder what modern controllers would think if they could have seen a radar plot of 1,000 aircraft bombing one target within one hour, all at roughly the same height!

On one occasion we were approaching the target area and George Downey, my rear gunner, who had eyes like a hawk, called up, 'I can see a single engine aircraft flying on our starboard side, I'm sure it's a 109 or an FW, I don't think he's seen us, shall I have a go at him?'

I thought for a moment and said, 'Better not George, as you might miss him and then he'll probably come and get us.'

'He's a sitting duck, Skipper, I couldn't possibly miss him.'

We were then entering the flak area and I was about to tell George to go ahead when he said it had peeled off; they very rarely entered the flak in the target area.

Although most of us smoked cigarettes in those days, I never allowed it in the aircraft while flying, although I believe some crews did smoke while on ops. This made landing all the more enjoyable: when you stepped out of the aircraft, you lit up and smoked about three cigarettes running, then more during debriefing, followed by bacon and eggs usually at five or six in the morning. We used to go to bed at about 8 am and get up in time for lunch.

For the last few weeks, during the very hot weather, I used to go off most afternoons to swim in the river about five miles from the aerodrome, leaving 'Timber' or 'Dave' in charge of the flight.

At about four o'clock in the afternoon of 25 July I was lazily swimming downstream when I saw an erk coming down the towpath on a bike and to my horror he stopped and called to me, saying I was wanted at the aerodrome immediately. As I knew very well I should be on the aerodrome looking after my flight I visualized a colossal 'strip' from the CO and asked the erk how he had known where to find me. He grinned and said: 'Well Sir, the CO gave me an idea as to where to look for you.'

My apprehension was increased and I hurriedly dressed, leapt into my van and told Vicki my WAAF driver to step on it.

To my surprise 'Eddie' [Wing Commander D.W. 'Eddie' Edmunds DFC, the CO] apologized to me for interrupting my afternoon and told me that as one of my pilots had gone sick for ops that night, would I produce another crew.

'Sure,' I said, 'if I can find the rest of my crew I'll go myself.'

I knew very well that officially I should not operate any more as I had finished my tour and was awaiting posting; however, my crew was pretty keen and as there was a lot of rivalry between 'Timber' and me and our respective crews, I thought this would be a good chance to get one ahead of him, as he was on leave.

By phoning up various haunts in York, I collected all of my crew except one and they managed to get to the station in time for briefing.

I borrowed a bomb aimer from another flight.

'Your target for tonight,' said the Intelligence Officer with a sly grin, 'is Essen,' a fact which I had already ascertained from the station commander, who said he was coming with me as second pilot, just for the ride. Officially the station commander was not supposed to do any more operations, but 'Jimmy' seemed to thrive on excitement and a trip to the Ruhr was meat and drink to him.

An American general, who was staying with him, also wanted to come, as he had not flown on night ops before, but Jimmy wouldn't allow it, so the general said he would wait up for our return.[24]

After briefing we assembled in the crew room and collected all our gear. While the others clambered into the transport, Vicki drove me off to collect the CO and on to 'V-Victor'. There we found the rest of the crew standing around having a last smoke while the armourers and fitters were checking the aircraft.

'V-Victor' (Halifax II Series I (Special) JD207) was a fairly new Halifax, slightly faster than my previous one and with a better ceiling.

Just as we were about to climb aboard a limousine arrived and the AOC from Group HQ got out, grabbed Jimmy and bundled him back into his car, so we took off with a reduced crew, consisting of our borrowed bomb aimer and my permanent crew; Smithy, my wireless operator, 'Jonah' my navigator, 'High' my Canadian engineer, 'Al' the mid-upper and George my rear gunner.

---

24 Brigadier General Fred L. Anderson commanding the US VIIIth Bomber Command flew as an observer on this raid. Canadian Flight Lieutenant 'Rick' Garvey's crew on 83 Squadron had the honour of flying the general on *Q-Queenie*.

George was a real character, who had run away to sea as a lad and sailed before the mast in a square rigger. His life had been one long adventure story and we used to listen to his yarns for hours over pints of bitter on the nights when we were not flying. He had had to knock about fifteen years off his real age to qualify for flying duties.

I considered him the best and most reliable rear gunner in Bomber Command and so did several others, including the flight commander at my last station who had tried to get George to leave me and join his crew.

George had two Jerries to his credit and was always icy cool when giving directions to me for avoiding action from night fighters or master searchlights.

'Just coming into the fighter zone,' came Jonah's voice over the intercom.

'OK, keep a good lookout everybody.'

We were still climbing and reached 20,000 feet as we saw the Dutch coast coming up.

'Should be able to reach 21,000 feet,' I said.

'Whizzo,' came from George.

'Another two minutes on this course, Skipper,' from Jonah.

At that moment I saw the Pathfinder's turning-point flare go down on our port bow and informed Jonah. He gave me my next course and I set in on the compass grid-ring, so we came abreast of the flare and turned onto the new course.

Already we could see the glow of the Ruhr, caused by the searchlights, Pathfinder flares, incendiaries burning on the ground and the layer of flak.

We were at 21,000 feet and 'Victor' was sluggish. I was flying straight and level to maintain height, as jinking, in my opinion, was unnecessary when 'Monica' (our night fighter detector) was switched on. Taking unnecessary avoiding action also lost one a lot of height and speed, which was so important on approaching the target area.

The intercom had been silent for some time, but now, as was always the case, everybody started to speak at once.

'Gosh, look at the searchlights; they've got more than ever!'

'There are six separate cones going, with about twenty searchlights to each one.'

'Look at that poor devil in the cone on our port beam – he's had it.'

Sure enough, he had 'had it'; they had been pouring flak into the apex of the cone and we could see him quite plainly, a tiny silver plane twisting and turning but seeming to remain stationary in the sky.

A bright yellow glow appeared and went down diagonally, very slowly, the cone gradually collapsing and following him down.

The flak layer, caused by countless little flashing stars, seemed to be slightly below us, covering heights from 15,000 to 19,000 feet at its densest; everyone who could see it, the bomb aimer, myself and 'High', commented on it, exaggerating its intensity. This was our usual custom, a game we'd play to try to put the wind up George, who couldn't see what lay ahead. George had nerves of steel and, I think, the hotter the reception, the more he enjoyed it.

We were now well in the searchlight area and I had picked a gap between two cones, flying on a course which would take me about five miles from the starboard cone and a mile from the port.

The machine on the port side, as we came abreast of him, was twisting and turning and we were watching him with interest; when suddenly, with no warning, we were temporarily blinded, as the whole cone switched across to us!

I had been taking slight evasive action, but I suppose as we appeared on the detector screen alongside their first victim, the operators thought we would be easier to hold.

'Hold tight all,' I yelled down the intercom, as I pushed the stick hard into a diving turn to the right.

We had been coned by searchlights several times before and had formed various conclusions and learnt several lessons.

Once caught and held, it was almost impossible to get out of the cone until you got away from the area. Even if you dived vertically downwards, as several people had tried, the searchlights had no difficulty in holding you. So the only course open was to attempt to avoid the flak, which was on its way up to you.

I had always adopted the same tactics, namely, dive 1,000 feet to port or starboard to gain speed and then turn onto different headings and hold each one for twenty seconds or so.

We could feel the four bumps as the flak got nearer and every now and then hear a series of 'crumps' which means that it is very near. After one particularly loud crump there was a rattle on the fuselage like hail and my heart skipped a beat.

I had my head well down in the cockpit so as not to be dazzled by the bluish-white light; my eyes were glued to the instruments and I was sweating like a pig as I hauled on the controls.

For the brief time one is caught in a cone (usually just a few minutes – our longest period was 7½ minutes) one lives a thousand ages and I cannot imagine anything more exciting. One's nerves are strung to maximum tension and every second seems an hour as one realizes that one is the visual target for a score or more gun crews.

Resisting the temptation to throw 'Victor' into the wildest acrobatics, I kept the air speed at 200 mph turning onto different headings, but all the time working my way in a certain direction, until at last, after just over three minutes, according to Jonah, the glare lessened, the 'crumps' became fewer and eventually the last light flickered out.

Remembering the ominous rattling, I called up everybody by name and told 'High' to check his instruments carefully.

'Hullo, Skipper, 'Monica's u/s,' came Smithy's voice.

'OK, keep an extra good lookout everybody.'

We had lost 3,000 feet of precious height and were well off course, so we came in to attack the target from the north-east instead of north-west and I felt some apprehension, picturing the 500-odd other aircraft flashing across our path in a series of near-misses.

'Hullo, bomb aimer, running up, bomb doors opening.'

'OK, Skipper.'

'Bomb doors open.'

'Left, left.'

'Steady, hold it.'

This was usually one of the tensest moments of any bombing raid, as you have to ignore the flak and fly as straight and level as possible, obeying the bomb-aimer's instructions. And yet, with full bomb load and bomb doors gaping wide, the aircraft is at its slowest and most vulnerable. However, I always took the view that as the run-up lasted only a few minutes, we could rely on our luck not to be hit at that time.

Also, I and some of my crew had felt all along that our luck was going to hold and had a sort of blind intuition that we'd finish our tour safely.

'Bombs gone.'

'Steady, steady.'

We had to keep her on course until the camera had recorded our aiming point and I held her steady with my left hand as I flicked up the bomb door lever with my right.

The red camera light flashed on and off and I pushed the nose down, going into a steep turn to the right, noting with satisfaction the ASI reading 220 mph.

We still had to pass through the searchlight area, but now we were light, had plenty of speed and had no difficulty in evading the master searchlights.

'Searchlight coming up astern,' said George.

I turned 90° to port, glanced left and saw the beam moving slowly along our original course, radar controlled.

'OK, Skipper, it's stopped. Now it's gone out.'

'How many fires, George?'

'Six large separate fires with a healthy red glow and a mass of incendiaries to the south of the target area. Smoke is up to our height. More incendiaries about ten miles south-west of target.'[25]

'Probably Jerry diversions.'

'PFF flares still going down. Four cones of searchlights.'

'Machine going down on our starboard quarter.'

I turned starboard and saw a yellow glow increasing in size and going down at a slant, like a very slow comet. We watched its leisurely progress in silence and after a few moments a series of sparks appeared and the glow split into two or three separate flames. You can never see parachutes at night unless you are very close. We always like to think they all got out, although in fact this is very rarely the case.

'Hullo, Skipper, turn on to 342°,' came Jonah's clear voice.

'OK.'

'We keep this course for eight minutes, if you can hold her at 180 mph.'

'OK Jonah, I'll keep her at 180 and 17,000 feet. Everybody keep a good lookout, as 'Monica's u/s.'

We had been flying steadily for about five minutes and everybody was slightly relaxed as the danger area was past. At this period you always experience a feeling of relief, your nerves return to normal and you get the feeling of having accomplished something; a similar sort of feeling, I imagine, as a mountaineer reaching the summit after a hard morning's climb.

'Just getting a fix, Skipper.'

'OK.'

I kept my eyes strained into the darkness ahead and above. 'Got a fix, Skipper. We're on time and right on track, in the middle of the stream.'

'Whizzo,' from George.

---

25 In all, 627 aircraft out of 705 despatched dropped 2,032 tons of bombs on Essen. Harris was not exaggerating when he said that 'they inflicted as much damage in the Krupps works as in all previous attacks put together'. Twenty-six aircraft: ten Halifaxes, seven Stirlings, five Lancasters and four Wellingtons were lost.

Suddenly, with no warning at all, our peace was shattered by a series of deafening crashes, which developed immediately into a loud roar. The plane rocked and pitched forward and I felt the stick go dead in my hands.[26]

'Christ, it's happened,' I thought. 'But it just can't be, it can't possibly happen to us.'

Long training came to my aid and although I felt like jelly inside I tried to keep my voice quiet as I came out with the formula, 'Prepare to abandon aircraft.' Not a sound from the intercom.

The cockpit was glowing bright yellow as the starboard wing had caught fire.

I knew a night fighter had scored a direct hit on us as I had seen a yellow stream of tracer spreading fanwise in front of us and below.

The roar of the flames increased and, although I knew it was useless, I cut the starboard engines and pressed the extinguishers.

The perspex around me was shattered and a hurricane was sweeping through the cockpit.

---

26   'V-Victor' had been attacked by Major Werner Streib of NJG 1 at Venlo. (On the night of 11/12 June Streib flew He 219A-0R2 Uhu (G9+FB) a prototype version of the Heinkel He 219 'Owl' and claimed to have shot down four Halifaxes and a Lancaster in only 30 minutes. However, when returning to Venlo Streib misjudged the landing approach and used the flaps at too high a speed. The Heinkel crashed and was written off on on landing, Streib and Unteroffizier Helmut Fischer his funker escaping with slight injuries). 'V-Victor' was his third victory of the night, the other two being a Stirling 11 kilometres north-east of Eindhoven and a Lancaster 10 kilometres north of Helmond, which took his total score to 61st Abschüsse. Often called 'Father of the Nachtjagd' Werner Streib, born on 13 June 1911 in Pforzheim, helped develop the operational tactics used by the Nachtjagd and with the likes of Wolfgang Falck made the Luftwaffe's night-fighter arm an effective fighting force against the bombing offensive. After a spell in banking and finance, Streib had joined the Wehrmacht as an infantryman. A transfer to the Luftwaffe as an observer in a reconnaissance unit followed and later he trained as a fighter pilot. In 1937 he was assigned to Jagdgeschwader 2 'Richthofen' at Jüterbog-Damm. He then became a Bf 110 Zerstörer pilot in Wolfgang Falck's ZG1 as the war began. The first of Streib's 66 Abschüsse and the only one in daylight was a Bristol Blenheim on 10 May 1940. Werner Streib ended the war as Inspector of the Night Fighters with the rank of Oberst and was the fourth highest-scoring night-fighter pilot with 67 Nachtjagd victories (including 30 Viermots) in 150 sorties with NJG1, plus one as Zerstörer in I./ZG1. He was awarded the Ritterkreuz with Eichenlaub and Schwerter. After the war he worked in the grocery business before joining the Bundeswehr on 16 March 1956. For three years he commanded the pilot school in Landsberg am Lech equipped with the T-6 Texan which was responsible for training the beginner pilots in the Luftwaffe. Streib's military career ended with his retirement on 31 March 1966. His last position was Inspizient Fliegende Verbände (Inspector of Flying Forces). He died on 15 June 1986 and is buried in Munich.

'Jump everybody,' I yelled, but felt that the intercom was dead.

Victor was going down steeply. I could see the altimeter unwinding fast and started to panic.

At that moment another loud bang and more tracer appeared ahead.

'The swine's following us down and with the flames for a target he can't miss,' I thought.

I really panicked this time and tried to heave myself out of my seat, but found I couldn't move and thought, 'Machine must be in a spin and I'm being held down by centrifugal force.'

I sat back resigned to stay in, relaxed and then realized that I was still strapped in!

I pulled the harness release, lurched forward and started to climb out of my seat, pulling myself up by the hand-hold above the windscreen. I got my right leg over the flap and undercarriage levers and was starting to get my other leg out when the hand-hold broke and I fell down the steps into the forward compartment, my left leg just coming free in time.

I crawled back to look behind my seat. 'High' was slumped down in such a position that I realized at once there was nothing I could do for him.

Back again in the forward compartment it was dark and my eyes, dazzled by the flames above, could see nothing.

I groped for my parachute pack, found it and like a clumsy fool, on picking it up, must have pulled the D-ring, as I felt the pilot chute jump into my face. I hugged it to my chest to prevent the main chute coming out of the pack.

I could now see dimly and instead of seeing the hoped-for cavity in the floor, I saw the escape hatch was partly open and somebody struggling with it.

Holding my pack under my right arm, I tried to pull the hatch upwards, but found it would not budge and then saw that it was being held down by a parachute pack, the harness of which went through the gap and presumably it was somebody's weight outside in the slipstream which was holding it down.

A concerted effort on my and the unknown person's part (I presumed it was Jonah or Smithy) freed the hatch and the pack whipped through the cavity.

I tried to hook my own pack onto my harness. The string tying the straps in place had broken and the straps were hanging behind my back. As I struggled to pull them over my shoulder to the front, my pack slipped from under my arm and I could see the white chute start to billow out in the airstream coming through the open hatch.

I got hold of one hook from the shoulder strap at last, pushed the white silk to one side and after what seemed an interminable time, found the corresponding hook of the pack and snapped it onto the harness.

I looked up, saw no movement in the navigator's position and thought, 'Thank God, everyone's gone.'

As I slid through the hatch, feet first, I was immediately jerked upwards violently and thought for a moment that my open chute had been caught on part of the aircraft.

This was not so however, as the deep roar died rapidly away and I looked down to see the last of 'Victor', both wings on fire, spiral down and hit the ground with a muffled explosion about five seconds later.

I was swinging violently from side to side and as I had only hooked one strap onto the pack I felt I was slipping out of my harness to one side. I tried to climb up towards the bottom of the pack to hook on the other strap. It was about four feet above my head. But I gave up as a numbing pain started in my right shoulder which had been previously damaged in a plane crash.

The swinging was lessening and I looked around. Below me the ground was plainly visible in the glow of the fire and I noticed I was drifting away from it.

I judged the ground to be about 300 feet below and there came the thought, 'In all probability, in a few seconds, I shall break my right leg when I hit the ground.;' my leg was still weak, having been broken twice in the above-mentioned accident and I was unable to flex the knee fully.

I took a grip as high up the strap as I could reach and held my right leg out in front.

As the ground started to rush upwards, I pulled on the strap and hit the ground fairly gently, landing on my left leg and rolling over backwards.

I got up, ran around my parachute, collapsed it and rolled it up in my arms.[27]

My heart was thudding and my breath coming in quick gasps, so I went over to a bush and sat down to think things over and give myself time to recover.

I had plenty to think about and it took a few minutes to compose myself.

After the roar of engines in my ears for so many hours, everything seemed very still and quiet, except for a steady drone high above in the starry sky, which was gradually lessening as my luckier companions, the other 500-odd aircraft, were winging their way home to bacon and eggs and a comfortable bed.

I thought of the American general, whom I would not meet in the briefing room; of Jimmy, the CO, who so nearly came as my passenger and what a God-awful row there would have been at Group if he had.

---

27   He came down on Kampina Heath north of Oisterwijk.

I thought of Vicki, my faithful WAAF driver, who in spite of all my injunctions to the contrary, was always out at dispersal with the van at 0300, 0400, 0500 hours, whenever we were due to arrive back from a trip. Sometimes she had to wait an hour, or longer, if we were forced to land away. She never missed meeting us and would be waiting tonight, perhaps hour after hour, for a crew who had made their last trip.

I thought of my coming ten days' leave and the posting to Transport Command for which I was hoping.

And then I started to think of my crew. How many had got away? I looked away to where my plane was still burning about a mile away, like an enormous red bonfire, sending sparks high into the sky and with pyrotechnics, Very lights and ammunition dancing around the flame. Who, besides 'High', were being cremated?

I had seen one and only one other parachute floating down besides mine, but the others could well have been lost in the darkness.

I got up, buried my helmet, parachute and battledress blouse and started out to look for the others. I soon gave this up as being hopeless and, remembering all the escape lectures, started to run away from the wreckage to put as much distance between me and any German search party there might be.

After about twenty minutes I stopped to review the situation.

Luckily I had been wearing rubber soled shoes, which made travelling fairly easy. I had Dutch, Belgian and French money and enough food for about a week in iron rations. I took off my heavy white sweater and rubbed it on the ground so that it was not so conspicuous in the darkness.

I found that my watch was smashed, a bullet having passed through the side of it causing a slight wound across my hand, but the hour hand was still on and showed a time of approximately 1330. As near as I could judge, I was near the Dutch-German border, either in Germany or Holland, so I took out my silk escape map, studied it and reckoned that my safest course would be to make for the north-west, to make sure of getting into Holland before daybreak.

The country appeared to be flat marshy ground, with small trees and bushes, divided by numerous small dykes about four feet wide into which I kept stumbling.

I made off at a fast walk and travelled for about two hours without seeing a house or farm. I was using the stars for guidance; although I had an assortment of small compasses, it was easier to glance at Polaris every now and then, instead of stopping and waiting for an oscillating compass needle to come to rest.

I was fairly fresh, as having operated the night before I had slept until 1330 in the afternoon the previous day and reckoned I was making a good four miles an hour.

Somewhere ahead of me I heard a clock strike four times and seemed to be approaching a town or village as the houses on either side of the road became more numerous.

I left the road and took to the fields to try to bypass the town, but to no avail, as I soon found myself in its outskirts and unless I retraced my steps, more or less had to go right through it.

I thanked God for my crêpe rubber soles as I padded noiselessly through the empty streets of a fair-sized town, which showed not a single sign of life: no lights, no sound, no movement.

I knew about the curfew and was a bit scared at first of meeting police or patrols and stopped at every street corner to investigate before crossing.

I came to the cathedral square and was so interested in the building that I walked right round it, thinking all the time that I must be crazy to be examining architecture when I should be running for my life!

After a while the buildings started to thin out and I was through the built-up area.

The road ran beside a large dyke or canal and I scrambled down the bank to fill my water bottle. The water tasted filthy, bitter and brackish.

It was starting to get light and high time to look for a wood in which to hide through the day.

I found a signpost which read 'Voor'. I knew this could not be a German name so now I knew for certain that I was in Holland, much to my relief.

Passing a cornfield I rejected the idea of hiding in the corn, thinking it might be awkward if they decided to reap the harvest that day.

Eventually, in almost broad daylight, I found a wood, not as thick as I would have liked, but I thought it would be unwise to travel further and crawled into it and settled down under some brambles. It was wet with dew, but I had thick long woollen underwear (we always wore them for night flying) and shirt, trousers and aircrew sweater, so expected to be warm enough. The clock struck five.

I woke up stiff, aching all over and very cold. The mosquitoes were buzzing around and had bitten my face, neck, hands and ankles. In fact they tormented me for the rest of the day.

That day was one of the longest I have ever spent.

I heard the clock strike seven – I'd been asleep for less than two hours.

There was a small clearing close by and I took off all my clothes, spread them out to dry and lay down in the sun to get warm, the mosquitoes not being so bad in the sunlight.

I must have dozed off, for when I came to I heard voices. I was a bit anxious in case I should be found with nothing on!

However, the voices went on and I discovered there was a road leading through the wood less than ten yards from where I lay.

I was not hungry yet, so contented myself with two Horlicks tablets and a drink of the brackish water I had collected during the night. I had only half a dozen cigarettes left and thinking it was no good rationing myself to one a day, I smoked the lot.

During the day an Me 110 circled the wood fairly low and I cowered under a bush, imagining that they were looking for me and my crew.

The day dragged on endlessly and it wasn't until the clock struck eleven that it became dark enough to start travelling. I had studied my silk map during the day and was appalled at the enormous distance which lay ahead – through Belgium, France and Spain; and I reckoned that the sooner I contacted the 'organization' the better. I knew I was in Holland, but where in Holland I hadn't an idea. Anyway I had decided to travel south and set off as fast as I could.

I passed some rather drunk farmers on the way, long after curfew time; luckily they didn't stop me. I covered about twenty-five miles keeping to small roads and lanes and eventually went to sleep under a haycock.

The next day, although I had intended to remain under cover, I was so bored that I set out about noon and went to one or two small farms to try to get help. When I told them who I was, speaking in German, they became scared and refused to help.

I slept that night in a barn on a pile of hay. It was so comfortable that I overslept and woke up to find a farmer looking at me enquiringly.

I tried to talk to him in German but he couldn't understand, so I mimed that I was eating a meal, by pretending to use a knife and fork and munching food, which he did understand and took me into his house, gave me a crust of bread and some buttermilk.

He didn't appear to be at all anxious, but his wife seemed nervous and waited around while I ate and then showed me the door.

I wandered on down the lanes all day. The weather was perfect and I was quite enjoying the experience, but rather lonely.

I called at one or two farms, ostensibly to ask for water (which they drew up from wells in a bucket suspended from a large beam like a see-saw) but really to try to contact the organization. At one farm I bought a farmer's light blue jacket so that I would not be so conspicuous. I saw it hanging up in the doorway and offered him ten guilders, which he seemed very pleased to have.

I had at last found out my whereabouts on the map, about thirty miles WNW of Eindhoven.

I passed an aerodrome and looked at the aircraft at dispersal longingly, but they were all well guarded. If I could only get into one of those I could be back in England in two hours! Instead of that, by the route I was taking it would probably take me six months! However, there wasn't a chance.

I spent the next night in a wood and the next day plucked up courage to go into a village and have coffee at a café. My iron rations seemed to satisfy my hunger all right, but it was company I craved. I knew it was reckless. I left without arousing suspicion, but I was pretty nervy and decided not to do it again.

So far I had not seen a single German.

I was looking unshaven and was very dirty, not having washed properly since I landed. I wanted a cigarette badly, but there seemed no hope of getting any. My right shoulder ached, especially in the mornings and I was feeling rather depressed.

I called at a large farm the next morning, but they couldn't help me. There were two Belgian lads working there and I had quite a long talk with them in French. They came across the frontier every day to work on the farm and said it was only four kilometres away, so I resolved to cross that night. They said it would be pretty easy.

I was approaching a village and as I entered it I thought I would try to get a shave and a wash. People had been eyeing me dubiously of late and I didn't blame them, feeling the quarter-inch stubble on my chin.

I had gone right through the village without seeing a barber, so resolved to call at a small house and picked one with a little garden in front, went down the path and knocked on the door.

It was eventually opened by some sort of official in a greenish uniform. He looked at me queerly as I asked in German if I could borrow his razor.

'*Eenglisch?*'

I nodded.

He took me by the arm, piloted me into a living room and proceeded to go through my pockets, fishing out compasses, maps, food, etc.

He went out of the room and I started to feel a bit apprehensive, opened the door to leave and met him coming out of the kitchen with his wife.

In slow, halting German, he explained that he would help me across into Belgium, but I was to maintain the utmost secrecy and not tell anyone afterwards about him helping me.

FINAL FLIGHT

'*Sonst* ...' and he drew his hand across his throat.

'At last,' I thought, 'I've found the Org.,' and was filled with relief.

His wife gave me a meal in the kitchen and I gave his children the sticky toffees I had been carrying in my pocket. They were delighted, as I suppose they were the first sweets they'd had for a long time.

During the afternoon a pal of my host's arrived and went into a discussion, none of which I could understand. Eventually he motioned me to follow and we went off down the road, me sitting on the carrier of his bicycle.

We came to a wood and he told me to get off and wait in the wood. I waited about half an hour while he waited on the road and thought to myself, 'now is the time to sneak off if I'm not quite sure of him.' However, he seemed genuine, so I waited until another man came along on a bike and stopped to talk to the one in charge of me.

Eventually he beckoned to me again and we carried on down the road to another village, which I reckoned must be on the frontier. We stopped and went into a large house and he took me to a room which looked suspiciously like a cell and told me to wait.

'He's gone to get me fixed up with papers,' I thought and sat down to wait.

After about twenty minutes nothing had happened and, growing apprehensive again, I went and opened the door.

To my horror, outside I saw a guard with a rifle slung over his shoulder and asked him what was going on.

'*Warte herein! Die Deutche kommen in einer halben Stunde.*'

The Germans were coming.

In a flash I realized the whole thing. My man had lost his nerve and betrayed me, bringing me to this place, which was, I imagine, the local police station!

I made a dash past the guard down the corridor and the guard gave a yell. Rounding the corner into the hall I was confronted at the main door by another sentry, who was in the act of unslinging his Tommy-gun.

I stopped and went back into the cell.

After what seemed an endless wait, I heard boots coming down the corridor. The door was flung open and I had my first sight of the field grey Luftwaffe uniform as two sergeants came in.

Komm!

We got into a saloon car, drove off to Eindhoven and got out at a large building with guards on the door. Inside the walls were covered with huge swastika flags, eagles and portraits of Hitler. I was now well and truly in the hands of the enemy.

Squadron Leader John Hartnell-Beavis was incarcerated in Stalag Luft III until the end of the war. Because he had studied architecture before the war he helped in the creation of the monument designed by Wilton Todd for the fifty escapers murdered by the Gestapo on 6 April 1944 following the Great Escape from Stalag Luft III by seventy-six airmen on the night of 24/25 March. This monument was named 'The Fifty' and was placed in the local cemetery near Stalag Luft III on the road leading to the entrance to the former camp. The three stone blocks with the fifty names were engraved by Dickie Head and Squadron Leader John Hartnell-Beavis. He died in July 2007.

Sergeant Ray Smith was the only other member of the crew to parachute to safety. He landed in a forest about five miles from Tilburg. There he received help from two English-speaking Dutch and was taken to Rotterdam. He was hidden in Holland at various places between 26 June and 9 October when he went to Paris by way of Amsterdam where he stayed until 14 October. He left Paris on 14 October and travelled to Bordeaux and Bayonne. Along with a few companions he reached Dax in southern France where he spent a day in a hotel. When they wanted to travel to the Irun in Spain by train they were warned in time that the train was full of enemy troops. They were able to hide underneath the train carriage by clinging onto the cross girders with their hands and feet. It was a hazardous journey but they reached Hendaye near the Spanish border, crawled from underneath and ran up the tracks in search of the train to Lisbon. It had already left so they spent the day hiding underneath a train again. In the end they were able to board a train to San Sebastián where they arrived on 16 October. Since they did not have any tickets they managed to get out of the station by walking through the goods entrance while wearing berets and overalls. In the main street they asked a man the way to the British Consulate. The man showed them the way and the next day they were taken to Madrid and from there to Gibraltar where they arrived on 25 October. Two days later Smith arrived in England.

John Hartnell-Beavis was awarded the Distinguished Flying Cross as per London Gazette *dated 15 October 1943. His Citation in* Air Ministry Bulletin *11720 stated: 'As captain of aircraft Squadron Leader Hartnell-Beavis has flown on many operational sorties and although his aircraft has, on several occasions, been hit by anti-aircraft fire, he has continued to display exceptional keenness. An excellent flight commander, his fine fighting spirit, courage and determination, have been an inspiration to the other members of his squadron.' In 1946 he married and settled in Totnes, where life was pleasant but work was scarce, so after a year they moved to Birmingham, where work was plentiful and stayed there for twenty years before settling in Lymington, Hampshire, starting his own architectural practice.*

Chapter 5

Warriors for the Working Day

On the night of 31 August/1 September 1943 622 bombers – 331 Lancasters, 176 Halifaxes, 106 Stirlings and nine Mosquitoes – assembled in a giant stream and headed for the 'Big City' once more. Three heavy bombing raids in ten days by Bomber Command on Berlin resulted in the loss of 137 aircraft and great loss of life to Berliners. It was but a prelude to sixteen major raids during 18/19 November 1943 to 24/25 March 1944 which have gone into history as the Battle of Berlin. One of the Halifax crews on 77 Squadron at Elvington that took part in many of these raids was JD462 'N-Nan' ('Naughty Nan') skippered by Flight Lieutenant Peter Cadman who hailed from Canterbury in Kent. Flying Officer Gerard 'Mac' McClorry, the navigator, was from Lancaster in Lancashire and Sergeant Harry 'Clay' Clayton, the bomb aimer, was from Wigan. Both were ex-policemen. Flight Sergeant Arthur 'Smokey' Powell, the wireless operator, came from Leeds; Sergeant William J.W. 'Scats' Batty, mid-upper gunner, was also from Leeds and Sergeant William F. 'Triv' Trivett, rear gunner, who relates the events of 31 August 1943, was a Londoner.

31st August: 0600 hours.
With hands behind his head Sergeant 'Triv' Trivett lay on his back staring up to the ceiling, listening to the fading pulsating roar of the low flying bomber aircraft that had awakened him. His immediate thoughts were of the previous night's events, on 30/31 August, when during a test run up of their aircraft's engines before take-off; one engine had overheated far in excess of the acceptance level. It was the port side engine which supplied energy to his rear turret. Despite frantic and heroic efforts by the ground crew to get them airborne, they had missed their deadline of extended take-off time and were ultimately 'scrubbed' off the night's flying operation when 660 heavies targeted the twin towns of Mönchengladbach and Rheydt; the first major attack on these cities since 11/12 August 1941. Over 2,300

buildings were destroyed. About half of the built-up area in each town was devastated. Twenty-five aircraft failed to return. Cadman's crew, who presented themselves back at Flying Control in full flying kit, were dejected and disappointed. So much effort had gone into the day's preparation by all trades for this operation and with the rest of the squadron airborne and on course for Germany they felt like imposters. Trivett's frustration showed to the extent that a veteran of two Bomber Command tours, now working in Flying Control, came over and placed his hand on his shoulder. 'Take a tip from me,' he offered, 'Don't ever get upset over being scrubbed from a flying operation. Remember, that could have been the op you were supposed to go missing!'

'The sound of the low flying aircraft's engines had died away,' recalled Trivett. 'I turned my head to look down the line of beds in this RAF aircrew Nissen hut. Three were empty. This was ominous and boded ill for the crew that had apparently gone missing on last night's raid on Mönchengladbach.[28] Their stay on the squadron hadn't been long – just two days – and they had gone missing on their first op. It wasn't an uncommon happening either. It was recorded your first five ops were to be your hardest, after which luck was needed in heavy doses. I tried hard to place the missing faces – but really, I hadn't had time to get to know them.

'Soon their kit bags and belongings would be removed to the guard room for safe keeping, to await the Padre's attention and his helpers to sort any dubious correspondence, leaving only personal effects if needed to be sent home. Soon the next of kin would be receiving those dreaded telegrams; "The Air Ministry regret to inform you that..." giving cold comfort to shocked and tearful relatives.

'To the Air Ministry the missing crew would be just another statistic in the mounting numbers of air crew who failed to reach that coveted tour of thirty flying operations. Tomorrow a new replacement crew will arrive from a Conversion Unit to fill their places, yet, even more tragic, few people will have known of the missing crews' existence on the squadron.

'To be remembered on a squadron fell to a select band blessed with an abundance of luck that enabled them to stay alive long enough to complete their thirty operations. Distinction would be bestowed upon

---

28   Halifax II JD460 KN-D skippered by Flying Officer John Goulding RNZAF crashed in the target area killing the pilot and three of the crew. The three others were taken into captivity.

them when during a riotous night in the Mess the celebrating crew by custom would be allowed to write their names on the ceiling. Sadly I recall that this occasion wasn't shared by too many crews, for during the period about which I write (1943-44), when 'Maximum Effort' was the byword of Bomber Command, only one in three aircrew survived to complete a tour. That was when a meticulously planned night flying operation deep into Germany would return minus thirty or forty, maybe even fifty of Bomber Command's aircraft; there was a loss of 76 on Leipzig and 96 on Nuremberg.

'0700 hours.

'No more time for day-dreaming or reflections. I am on my feet half-dressed and on my way to the ablutions for a warm water wash before the masses get up and drain the heating system cold. The fresh air, damp dewy grass, the invigorating early morning chill; oh it's great to be alive.

'0730 hours.

'I return to tidy my bed. Re-entering the Nissen hut was like walking into a foggy swamp. Stale breath, burning cigarettes and the accompanying blue hazy smoke, plus a few bods who it appeared had lost the knack of controlling their surplus wind culminated in a smell most foul. I give an exaggerated consumptive like cough that bends me over and the effort rasps my throat and brings moisture to my eyes. A muffled voice from beneath a blanket part surfaces to say, "Cough up and die you - - - - -"

'In this NCO aircrew hut I am billeted with my bomb aimer Harry Clayton, wireless operator 'Smoky' Powell and mid-upper Bill Batty. The rest of the crew, being commissioned, slept in the officer quarters.

'0745 hours.

'Off to the mess for breakfast before its closure at 0830 hours, but before leaving the hut I linger long enough to glance back at those three empty beds and I ask myself, "what was that profound prognosis that I found hard to accept last night?" Don't worry about a scrubbed operation; it could be the one on which I was supposed to go missing!' I readily accepted it now and silently counted my blessings.

'0800 hours.

'There is no queuing for breakfast (only at dinner time). Straight in for porridge and beans on toast with a splat of tomato sauce from a pressurised bottle.

'0830 hours.

'Breakfast tucked away inside me, I stroll to the "Flight offices". Here air crew assemble in their respective sections, i.e. wireless, navigator, flight engineer and gunnery. I take notice of an information board laying out the procedure and programme for the day. From the gunners' point of view it could be a film on safety and escape, aircraft recognition, dinghy drill, night vision techniques and observation, FFI, medical parade, sport, clay pigeon shooting, anti-anything injection (nothing for anti-war) and the odd lecture pushed in the programme. The working day will end at 1700 hours. More often than not many bods are skiving and you would be lucky to find a full house after 1430 hours. Just half an hour into a lecture on aircraft recognition, a head pops around the door and informs the lecturers that all outside phone lines are dead. We are geared to know the significance of that. Eyes look out of the window and there on the perimeter track a WAAF drives a tractor pulling a trolley-load of bombs. A couple of armourers sit astride the load.

'I feel deflated and disappointed. There goes my celebration drink tonight. My heart was set on catching the 1900 hours off-duty bus into York and eventually 'Betty's Bar', the Mecca of 4 Group aircrew squadrons. It was a safety valve from flying operations. Visits and acquaintances were made in almost every pub in this lovely city of York but 'Betty's Bar' took pride of place. Many has been the greeting across the bar to somebody apparently back from the dead – or even mistaken identity. "Hello stranger, am I glad to see you. I heard you went for a Burton." It would be passed off with a laugh and after a drink – well several – arrangements would be made to meet again, the next free night, why not?"

'But aircrew could only plan one day to the next. Although operating from different stations both would be flying on the same mission. After returning, on your first free night you'd make for 'Betty's Bar' to renew acquaintance with your long lost pal. You stand by the entrance door. Even on a crowded evening you could see them all come in from here aided by an exceptionally long mirror on the wall. The mirror carried hundreds of aircrew signatures, but there was a suspicion that one signed your life away. While there was that fraction of doubt, my name never went on that mirror. You wait for your friend because you knew he also wanted to make this meeting. But before the night and its drinking time had flown away someone would tell you what you already knew in your gut: your friend had 'gone for a Burton' on last night's flying. But grieving and sorrow was only for close relatives. It was an accepted fact that every night raid would suffer casualties. What a great comforter that in-built feeling that told oneself that it would always be the other crew who would go missing.

'Since being stationed near York I have secretly wished when my 21st birthday came around to celebrate in 'Betty's Bar' in the companionship of my own crew and our faithful ground crew who service our "N-Nan". I am sure it would be a riotous evening to remember in my future years. I hoped I would make it but there was always the uncertainty in war. The sadness of missing and killed young aircrew was seldom dwelt upon; there was too much living to do in maybe so short a time. Many of these lads could relate terrible experiences i.e. near misses, crash landings, lumps blown out of aircraft – but sometimes, only in select company, a life and death situation would appear to have been a hilarious experience.

'1115 hours.

'Our training day had finished early. We were dismissed from the Flights to carry out the usual pre-op inspection of our aircraft. The armourers had already seen to the turrets, but it was always good practice to let them see we cared. The perimeter track was busy with transport running aircrew out to various aircraft. I rode with Bill Batty my mid-upper gunner to our Halifax JD462 'N-Nan' on its dispersal pad. Bill and I had harmonised our guns and turrets yesterday for the raid on Mönchengladbach but that was scrubbed, so we got off lightly. Our ground crew had attended to last night's offending engine and after their test run-ups stated that it would be OK for tonight. All around the perimeter track trailers of bombs were being delivered at different dispersals and petrol bowsers seemed to be in plentiful supply. Such was the lead up to the start of an operational day in Bomber Command and at 77 Squadron, Elvington, Yorkshire, in particular.

'1205 hours.

'A steady stream of aircrew were now making their way back to their Messes ready for lunch.

'1230 hours.

'Back in the anteroom of the Sergeants' Mess many were smoking cigarettes. Some hiding behind newspapers, others playing cards or telling jokes. At the far end of the room a navigator plays on the piano, but for all the attention he is getting he could have been in solitary confinement. Amongst the remaining aircrew the usual guessing game starts.

'It is in whispers first:

"Where's the target then?"

"Nobody knows."

Nobody will know till briefing but in helping to pass the time, the guessing game goes on.

"It's full tanks, so I'm told."

"Who told you that?"

"Well I think it is!"

"There you go again! Sounds like a long trip then!" A head pops around a paper to join in the conversation: "Where do you reckon then - the Ruhr?" The commanding voice of a gunner: "You twit! Get back behind your paper and cartoons, that's only just past Southend!" Another bod picks it up and refers directly to the chap with the paper: "It's full tanks remember!" he mocks.

'Not to be belittled, the "paper man" came right back: "So what – I remember once before – we had full tanks – and when we got back there was plenty unused in the tanks." It went awkwardly quiet for a couple of seconds before a razor of wit sliced through the Mess: "Cor blimey surely ain't that what you'd expect if you abort when you see the enemy coast?"

'It was play-acting and teasing at its best. For two or three crews in this room, it could be the last laugh they would have. An orderly entered the anteroom and as of one accord the aircrew rose from their chairs, the battle order was being pinned to the notice board. For those at the back necks grew as they stretched to read the crews detailed for tonight. I picked out the name of my skipper: Flight Lieutenant P.M. Cadman – and read the six names below his; my eyes lingered a little on the last one: Sergeant W.P. Trivett, rear gunner. Not that I didn't want to go, but my heart was set on having a good drink in Betty's Bar in York tonight.

'1500 hours.

'Dinner is served. Into the Mess, which seems a little quieter than usual. The Tannoy crackles and a WAAF's voice carries through the Mess. "Will all detailed pilots and navigators report for Briefing at 1430 hours." Short and to the point. A buzz of expectancy in the air. 1400 hours. Dinner is over. Crews saunter back to the anteroom to await the call. It isn't long in coming. "All detailed crews report for main briefing 1600 hours." If one has any uneasy feelings or any secret thoughts then this is the time to shed them. Now you have spare time to write a letter (sometimes called a last letter), play cards, walk back to you billet, a quick wash and shave, press your uniform, or in aircrew parlance, have a tom tit!

'1545 hours.

'Crews are walking towards the briefing room. Outside its door three or four service policemen with Alsatian guard dogs patrol the entrance. Who looks the more ferocious twixt police and dogs is debatable. Crews are assembling outside. On the grass forecourt an aircrew bod deep in thought picks his teeth with a matchstick. A few appear loud of mouth and confident. Some give a nervous laugh to any conversation, while those with more than a few ops to their credit talk quietly in small groups, occasionally looking around at the tell-tale reactions, for they have been through these stages themselves.

'1600 hours.

'The doors of the briefing room have opened and we file in while being scrutinised by the 'door men'. Inside are the pilots and navigators who have been plotting the routes and times. There is a heavy feeling in the air accentuated by the mist of blue smoke from cigarettes. All curtains are drawn and the lighting that adds more warmth to the bodies now crowding in causes its own problem. The long slatted wooden forms are soon hidden by the sitting aircrew. We await the arrival of the Station Commanding Officer. Shuffling of feet and knocking over of the odd form herald his presence as 130 air crew come to attention. It needs only the customary wave of his hand in acknowledgement, a nod to the Wing Commander to uncover the target and the show is on.

'All eyes focus on the target area. A few 'Cor Blimey's, 'Good God's and a single 'Oh I do say old chap' release the tension of the day.

'So there it is, the Big City – BERLIN. The sounds are of gum chewing, biting the ends of pencils and of the virtuoso who could beat a tattoo with pencil between his teeth; hearts beat faster and I would suspect a few nearly stopped, a buzz of excitement.

'The flight officers give us a collective briefing i.e. what to look for and so much to be stored in the head. Times, routes, turning points, bomb-loads, petrol quantities, heights, timed waves of aircraft, flare markers, expected temperatures during flight, speeds, flare codes, aiming point colours, allotted time of take-off, what time one would go through the target. Oh, I almost forgot of course: the weather, on which the whole operation depended.

'The briefing ended with Carr, the Officer Commanding, telling us in a rather haughty voice of the significance of this operation. He offers his best wishes to one and all for success and returns and concludes with, "I wish I was coming with you." Well if ENSA visit the station, they need not look far for a stand-up comedian!

'1730 hours.

'Briefing over now, all pockets are emptied of letters, photographs, old bus tickets, landladies addresses – anything that would give the enemy information. All is placed in your own numbered bag and collected on return. In this packed room, the heat of bodies, the cigarette smoke and the enforced security closure of windows is overbearing and suddenly daylight is seen through an opened door. Cooler air drifts in and kisses ones face. Ecstasy.

'1745 hours.

'Now back in the mess for an operation tea of fried egg and chips which in these days of rationing is considered a delicacy to many back home.

I enjoyed my meal, as I always did and I was determined to enjoy the other egg that I would receive on return despite the usual requests from others asking could they have my other egg if I went for a Burton. This apparent callousness was commonly accepted by most crews – behind it was a little nervousness. One cocky sod once asked me if I thought I'd ever finish my tour! I replied, "I don't think you should be asking me that because you won't be here to see it." Unfortunately, that was a case of many a true word spoken in jest.

'1815 hours.

'Meal over, back to the billets to put on extra woollies for night flying then back to the Mess to get transport to the flights. Most aircrew take a casual walk, but I'm a bit bulky with my extra clothing and there is no point in sweating unnecessarily, so it's a ride for me.

'1830 hours.

'At the flights, prepare to inspect my flying gear. Shall I wear an electrically heated suit or an Irvin sheepskin jacket? The electric suit is not so bulky. I plug in the suit and make sure it works. One suit I didn't pre-test and on the trip the left side remained cold, as did the right leg and foot, but there was a smell of burning and my left foot got so hot I had to unbutton the connecting studs to take it out of circuit. Try that with three pairs of gloves on: silk, woollen, leather. For a short while I could have taught St. Vitus a few hops, but also I nearly had frostbite. I'll make sure that doesn't happen again.

In spite of a pleasant day, the met forecast is very cold at 20,000 feet. In the locker room there is a quietness as private thoughts come uppermost. Hands go in and out of pockets in search of any overlooked item that could give Jerry a lead on information. I am wearing a pairs of socks as well as heavy white sea socks, vest, shirt, pants, long johns, trousers, pullover, battle dress, flying boots, gloves and an electric flying suit – and that's just to get out to the aircraft. Before getting inside I shall don a Mae West buoyancy jacket and over all this a parachute harness to keep it all in place. The rear turret is a very cold and lonely place.

'1900 hours.

'All crews are togged up and assembled outside flight control awaiting transport to take them to their respective aircraft. (At this stage most are saying, "please God don't scrub it"). While waiting for transport I have time to look around and I see Freddie Cox, a rear gunner. I'm sure tonight he is doing his last op of his second tour!? There's Daffey and his crew. Freddie Taylor my gunnery leader has no crew and picks the op as it comes along.

He's certainly picked a right one tonight. There's Warren's crew. We joined the squadron the same day as them. There's Robinson's crew and Mansoon's and not forgetting my own skipper Peter Cadman. Hang about, who do I see talking to the Officer Commanding? Air Commodore Gus Walker, an ex-English Rugby international of course.[29] There's so many well-educated people amongst this lot, at any other time and place in the world, with my council school education I would have felt awkward and out of place. But, as has been said before, war and death are great levellers. There are lads with gaudy scarves, another with a balaclava under his helmet, while two I see with sheath knives strapped to their legs. I carry one inside my sock and leg, worn with the thought that it might be vital some time.

'1915 hours.

'My skipper jumps aboard the tailboard of a transport bus and calls his crew to join him. I make a spirited effort to follow; my bulky clothing holds me back. Somebody takes my arse in his hands and gives me a push upwards and I am up on the wagon. We are driven half way around the perimeter track and dropped off at the dispersal of 'N-Nan'. Inside the aircraft, testing oxygen and intercom to all stations and that the illuminated gunsight is OK.

'Engineer converses with pilot and the engines are given a quick burst. Gun turrets are operated under power, gauges are checked up front, revs, vacuum and power, all engines switched off. The skipper accepts the aircraft and signs the Form 700. All outside for the odd joke with the ever-faithful ground crew. The last smoke and then the ritual watering of the grass. I could be sitting in that turret for 8½ hours.

'The evening sun is low over the airfield, a lovely breeze and I can feel the first chill of the evening. All is quiet. It is the perfect setting to end the day. The minutes tick by slowly; the skipper glances at his wrist watch and says "OK chaps, time to pile in" as I crawl through the fuselage to reach the tear turret. I sweat from the exertion as I squirm into my turret. I secure my parachute in the fuselage outside the turret – there is no room for it inside with me.

---

29   On the night of 8/9 December 1942, 133 bombers and Path Finders including 108 Lancasters were ready to be dispatched. While bombing-up at Syerston, incendiary bombs fell from the racks of a 61 Squadron Lancaster, exploded and set fire to the aircraft and the inhabitants of Newark and district were able to hear for themselves the explosion of a 4,000 lb bomb. Group Captain Clive 'Gus' Walker, the Station Commander, went out to the bomber on a fire tender and the Lancaster blew up killing two men and blew the Group Captain's arm off. 'Gus', who had played rugby for Yorkshire, Barbarians and England, returned and post-war became AVM Sir Gus Walker CBE DFC AFC.

'2000 hours.

'A bright green flare fired from a Very pistol arcs gracefully over the airfield. The silence is rudely shattered by the first aircraft to start its engines, followed by another and then it's our turn and the air fills with a cacophony of warlike intent. Engines are now revving and we are taxiing from the oil-stained apron of our dispersal, making our way around the perimeter and as the aircraft rolls slowly by, the faithful ground crew I notice are giving me in the rear turret a two fingered victory salute – well I do have my doubts – for I've never seen a salute performed as energetically as that! One thing I can be sure of, if and when we get back, however inclement the weather, you can bet your last sixpence some of those lads will be on duty directing 'their' aircraft to the dispersal. Having arrived at the end of the runway, we turn into wind, waiting the off. Flying control has an assembly of viewers waving away each aircraft: wives, girlfriends, some you can bet with watery eyes, seeing off their aircraft that is carrying someone special. They stand with their thoughts and maybe a short prayer.

The engines vibrate and the aircraft laboriously trundles down the runway and gathers speed. The tail becomes airborne, anxiously I watch the runway become longer and longer and suddenly the rumbling of the tyres ceases and we are airborne.

'2015 hours.

'I take the safety catches off my guns and I'm now in business. The pilot and bomb aimer with engineer are going through their cockpit drill. Over the intercom I hear "wheels up, flaps up, revs 2,650". The navigator takes his cue: "Skipper set course 065° now."

"Wilco 065."

'Some short time later the bomb aimer comes in. "Navigator, we are crossing the coast NOW!" The message is acknowledged. The sky is still light, much too light for my liking. My thoughts run riot: What if Jerry had sent out intruders – Ju 88s – he'd have a field day. I look down under the tailplane of this Halifax. I see a wide expanse of North Sea and shudder to think how cold and unfriendly it seems down there. Some ships can be seen. I wonder, are they ours? How do they view us up here? Do they say "Good Luck" or do they say "Achtung!" The enemy sea-going wireless operator would by now be tapping out his coded messages to German shore base as we make our way in. By the time we arrive those night fighters could be airborne.

'On this raid there are 700 aircraft detailed carrying 4,900 aircrew. Perhaps they are too occupied in their jobs to ponder on the outcome. How strange it seems that one never really sees the cards stacked against oneself.

'Our height is now 10,000 feet and we are now all breathing oxygen and with the aircraft climbing steadily and the sun having now gone down I am left with my two companions of loneliness and coldness, conscious of the growing darkness and grateful for the reassuring throb of our Rolls Royce Merlin engines. There is no idle chatter now, only orders, observation concerning safety and relevant information. My eyes look deep into the dark sky searching. The mid-upper gunner Bill Batty will be looking after his search area. We are aware that the aircraft is vulnerable from below. For this reason the skipper often asks to move the aircraft to have a good look below.

'A call from Harry Clayton jolts my senses. "Searchlights ahead navigator".

'I hate searchlights. It's not a pleasant feeling flying along in a cone of searchlights, blind to the outside world and everything being fired at you. Tonight we have been promised some cloud. Various four-engined aircraft are seen dimly heading for the enemy coast dead on track. I look through my gunsight. Its red illuminating sight ring now stands out strongly against the darkened sky. I dim it down on its rheostat control so it does not ruin my night vision. The familiar crack that accompanies the switch-on of the intercom stabs at my ear-drums as the bomb aimer informs the navigator 'Mac' McClorry of our pinpoint on the Dutch coast which puts us dead on track. However, the 'nav' is anxious about the absence of a route marker, working on ETA (estimated time of arrival) we make a slight deviation of course and are now starting a long run-in across Germany and its defence. The bomb aimer warns us gunners of a fight drome lit up to starboard. There was also another drome which had just lit near the Dutch coast. They are waiting for us tonight. Many night fighters would be off the ground now climbing high, hoping to get into the bomber stream. Then the fireworks will start. They will be looking for the odd straggler or even those of a later wave. The thin stretch of cloud seems to be widening and searchlights are gathering in concentration. We level off at 18,000 feet. As I look down my heart is in my mouth as the searchlights play on the bottom of the thin cloud.

'To a fighter patrolling 1,000 feet above us we must be easy prey, silhouetted as we are above these illuminated clouds. My eyes are hanging out like organ stops as I scan above and to the sides, praying that I won't see the flicker of tracer fire that will reveal a Jerry fighter.

'A few miles astern and below us a bright flash leaves a red patch on the cloud. It dies off in a few seconds and is gone as though it never happened. It could have been flak, a collision, or a fighter.

'It's folly to look into the light for too long. We must be visible from miles away. I ask the skipper to weave gently to make it a little more difficult for 'them' and for us gunners to have a quick look below the aircraft. He is only too willing. We are past that searchlight belt – there will be others. I feel a little more secure, but I know we are visible because I can see the red-hot exhaust engine stubs of other four-engined aircraft. I call up my navigator to tell him of these aircraft's movements and he replies in another ten seconds we will be turning. He thanks me and casually gives the skipper a new course. Nice fellow. Snag is if he gets lost, so do I. However, being able to cooperate with one another is the recipe for a competent crew.

'Way out on the port quarter an aircraft has jettisoned its load. It sparkles as it hits the ground.

'Suddenly a stream of coloured tracers cut across the sky and at the end they grow into a red ball of fire. First blood to the fighter. The intercom cracks: "Keep a sharp look out gunners." The skipper's order is unnecessary. My eyes are attracted to that unfortunate aircraft and seven crew which are now racing down to basement level – it resembles a shooting star. It's too dark to see parachutes but I am looking. There may be survivors, but there are not many from the North Sea.

'The flak is getting thicker now as we penetrate deeper into Germany and as I change my search to port, a vivid flash brings daylight momentarily to the sky and I discern the disintegration of a four-engined aircraft. A lucky shot or directed flak? Surely a hit in the bomb bay? Darkness has closed around me. The intercom is switched on, above the amplified engine roar I hear the skipper:

"What was that flash rear gunner?"

"A direct hit – a blow-up skipper."

"You OK?"

"Yes."

"Good." End of conversation.

'There are times when I think our aircraft is all alone, but for a brief moment when that flash rent the sky I could see aircraft all around us. Lucky wireless operator and navigator who can in a minor way cut themselves off from the outside world by just pulling their curtain closed in their little compartments. Thankfully there seems to be a lull in ground-to-air activity. It must be fifteen to twenty minutes that we have been flying in darkness, but experience warns me that Jerry has eased up the flak to give his fighters a free run around the sky. We can be lulled into false security. Vigilance is the watchword – always. The intercom comes to life. The engineer says:

'Blue searchlight on the starboard side gunners.' I turn my head. The blue beam slants 60° forward parallel to our track. Fighters orbit this beacon during a lull in their bomber contacts, the angle of the beam laying off in the direction we are travelling. There is no let-up in this search of the night sky. The cold air comes into the turret through the open clear view panel and I am thankful for the small warmth of my heated suit. We are getting nearer the target area now. The sky is taking on a strong violet/blue mantle, the effects of searchlight activity welcoming the PFF. The engines roar through the intercom.

"Nav to Skip, target ten minutes."

"Roger."

'I can just hear the rumbling sound of exploding shells. Sometimes this Halifax trembles and occasionally even staggers as though it has received a punch in the belly and the smell of cordite and smoke that filters through my oxygen mask is a difference between war films and reality. The reassuring voice of the skipper on the intercom breaks the silence inside this aircraft.

"Everyone back there OK?"

'We go through a set procedure. I take a deep gulp of oxygen before answering in case my voice sounds high pitched. "Rear gunner OK Skip."

"Mid-upper OK?"

'And so down the line through the crew. The bomb aimer has moved into his prone position and from now on it is all his. He holds a short conversation with the skipper about grouping of the target indicators etc. Sitting in the rear turret I have my back to this vista of searchlights but my turn will come when we are moving through the target area. The clouds are illuminated by the searchlights beneath them and we in Halifaxes, Stirlings and Lancasters are like black birds of prey moving across this background. The sky seems full of red darting lights, some bursting yellow, some orange. The lazy way tracer shells have of climbing to the heights, then shooting past at incredible speed – it's uncanny. Sitting in my turret and scanning all around – I want to look in a dozen directions at one time. My eyes seem to be on extended spring wires, rigid in concentration. The quiet voice of the flight engineer comes through on the intercom as from somewhere afar.

"Lanc coned in searchlights over there Skipper."

'A laconic "his luck" ended that informative conversation.

'The bomb aimer is next on, his breathing laboured and come to think of it I'm not doing too bad myself. The flak is a bit heavy now and the occasional whomp, whomp through the open turret window comes to my hearing more often. Path Finders have put down their target indicators – red flares dripping in brilliant green. The mauve sky is now tinged with pink as the raging fires below reflect on the clouds. As I carry out my search, I can see a Lancaster and a Halifax emerging from sinister black shadows, their tail fins and wing edges tinged as though touched by an artist's brush and a glint from a perspex cover as a searchlight sweeps over it. The bomb aimer has taken over.

'A series of "Left, left" – "Eight a bit" – "Steady, steady": that agonising ten-second run seems like an eternity. We are so vulnerable on this run. A Lancaster is high above us on the near port quarter, his bomb doors are open and I am looking up into a cavernous bay with a neatly laid out armoury. It worries me. SURELY he can see us down here? He can't be that stupid – can he? And suddenly the deadly cargo is spewing out and falling like lemmings going over a cliff. I don't suppose I'm the only one muttering, "Come on – sod the bombing picture – let's get out of here!" In the middle of my muttering I hear, "Bombs Gone Skip." The time is 2342 hours.

'Ten minutes later we turn to port on our first leg home that will take us clear of this conflagration. As we turn I am sitting on top of the world with a grandstand seat apparently sailing through space in a glass bubble. As I survey the scene before me I am left speechless with awe. It's like a hornet's nest. The searchlights have almost been subdued – the part cloud cover kept the searchlights down. At times I felt I could have put out my hand and cast shadows in the beams. Other aircraft ran out of luck. I saw a Halifax caught by a few searchlights who froze on it. The Halifax was doing a series of corkscrews. The pathetic aircraft was surrounded by bursting flak twisting and turning like a silver moth around a flame. He could elude his captors no longer as cannon shells from fighters set him ablaze. Parachutes were seen to emerge and descend into the target area. Not for them a decoration – perhaps not even survivors' leave.

'The clouds were now awash with a crimson glow. From my position in my turret, I am confronted with a truly awesome sight of pure wanton destruction of a city, with brilliant white incendiaries starting fires, searchlight fingers like a spider's web, red and yellow shell burst leaving blobs of black and grey smoke. They disfigure the panorama yet are an essential part of it, mingling with the invisible hanging of the brilliant red and green target indicators. Drifts of rising smoke can be smelt through my clear open view panel. In the middle of it all, Stirlings, Halifaxes and Lancasters who have survived half the journey scudding for the beckoning cover of darkness and home.

'We are through the target area now on our long leg return. The click of the intercom galvanises me instantly.

"Fighter below crossing to starboard gunners."

'I recognise the bomb aimer's voice. Looking out to starboard I see the single-engined fighter. He came up level, slightly behind the starboard beam. He flew parallel for a few seconds – enough time for standard evasive procedure. Prepare to turn to starboard. His wings flip up giving a plan view. He is turning in and I conclude starboard: GO! The next second my stomach goes into my boots as the Halifax goes into a tight turn. I didn't see him go, but coming back on course we never saw him again. The time taken to relate far exceeds the time of action. I don't think he worried too much in missing us – his pickings tonight were probably plentiful.

'We are in darkness again with the target fifty miles back. Suddenly we are bathed in a brilliant white light. I can see from above possibly a mile either side of us two rows of hanging white flares. It has turned night into day and they are cascading right along our track home.

'All around us four-engined aircraft are zigzagging. We have never experienced this tactic before. There are aircraft all around us in this almost daylight sky. I am standing up in my turret but leaning forward to get a view below. All eyes in these aircraft must be hanging out. After a long 15-20 seconds the flares burn themselves out, darkness descends and once more I am alone with my private thoughts. God, there must have been some very frightened men in those bombers.

'We are now in and out of cloud and mighty thankful for the relief from going from darkness to light and back again. My eyes are beginning to feel like two balls of fire, searching the sky as I have for these last five hours and base is still almost four hours away. Looking astern, the glow of a red spot can be seen in the distance. It must have been sheer hell there in Berlin. Two thousand tons of HE and incendiaries in forty minutes by 700 aircraft. A few miles to starboard, searchlights have picked up an aircraft absolutely surrounded by bursting shells – he's so selfish: he's sharing it with nobody! The aircraft has strayed over a town. I glance back at him every minute or so: he's still there twisting and turning, until suddenly he makes the break. There is no aircraft but plenty of searchlights and they seem so mad; they are waving in all directions. When they get home the ground crew will have their work cut out. Some minutes later all the searchlights in the distance have been extinguished. Once more the safety of darkness closes in. In the loneliness and coldness of the rear turret I count my blessings and think how lucky we are in this crew to have a navigator and pilot who together keep us on track.

'The journey back to the coast is uneventful. The German fighters have had their fun; tomorrow we'll hear how successful they have been. On the intercom I can hear that the searchlights are active on the coast. Jerry will put up his usual coastal barrage hoping to catch low-flying damaged aircraft and those who have drifted off track. They need not worry about us; we are going home.

'Our route tonight has been a long curving track across Germany, Belgium and France and we are now crossing the French coast to make our way to Beachy Head.

'The excitement of the night is now draining away and I feel shivery. We are slowly losing height but this is not the time to lose concentration – many a crew, thinking they are home, have been shot down by an unexpected intruder. Over the intercom I hear, "English coast ahead." I wait impatiently for Beachy Head lighthouse to pass under the tail plane and as it does so I see the sea pounding the foot of the cliffs. Once again the engines are amplified through the microphone as the skipper says: "Well done all." But we are not home yet, there is still a vigil to maintain and we have still to get down in one piece. Nevertheless, I'm in a happier frame of mind. If I do have to bail out, at least I shall land in my own country.

'Flying north we pass London on our starboard side. I give a thought to my family down there and think of them asleep in their shelter. The time is 0345 hours. They can sleep soundly tonight for we have repaid a little of what we owed to Berlin, with interest. They weren't too particular when they dropped bombs in our back yards during the London Blitz. We even had a mine in our own street plus HE bombs, not to mention a few incendiaries. There were no military targets where I lived. While still carrying out my search from the turret, I recall the consternation that mine caused. Had it dropped another fifty feet it would have blown us all to kingdom-come. Its parachute had caught on the corner of a building and the mine hung below it resting against the wall. My father and I, during our "after air raid inspection of the local area", had walked along the pavement right under that hanging mine and didn't see it until a very young sailor came down a little later turfing us all out of our homes, after which they disarmed the mine and took it away to Hackney Marshes.

Flying now near London set off a train of thoughts. When the German bombers set fire to the City and Londoners saw clouds over their heads tinged with crimson and fires on the ground that turned night almost to day, that is how we left Berlin tonight. That weekend when I came out of the Trocadero cinema at the Elephant and Castle and was confronted with blazing buildings all around me, with smoke in my nostrils, heat on my face and fire engines gasping for more water, crisscrossing fire hoses losing pressure where punctures created their own small founts, I at 17 years of age selfishly shrugged off an elderly man in Bermondsey Street who wanted me to take him home in the opposite direction because he was afraid to walk alone. I wasn't to know he had just two minutes to live – to be killed by the very next bomb that screamed down. I have been tormented by that many times. I ask myself, was that providence or the benevolent love of God that saved me?

'We have now long passed London and I am keeping an eye open for our drome at Elvington. In all directions on the ground various airfields are lit up by the white circles of Drem lighting and many are receiving their returning aircraft. There are so many airfields the country is like a floating aircraft carrier. Bill Batty, our mid-upper gunner, has sighted the predetermined flashing letter and the skipper joins the left-hand turning circuit around the air field awaiting permission to land. Dead astern a distant white flash lingers a second and momentarily lights up a fair stretch of the sky. How ironic it would be to have survived the German defences then to crash in mid-air, or to land with a hung-up live bomb in the bomb bay. I hear my skipper acknowledge Flying Control's "N-Nan OK to land" with "Wilco, out". The trailing aerial is being wound in and there are the trees and hut and, with a slight bump and a bounce, we are home. The time is 0415 hours.

'We taxi to the dispersal guided by the airman with a torch in each hand making mystic circles with his arms. It is a treat to leave the aircraft and stretch ones legs. 8½ hours is a long time to be cramped up in one position. We chat to the ground crew. Theirs is a thankless task, hanging about in all weathers waiting for their aircraft to land. They are smiling tonight. Sometimes their aircraft and aircrew go missing. Next day a replacement aircraft will be delivered. Unfortunately the old crew cannot be replaced and they, the ground crew, will have to get used to new names and different characters.

'The wagon is here to take us to debriefing.

'In the smoke-filled room, the debriefing is underway and while waiting our turn, tea, coffee and a cigarette are taken eagerly – and we don't forget to make our way to the man issuing the rum ration. It's said the rum helps the coffee go down.

'You can notice the difference in the aircrew since beginning the operation. Some have grown a stubble of beard, some are showing a tensed face with fatigue. Maybe those advanced into their tour are just tired of the proceedings and wish they could go straight to bed and get the sleep they crave. A new crew who have just completed their first op are being debriefed. They are glad to be back and letting it be known they have been over there and successfully returned. With lots of luck and God's blessing they will be able to go over there and back another twenty-nine times and entitled to write their names on the mess ceiling on a future riotous night in the Sergeants' Mess.

'It is now our crew's turn to be debriefed. A set pattern of questions is asked by the intelligence officer: "Anything special about: the fires, flares, searchlights, flak, fighters, explosions in the target area, smoke, position of aircraft going down (from navigator's log). Any parachutes, etc." It doesn't take long. While drinking our ration of rum and coffee, I quietly confide in my navigator that it hadn't been a bad trip for my 21st birthday; in fact it was a piece of cake. However, my navigator betrays my trust by informing our CO, Wing Commander Lowe. It is suggested by him that now I am a man I should start drinking like one and I gulp at a large mug full of neat rum while tired voices sing "Happy Birthday to you." I step outside to breathe the invigorating fresh country morning air. It tastes good, God, it feels great to be alive.

'The Flying Control building is just a short distance away. Here officers and WAAFs are logging the return of aircraft. At debriefing we heard there were still four more to come in ("outstanding"). There was always the hope that they had put down at another airfield through petrol shortage or damage and information was late in coming through. Tomorrow we'd count the cost. There seemed to have been a fair share of aircraft under attack in the target area and there was more than usual tracer fire during the run home. I wonder if the new flare-dropping had anything to do with that?

'The early morning air was playing havoc with the rum inside me. I had finished the double neat rum issue, as expected. My head was dizzy. Enjoying the luxury of a couple of stout supporting arms, we all made for the Sergeants' Mess.

'It's at the returning operational meal when one sits at the table and casts furtive glances at the empty spaces. Names of the missing are seldom spoken. One tries to picture an aircrew person who you shared a joke with at early tea time: "Can I have your returning egg if you don't come back?" Although the bad taste and bizarre joking was accepted, it suddenly hit home when crews went missing and you wish you had bitten your tongue at the time.

I always enjoyed my egg on return from ops, but the thought of a greasy egg on top of the rum was too much for me. I offered the egg to another gunner sitting opposite me. He hesitated before answering, "No! No! It wouldn't seem right – after all you've got back from your op!"

"But I don't want it – it's yours!"

'I knew there was a punch line somewhere and it came:

"Now if you had gone for a Burton, well, then I would have enjoyed that egg – *but not now!*"

'0455 hours.

'It was a short walk from the Sergeants' Mess to the billets. I was apprehensive when opening Nissen hut doors after ops – I hated those empty missing beds – but the hut had a full complement tonight. The missing were from elsewhere on the station.

'0505 hours.

'I lay back on the top of my bed with arms behind my head staring up to the ceiling, listening to the rising drone of an aircraft with a miss-beat labouring engine. The inside of the Nissen hut was brighter with the airfield Drem lighting having been switched back on. It muttered to myself, "Good – one back, three to go."[30]

'My head was feeling heavy as I lay fully clothed on my bed. I remembered I should be thanking someone for allowing me to come home safely home on this, my special day. Whether I did or not I'll never know, for the rum obliterated everything from my mind for the next six hours. I needed that rest. There may be another "maximum effort" tonight!'

From this operation of 31 August 1943, of the 613 Lancasters, Halifaxes and Stirlings, 86 aborted and 47 aircraft carrying 329 aircrew were missing.

On 1 November Flying Officer Matt Holliday, from Keighley in Yorkshire, known as 'Curly', joined Pete Cadman's crew on his second tour as flight engineer and would complete thirteen ops with them before they were screened. 'Flight Sergeant 'Titch' Quine DFM and I arrived at Elvington about 22.30 hours after imbibing a jar or two in York and we progressed through the camp singing very loudly, *Fly high, fly low, wherever you go. Shiny 10 will give a good show.* Both being proud of having served on 10 Squadron we thought we would fly the flag a little.

---

30   Halifax II JB851 KN-J captained by Pilot Officer Harold Evans Vivian Gawler was lost with six crew members and the 'second dickie' killed and one survivor taken prisoner. Halifax II JD413 KN-G captained by Flight Lieutenant John Leslie Wilson RAAF was lost with four crew members and the 'second dickie' killed and two men taken prisoner, one of whom died on 4 September. Halifax II JD418 KN-A flown by Flight Sergeant Ralph Owen Chester was lost with six men dead and the two gunners taken prisoner.

Luckily we weren't lynched and I went on to become a proud member of 77 Squadron.

'The Irish Medical Officer at Elvington was a bit of a character. When I joined 77 I went to him to have correction lenses fitted in my flying goggles. He bluntly told me that by the time the lenses were ready I would have "shuffled off this mortal coil". I thanked him for his good wishes and, with God's grace, went on to prove him wrong.

'Wing Commander Roncoroni had taken over 77 Squadron just before I was posted there. An excellent squadron commander and another great man, in more ways than one: it was said he was the baby of a family of boys, the smallest of the lot, he was only about 6 feet 6 inches tall and broad with it. I never saw anyone who could 'chug-a-lug' as he could. He once jumped from a scaffolding being used in the mess for painting the ceiling into the mess carpet being held by the rest of us 'à la fireman' – I still remember the sound of his knees banging the floor as he landed in the carpet, which slipped from our hands – he didn't turn a hair. When I was awarded my DFC he was one of the first to congratulate me; when he won his gong he said it was an award to the squadron and not to him – the modesty of the man! His award was well earned and well deserved. He was killed in a motorcycle accident in the fifties.

'The squadron was called to make a maximum effort for a raid on Düsseldorf on the evening of 2/3 November. The Engineer Leader was flying with Pete Cadman on that one and as we walked round the flight offices he was complaining how difficult it was to make up crews when someone was ill. I was making the appropriate noises, commiserating with him on his difficulties, when he suddenly looked me in the eye and said, "Will you go?" Assuming what I hoped was a nonchalant air I said, "Of course". I hadn't flown in anger for many months and here I was about to be thrown in the deep end on my second day on the unit. I was to be flight engineer to one of the flight commanders Squadron Leader Badcoe and the aircraft was to be 'C' JD385 – take-off 1700 hours.

'All went well until about a quarter of an hour's flying time from the target when, as we were gently weaving along, the words "Fighter, fighter, starboard, go, go, go" resounded through the intercom. With a sickening lurch we dived down and to the right and then up and to port while I could see tracer bullets shooting between me and my instrument panel. Within seconds, down and starboard again and up and then to port in correct fighter evasion drill, the fighter still sticking with us until suddenly I was jammed up in the astrodome unable to move. The aircraft had stalled and we were upside down and dropping rapidly. The bag in which I carried my equipment slowly rose up and went leisurely down towards the rest position.

"This is it," I thought and then remembering an H.G. Wells film I had recently seen, "That reminds me of the glass going across the room in *The Invisible Man*" – a curious thing to be thinking as we were plunging to earth expecting the end at any second. Suddenly we were on an even keel. Badcoe had managed to get his feet up on the instrument panel and with superhuman strength succeeded in gaining control. We had fallen from 24,000 to 9,000 feet and all loose equipment had made the inside of the plane a shambles. The navigator in particular had the difficult task of trying to sort out maps, flight plan and his navigation equipment; not easy in the dark.

'Checking on all crew positions and finding everyone and everything in good order Badcoe decided to press on towards the target. Although we were behind schedule we knew we would have to bomb when everyone else had departed for home and could not possibly make our bombing height. Checking on engines and fuel state and deciding that as my log was in a torn and crumpled condition I would have to calculate on the fuel gauges, I began to cogitate on our reception over the target area. We would be bombing late, everyone else would have left for home: unless the enemy fighters had already landed back at their bases, we would be sitting ducks for the flak.

In the event, we gained height, bombing, from 14,000 feet, a brightly lit Düsseldorf – not a shot fired at us, the defences swamped by the power of the Main Force – and turned for home.

'Shortly after leaving the target area I went aft to check that all bombs had gone and then made my way in the dark to check the flare chute – in the hooded light of the torch I could see that it was empty, so I returned to my position and we closed the bomb doors. Remembering the tracer bullets I had seen passing between myself and the instrument panel I checked for bullet holes in the side of the aircraft, couldn't find any and realised that what I had seen was the reflection of the tracer bullets going past the plane showing in the glass of the gauges: all illusion and a vivid imagination.

'Returning over The Wash one of the crew went back to use the Elsan. "Hello skipper, the photo flare is inside the kite!" When the aircraft had turned upside down the flare had fallen from the chute onto the floor. Not thinking of that I had assumed that when the chute was empty the flare had gone out – the safety split-pin had been pulled – if a draught had removed the arming propeller! We opened the door and threw it out over the water.

'Home and Elvington – on the final approach we had to overshoot and the port inner exhaust stubs exploded in a huge flash and bang which added to the grey hairs of age and experience. Upon examination we found a hole made by a cannon shell in the starboard mainplane. It had removed most the end of the wing, missing by a whisker No.6 petrol tank and the aileron. The back of 'C' JD385 was broken; she'd got us home safely but she herself was consigned to oblivion. Squadron Leader Badcoe was awarded an immediate Bar to his DFC and at the crew conference a general Group signal was read to the effect that when taking evasive action pilots should take precautions to avoid stalling.

'I was to join a wonderful crew with eighteen trips to their credit, all of them done in the maelstrom of fire over Germany in 1943 and led by Flight Lieutenant Pete Cadman. He wore a ceremonial cap on which the cloth covering the peak was worn, with the result that in a slight wind he had a flap flopping away above and below the cardboard; his battledress was also a little scruffy to put it mildly. I usually flew wearing an engineer's boiler-suit over my battledress. The pockets came in handy for carrying escape gear etc. I used to joke that if I were shot down I could grab a shovel and begin to clear away some rubble somewhere and be taken for a workman. The effect was rather spoilt by the legend 'von Holliday' in huge letters in yellow chinagraph pencil on the back. We probably all relied on some mascot or other to ward off evil spirits. I always carried a small brass Lincoln Imp which I had purchased in Lincoln during my sojourn at Cranwell in 1939. In fact as time went on I collected an assortment of talismans and ended up with 'Doomy' (a Mr Chad-type figure), a small lion and a chromium-plated horseshoe; but the only one I always carried was the Imp, suspended from my battledress pocket. Pete Cadman had a mascot, his childhood teddy named 'Flight Sergeant Wakey-Wakey'. What a character – harum-scarum and full of fun on the ground – in the air calm and cool as a cucumber – a leader and a first-class pilot – you could go anywhere with him because he imbued you with a feeling of confidence in his and your own ability.

'My first op with him was on 18 November. Mannheim-Ludwigshafen. Take-off 1645 hours. 'N' JD462. On return we got lost amongst the balloon-barrages at Liverpool and Manchester.

"Right, Mac," Pete said, "I know where we are."

"Right, Skipper;" starting to complete his chart and pack up.

"That's not it Mac; can you give me a bearing?"

"OK. Fly on a heading of 270 till I get a fix."

"Righto Mac, I can see the drome."

'This carried on for quite a while, Mac giving Pete a heading, Pete flying it for a while then saying he could see base, finding it was not Elvington and requesting another bearing, but not giving the navigator time to get a fix before haring off in another direction. The result was that we got hopelessly lost – and we did not have an unlimited supply of fuel. Eventually we spotted a pundit (a beacon flashing Morse) for which we had no information – circled it and called up 'Darky'. "Hello, Darky, hello Darky, this is 'N-Nan', request a bearing." After repeated requests we eventually received a reply asking us to repeat our message – this happened about four times before they finally told what station it was: Squires Gate.

'Flying back to Elvington was no difficulty and we landed safely – although fuel was a constant worry and we arrived with a minimum amount remaining. The other members of the crew were at pains to explain to me that "Pete wasn't always like this." Having always assumed, like most of my contemporaries, that if you landed back in one piece you were lucky, I suppose I said something to the effect that I was quite happy and would not wish to make any judgment on a pilot who had brought us safely through a raid over Germany. Mac was not so lucky however, despite the fact that the incident was not of his making and I believe he had his leg pulled shamelessly by the other members of the 'Navigators Union'.

'On 19 November we did a trip to Leverkusen. Intense barrage flak – stepped up to force us to fly higher. We were hit numerous times without being seriously damaged. On 22 November it was Berlin. Cloudy conditions – ice in clouds – plenty of flak. A 77 Squadron Halifax and a 102 Squadron Halifax crashed into each other as they circled to land at their respective dromes. All were killed. Strangely, both were lettered 'K-King'. We saw the flash in the sky as they collided. It gave us a scare as we prepared for an overshoot on our approach.

'Four days later, on 26 November, it was Stuttgart. There was thick cloud over target and many fighter-flares illuminating our route to the city. All Yorkshire aircraft had to land elsewhere because of thick fog in the Midlands and we were BFX'd to Tangmere. We returned to Elvington on the 28th. Lancasters had used the Yorkshire bases and there were crashed aircraft everywhere around York – a terrible sight from the air – one had made a huge hole just off the end of the runway as it crashed and exploded. Some of us used the opportunity to have a look round a Lancaster. A crew member of one remarked, "There's only one aircraft in Bomber Command and this is it." We looked at him in amazement, too flabbergasted to reply. We discussed him later, wondered how many ops he had done and where he was at the beginning of 1942. Thus was the myth of the Lancaster begun and has been carried on ever since. It was a great aircraft and much loved by its crews, but so was the Halibag; it performed very well, but the Halifax III equalled if not surpassed it in many ways. What's more, the Hally alone could use the motto *Ubique*. It performed all kinds **of** duties in all theatres of war – a truly remarkable aircraft. I flew in Lancs across the Atlantic in 1945 and liked it immensely, but the Halifax brought me through two tours of ops and eight months as an instructor. However, we all know that only the Spitfire and the Lanc existed in WW2.

'On 20/21 December when we went to Frankfurt many combats were seen. I saw an aircraft flying with its navigation lights on, attracting searchlights and flak, but did not see it go down. A Lancaster was on fire over the target area, gently weaving in a flowing manner as though it was on an exercise. I got the impression that the crew had bailed out, leaving 'George' or a ghostly hand at the controls. 'Titch' Quine was shot down over Frankfurt. He survived the crash we heard and his commission came through later. We said, with typical aircrew humour, he would be moving from a Stalag to an Oflag!

'After our briefing for Berlin one night, 'Titch' Quine pulled the legs of the rest of the flight engineers who had not been to Berlin before... to say the least he inferred we would not like it over there. He was right, although we did not appreciate him telling us. I remember he had just bought a Morgan 3-Wheeler and parked it outside the ops block. In the usual manner of aircrew I said, "Can I have that if you don't come back?" It felt strange seeing that car stuck outside Ops until a corporal disposed of it.

'In his capacity as Deputy Engineering Leader, Curly's duties included organising flying duties, ascertaining petrol and bomb loads, ensuring relevant sections were given this information and checking all the flight engineers' logs after each raid to ensure engine controls were used to maximum efficiency. This was a particularly arduous job on the Halifax, which had six petrol tanks in each mainplane and a system of cross feeds to ensure the fuel could be fed from each tank to any of the engines – necessary if any engines had to be feathered (if the bomb-bay tanks were fitted – three of 230 gallons each – the problem became more difficult still). The flight engineer's log had to be filled in and petrol use calculated every hour and each time revs and boost were altered, so that we knew how much we had used and were using with the present engine control settings.

'On 2 January 1944, after the powers-that-be suggested that 'N-Nan' had had its day, we were horrified, so Pete decided we would take her on a test to prove otherwise. So we climbed as high as possible (32,000 feet) and then went into shallow dives to build up speed, then climbing after each dive to attain a further height increase. We were rather pleased with 'Nan'; we had shown her to be a superior aircraft. We went on leave next day and when we returned 'N' had been transferred to 1658 HCU and went missing on an air-to-sea firing exercise on 5 June 1944.

'On 20/21 January on Berlin a "scarecrow" exploded just above us on the starboard side. I was looking in that direction and saw it clearly. The Germans said after the war that there was no such thing as a shell which exploded in this manner, therefore what we saw was in fact an aircraft exploding after a direct hit, probably in the bomb-bay.

'On 21/22 January Squadron Leader Clifford John Farmery DFM failed to return from the raid on Magdeburg, this the first trip of his second tour. His aircraft was one of five Halifaxes on 77 Squadron lost on Magdeburg.

On another Berlin trip, on 15 February, a Bf 109 single-engined fighter crossed from starboard to port about fifty feet above us. He was clearly visible, as were many of our bombers. I kept a close eye on him as he passed over us, without warning the rest of our crew, as we were on the bomb-run. He made no attempt to attack us or anyone else and I had the impression he had run out of ammunition.

Four days later it was Leipzig. As we flew over the enemy coast we observed many navigation lights approaching on a collision course. The wind had veered round and instead of a headwind we now had a very strong tailwind and to ensure we arrived over the target on time it was essential for all aircraft to waste time. Some had done a 180-degree turn and were coming back through the bomber stream – a dangerous manoeuvre. Mac worked out a dogleg to port, resumed correct course later and reached the aiming-point dead on time. Brilliant work from an extremely able pilot, with navigation assistance from bomb aimer and wireless operator.

'On landing after an op, for a few minutes Cadman sometimes acted in a strange way, shouting and bawling at anything or anyone who displeased him. This didn't last long and was obviously the release of his pent-up feelings and who can blame him? Pete had his own party pieces, his favourites were *The German Submarine Captain* and the bloke in the burning building who was exhorted by his mates to Jump, Bill, we as a tarpaulin! I can see him now, standing in the mess at Elvington with Flight Lieutenant Wodehouse, both singing in a loud, discordant manner to the radio churning out The *Waiter and the Porter* and the *Upstairs Maid* or a Maori war-chant which sounded like *Whoooa! Whoooa*! Another favourite was *Java Jive – I love coffee, I love tea* etc being given a rendering never envisaged by the songwriter even in his wildest dreams.

'He was the instigator in the burning of the Mess pie. We returned from an evening in York to discover that certain members of the squadron had decided that the piano had had its day – small wonder after all the beer slops that had been administered to its internal organs – and they had proceeded to dismantle it and give it a decent Viking funeral by placing the pieces reverently upon the large open fire. Pete was one of the ringleaders and seemed to have enjoyed the exercise; that is until the pay-off. The 'Groupy' (Group Captain Bertram, a good station commander) failed to see the joke and ordered all concerned to pay for the damage. I forget the amount, but it seemed exorbitant at the time and would have cut down the beer intake of the culprits for many days to come. So it was decided to ask all the members of the Mess who wished to do so to let a proportion of the cost be added to their mess bill. Disaster indeed. I can still feel the pain as I appended my name to the list of assenters.

'Another time, after an evening in the local we ended up in the billet of 'Clay', 'Triv', 'Scats' and 'Smokey' where we dismantled the stove chimney to the detriment of selves and surroundings and for a finale Pete and I had a wrestling session amidst the carnage. Great fun!

'Always at debriefing a WAAF dispensed coffee while the padre dished out a tot of rum to each crew member, imbibing a tot or two himself in the process. Some of us didn't like rum so we passed our ration to one of the other lads who did and in their tired state they went to bed reasonably happy. And the padre? I have seen him tottering out of the room long before all the planes were back, too inebriated to continue and leaving the WAAF in full charge. I suppose he was living up to the title of 'sky pilot'!

'My favourite pubs in York were the Half Moon and the City Arms, but you name it and most likely we visited it at some time or another, including the Black Swan which we called the 'Mucky Duck' – a play on words only, it was always neat and tidy. On a 'stand down' the City Arms was a popular place for the Flight Engineering Section parties and the dances held there were always well supported. We also imbibed in the local village pubs, including Wheldrake.

'We were taken very much for granted. The only thing many of our own people could say as a welcome when they saw you on leave was "Hullo, On leave again? When are you going back?" And many the time I stood in a pub and listened to the sad tale of how many hours overtime had to be worked. It made me almost glad to be having such an easy time of it on a bomber squadron.

'We used our cycles a great deal – many of us took our own from home – to travel to York and the local villages and I often cycled home when I had a leave period, calling for a little light refreshment on the way. If you gather from this that I was a bit of a boozer then you're right; but then most of us were, we lived for the moment – 'We are but warriors for the working day.' It was all innocent fun and even our inebriated perambulations along the country roads were pretty harmless as traffic was almost non-existent and our night-vision was superb. Mind you, I did come a cropper once or twice, but I won't elaborate unless pressed. Sometimes in my cups I would have an almost overwhelming desire to go down to the Flights, get into our Halifax and take off by myself. How daft can you get? I also had this recurring nightmare in which I tried to climb into the Halifax and wasn't strong enough to lift myself through the hatch.

'We once were in a large roadhouse in the country; the place was absolutely jam-packed, noise and hubbub, conversation all around, when suddenly the landlord put on the wireless and over the air came an announcement of a Churchill speech to the nation. Deadly silence reigned while we all gained strength from his remarks. This may sound rather dramatic, but he had this effect during the war and whatever one might think of him I feel that without him the conclusion may have been different.

'One thing gave us great amusement and that was the crowds of ladies who descended upon the villages in the Elvington area and were to be seen parading on the arms of our gallant Allies – news travelled fast to shell-like ears whenever new males were in an area. I once observed the same phenomenon in Keighley during the war when the Durhams came to be billeted there – there's something almost frightening in the sight of a hoard of predatory females (God bless 'em).

'The 23rd of March 1944 was a sad moment for me. We went to Laon, France, bombed the railway yards and had the best aiming point in 4 Group – good work on the part of 'Pete', 'Mac' and particularly 'Clay'. This was our last trip together as a crew. We discussed whether to volunteer for the Pathfinders, or see if we could join Wing Commander Lowe on his glider-towing squadron, or took whatever fate had in store for us. I for one said I wished to stay in Yorkshire amongst my many friends. We took fate's path. I had completed thirteen trips of my second tour – they were screened and departed after a celebration evening in the local with the ground crew, those grand, conscientious, hard-working, loyal lads to whom we owed such a debt of gratitude.

'Two Free French squadrons came to Elvington during March/April 1944. Most of us were pretty annoyed at having to move to Full Sutton.

We liked Elvington and were near York. We RAF people always had to move to worse conditions to accommodate our allies – 10 Squadron had to move from the peacetime station Leeming to Melbourne; the Middle East detachment had to move from permanent billets into tents to make way for a Liberator Squadron; and then our French friends at Elvington – first the Canadians, then the Yanks and now the French! We envied them their huge salaries, but did we have to give them our beds?

'In May 1944 I was in the Mess at Full Sutton immersed in a newspaper when someone rushed up to me and said, "Have you heard about Pete?"

'My blood ran cold, "What is it?"

"He's been killed. They were doing single-engine landings in an Oxford and the other engine failed on the approach. Both the instructor and Pete bought it."

'Pete had been an instructor before he came to 77 Squadron and was doing a refresher course and relearning the patter before resuming instructing duties when the accident happened.

'What a loss. Pete's name is on the War Memorial outside Canterbury Cathedral.

Chapter 6

Adrift in a Dinghy

BBC Announcer: *Tonight we tell the story of a journey from the Ruhr – the story of a crew of seven young men in a Halifax, one of a great force of bombers which recently attacked Gelsenkirchen. Their captain was a sergeant pilot from Ayrshire.*

'Jock': *We were all sergeants in that crew and we were flying together for the first time. Three of us were Scots: myself – the lads called me 'Jock', of course – the wireless operator* [Sergeant J. Birrell] *and 'Sandy'* [Sergeant E.A. Gosling] *the bomb aimer. Sandy was 29, the old man of the party. Well, we got to the Ruhr all right, flying over thick cloud and the fun started as we were over the target...*

'Jock' (on intercom): *Now ready, Sandy. I'm going down. Then I'll straighten out, giving you a level run. Carry on.*

Navigator [Sergeant K.W. Smith]: *That's more flak coming up. Gosh! They ought to see us now all right.*

Mid-upper gunner [Sergeant L.E. Hughes]: *We're in a searchlight fix.*

'Jock': *Then we'll give 'em a present of this lot. Bomb doors open.*

'Sandy': *Bomb doors open, Jock. Just keep her like this.*

Flight engineer [Sergeant W. Watt]: *Look out! That hit us! The inner port engine's burning. Feather that prop, Jock.*

'Jock': *Take it easy now, take it easy. The engine's cut out, but everything's under control. Carry on Sandy and snap into it.*

'Sandy': *Steady Jock, steady. Hold her. That's it! Bombs gone*!

Gunner: *Boy! Did she buck when the lot left her.*

Wireless operator: *You won't see the bursts in that mess. There's hardly a dark spot left.*

'Jock': *And there won't be a dark spot left up here if we don't get out of it. I'm heading for home pdq. Hullo! The bomb doors have jammed. That flak got 'em.*

Flight engineer: *What about the emergency gear, Jock?*

'Jock': *That's jammed too. We're in for a nice trip back – on three engines and with the bomb doors slowing us down.*

Navigator: *That's fine. You could climb out and pick daisies at this speed.*

Wireless operator: *All we need, Skipper, is a good strong headwind, just to cheer us up.*

Navigator: *Don't worry my lad. We've got that too.*

Narrator: *So with the bomb doors open and the speed considerably reduced, the damaged Halifax sets course to England on three engines.*

Navigator: *We ought to reach the coast in about fifteen minutes, Skipper.*

'Jock': *It'll be a pleasure to see it. We'll be lucky to get back for a lunch at this rate.*

Flight engineer: *Try and boost it up Jock; I've got a date with a corporal after dinner.*

'Jock': *A corporal! WAAF or RAF?*

Flight engineer: *WAAF, of course.*

'Sandy': *A corporal! The man's slumming!*

Mid-upper gunner: *Mid-upper here, Skipper. Fighter closing in on the starboard beam.*

Rear gunner [Sergeant L. Trowbridge]: *It's an Me 110, Jock. Here it is!*

Effects: Bullets: MG fire.

Mid-upper gunner: *He's turning in again. Swing her to starboard, Jock.*

Rear gunner: *He's after our tail. Coming in now.*

Effects: MG fire; splintering noise.

Rear gunner: *Rear gunner here Jock* (grunts). *He's put the guns out.*

'Jock': *Are you hurt?*

Rear gunner: *Yes, I think so* (grunts). *A bit.*

Mid-upper gunner: *He's coming back. Better start weaving Jock.*

Effects: MG; splintering noises.

Wireless operator: *'Sparks' here. Fire in the oxygen tubes. The cabin's hit.*

Mid-upper gunner: *Keep her steady, Jock! He's coming round. Hold your horses!*

Effects: MG burst.

Mid-upper gunner: *Got him! Got him! He's burning! He's going down!*

Effects: Whine of plane going down.

'Jock': *Good work laddie. You all right back there?*

Rear gunner: (grunts). *No, I can't move. The turret's jammed.*

'Jock': *We'll dig you out. Upper, go along and look after him. How are you getting on with that fire, Sparks?*

Wireless operator: *The extinguisher's smashed. I can't get the flames out. I can feel the heat coming up through the floor.*

Narrator: *The wireless operator and the bomb-aimer eventually manage to smother the flames. The upper gunner hacks away at the jammed doors of the rear turret and releases the wounded rear gunner. The badly damaged Halifax drones slowly on, steadily nearing the French coast.*

Flight engineer: *Aircraft ahead, Jock. Looks like a Focke Wulf.*

'Jock': *All right. It's no good staying up here at this speed. We'll go right down and dust the waves off going back.*

Effects: Power dive, tapering into steady drone.

Mid-upper gunner: *That's shaken 'em off. Struth! What's our height? Six feet?*

'Jock': *I don't know. The instruments don't feel very well.*

Navigator: *Got any idea of a course? The compasses aren't working.*

Navigator: *What about getting a radio fix?*

Wireless operator: *With what? The set's full of holes.*

Navigator: *Well, your guess is as good as mine, Jock. We ditched the maps getting the fire out, but I'd say that if you keep her nose straight ahead we might cross the coast around Margate.*

Flight engineer: *Margate! Gosh! Put me down at Dreamland with that corporal, Jock. That's all I ask.*

Mid-upper gunner: *Hullo, Skipper, upper here. Land ahead.*

'Jock': *Good.*

Engineer: *There it is, Jock. I can darned nearly see that corporal.*

Jock: *Keep an eye out for a landing field.*

Mid-upper gunner: *There's a cloud bank over the coastline.*

Effects: Drone of engines; spluttering.

'Jock': *That's the port outer engine gone. It's seized up.*

Flight engineer: That would happen.

'Jock': Take your ditching positions. I'm going to try landing near the coast. In the drink.

Effects: Drone of engines; more spluttering.

Flight engineer: *Inner starboard engine cut out, Skipper.*

'Jock': *I know, I know. We've still got one left, haven't we? How far are we off the land?*

Navigator: *I'd guess a mile.*

'Jock': We won't make it. But we'll try.

Effects: Engine with splutter: engine cuts out.

'Jock': *Here we go!*

Effects: Wind rush of plane; crash of water; lapping of waves.

'Jock': *Open the escape hatch. Get on the port wing and get the dinghy out. Someone help the rear gunner.*

Sandy: *I'll look after him. Come on lad. Put your arms round here. That's it; you'll be all right.*

Navigator: *Dinghy's no good, Jock. It's in ribbons. It looks like a swimming job to me.*

'Jock': *You'd need to be a pickled herring to swim in a sea like this. That coast may not look so far in the moonlight, but it's too far for any of us. I'll try a Very light.*

Sandy: *That's a bad light for the complexion. You look quite green without your make-up on, Jock.*

'Jock': *If this wing doesn't stop rolling I'll be greener still in a few minutes.*

Mid-upper gunner: *I never did like being on the sea. I'd rather be in it. I'm going to swim. I reckon I can get that far.*

Wireless operator: *Same here. I'll come with you. We'll send you a rowing boat if ever we get there. So long!*

Gunner: *So long!*

Engineer: *Gosh! This is worse than a switchback.*

'Jock': *Just keep a good grip and don't worry. They'll have seen our light from the coast. They'll pick us up. How are you, gunner?*

Rear gunner: *I'm not so bad.*

'Jock': *You'll be all right. A few days in hospital, perhaps, but you'll be all right, laddie. Just relax; we've got hold of you.*

Sandy; *What's that, Skipper?*

'Jock': *Just another aircraft getting home, I guess.*

Sandy: *Wait a minute! It isn't. That's no aircraft! They must have seen us. That's a rescue launch. Send up another light.*

'Jock': *There she is! You can see the wake. They'd better hurry up. We won't float much longer. I wonder how deep it is. I never learned to swim.*

Flight engineer: *You'll get a free lesson now, Jock. That ought to appeal to the Scotsman in you. Send 'em another flare.*

Rear gunner: *Look out! I'm slipping!*

'Jock': *He's overboard. Chuck him a line.*

Navigator: *I'll go in; wait a second.*

'Jock': *Ahoy there!*

Sailor: *Ahoy there!*

'Jock': *Wounded man overboard. Can you help him first?*

Sailor: *We'll get him. Put that beam on, Jim. There he is. Give us a hand with him. That's right. Over you come. Mind his leg. That's it. Get some blankets on him. Hi there! Grab this line. We'll tow you in.*

'Jock': *Okay.*

Sailor: *You can wade ashore in another 100 yards.*

'Jock': *That's it, lads, back home and broke. We've grounded.*

Shout: (off) *Hi, there!*

Flight engineer: *That'll be 'Sparks' and upper gunner. Still swimming for it.*
'Jock': *They're picking 'em up alright. Come on. Let's get wet.*
Flight engineer: *I always did like a nice paddle. Here goes. Gosh! It's that corporal's lucky day. She darned nearly lost me.*
BBC Announcer: *That's how a crippled Halifax returned from the Ruhr.*
During the Bomber Command offensive the BBC made recordings of the experiences of crews on operations. This one features Flight Sergeant S.W. 'Jock' Liggett and the crew of Halifax III JD157 on 78 Squadron at Breighton, near Selby, Yorkshire, who ditched off Seaford Beach in Sussex at 2305 hours on 10 July 1943 on return from Gelsenkirchen.

On 27 September 1943 a Halifax on 58 Squadron flown from RAF Holmsley South, Hants, by Flying Officer Eric Leeming Hartley, was shot down during a U-boat patrol in the Bay of Biscay when he attacked U-221 in the Atlantic 400 miles south-west of Ireland. Hartley, who was on his 28th anti-submarine patrol, dropped eight depth charges that sank the submarine with the loss of all hands, including Kapitänleutnant Hans-Hartwig Trojer. One of the most experienced U-boat captains, Trojer, a holder of the Knight's Cross who was known as 'Count Dracula' because he was born in Transylvania, was on his fifth patrol as a captain. Hartley's rear gunner, 19-year-old Sergeant Bob Triggol, flying on his first operation, saw the U-boat rear almost vertically before it slipped beneath the waves with the loss of all fifty hands, but he was immediately ordered to his ditching position. Return fire had hit the starboard fuel tank and set the Halifax on fire. Hartley struggled with the controls and had to crash land on the sea three miles beyond the attack position. The tail broke off the Halifax and Triggol went down with the aircraft. One of the gunners, Sergeant Maldwyn Griffiths, was dazed and, despite gallant efforts to rescue him, he floated away and was lost. After the Halifax went down, Eric's commanding officer wrote: 'The area has been thoroughly searched without result. I am afraid that the chances of rescuing him are now not very great.' But Hartley had other ideas. He and Group Captain Roger C. Mead DFC AFC, station commander of Holmsley South airfield, who was acting as second pilot to gain experience, navigator Sergeant T. Bach, engineer Sergeant George Robertson, wireless operator Sergeant A. Fox and mid-upper gunner Flight Sergeant Ken Ladds who was on his 47th sortie, were able to scramble into the inflatable life raft, which had inflated on impact.[31]

---

31   *Hitler's U-boat War: The Hunted, 1942-1945* by Clay Blair (Random House 1998) and *U-boat Fact File* by Peter Sharpe (Midland 1998) and *Handley Page Halifax: From Hell to Victory and Beyond* by K.A. Merrick (Chevron 2009).

Due to the speed of evacuation from the sinking Halifax, the emergency rations and survival aids could not be recovered. With few provisions, 700 miles from home and with the likelihood of their SOS going unheard due to the low altitude of the bomber, the six survivors settled in for a long wait. Over the next two days they tried to make themselves as comfortable as possible in the overcrowded life-raft. They took stock of their situation and found that they had five pints of water and some emergency rations, which included Horlicks tablets, a few barley sugar sweets, chocolate and a tube of condensed milk. On the second full day they were able to dry out some clothing and each had two Horlicks tablets at 1800 and a mouthful of water, an event that became a nightly ritual. To conserve their meagre supplies they had decided not to eat or drink anything for the first 48 hours.[32] Here are extracts from Eric Hartley's remarkable log:

Sept 27: All crew wet and seasick, possibly through swallowing sea water.

Sept 28: Found we had four tins of emergency rations. Includes Horlicks tablets, chewing gum, piece of chocolate, tube of condensed milk and five tins of water. Aircraft heard. 10/10 cloud therefore no chance of being sighted.

Sept 29: Low cloud and drizzle at first improving. Dried clothes and made fishing gear out of wireless aerial. Crew excellent in body and spirits. A very little soggy chocolate was shared.

Sept 30: Long and cold night, one small piece of chewing gum issued to each in morning, later used for bait without success. Continued practice of morning and evening prayers for assistance.

Oct 1: Night was bad, with cold and wet and great discomfort. Atlantic swell 35' waves and an unlucky cross wave overturned dinghy, some kit was lost.

Oct 2: No fish caught and no water used. Drizzle which we caught on handkerchiefs and sucked dry. Drank first tin of water one-sixth pint each.

Oct 3: Cold night stiff and miserable. False alarm when Mars mistaken for orange ship's light. Two whales blowing at surface 50 yards away. 30 to 40 porpoises passed quite close, these had close fighter escort of seagulls. Constructed fishing net from bellows handle and Ken's underpants, still without any result, fish too scary. Relied on wind and current to take us eastwards. Decided to make sail out of two shirts on the morrow. We used net to catch jellyfish of which there were many. We squeezed jellyfish in clean handkerchief in hope of extracting water but result was so foul that we threw away this slimy mess.

Oct 4: Made and mounted masts and sail consisting of two shirts sewed together by thin copper wire. Sail was a success and gave more speed than expected.

---

32 *Shot Down and in the Drink: True Stories of RAF and Commonwealth Aircrews Saved from the Sea in WWII* by Air Commodore Graham Pitchfork (National Archives 2005).

Oct 6: Night very bad. Sea very rough and torrential rain falling. Everyone had a good drink by sucking sail and handkerchiefs. Robbie began to show signs of becoming delirious.
Oct 7: Last few days taken toll on stamina and throughout the night Robbie and Tom delirious and required constant attention. Still keeping up our hopes and morning and evening prayers.
Oct 8: All now fairly well exhausted. At 1430 hours Flight Sergeant Ken Ladds sighted mast of naval vessel. Fired three Very cartridges. About twenty minutes later all picked up by HM destroyer Mahratta. *Doctor and ship's company took charge of us, gave us excellent and undivided attention.*

The six survivors were cared for by the ship's doctor and crew at the end of their eleven-day ordeal. Twenty-four hours later they were taken ashore by stretcher to the Royal Naval Hospital at Plymouth. The crew could not have survived for much longer, but their determination was rewarded by what was a very lucky sighting. The destroyers were returning to England from Gibraltar and happened to pass close enough to the tiny dinghy for it to be spotted. The destroyer had discovered the dinghy by pure chance – they were not actually looking for it. On 25 February 1944 while escorting a Russian convoy, HMS *Mahratta* was struck by two T5 Gnat torpedoes fired by U-990 off the coast of Denmark and sank. Only 16 of the 236 crew survived.

The survivors took a few weeks to recover but all returned to duty. Eric Hartley received the DFC for sinking U-221 and for his leadership during the dinghy ordeal. Flight Sergeant Kenneth E. Ladds was awarded the DFM for his conduct. The ordeal did not seem to affect Mead greatly. When in June 1944 the Group Captain addressed Coastal Command personnel in the base theatre, writer Hector Bolitho, one of the assembled throng, observed that Mead was 'thirty-five but looked twenty-five, which was strange as he spent eleven days in a rubber dinghy last summer, drinking three ounces of water in six days and ending with such a thirst that the crew squeezed the liquid from jelly fish to drink.'[33]

Eric Hartley returned to active service after his ordeal. In 1945 he wedded sweetheart Maud. He became a bank manager and lived in Oldham. When he died in 2003 he left his medals and memorabilia to daughter Kathleen Walker. Eric's family sold his DFC for more than £3,000. Mrs Walker, 67, said: 'We have no children to pass it on to and you begin to wonder what would happen to it after I die. I have got my memories of him and that is what counts.'

---

33   Roger Mead remained in the RAF after the war and retired in 1958 as Air Commodore Mead CBE DFC AFC. *Task For Coastal Command: The Story of the Battle of the South-West Approaches* by Hector Bolitho (1944).

Chapter 7

Halifax Heroes

I hope you never receive this, but I quite expect you will. I know what ops over Germany means and I have no illusions about it. By my own calculations, the average life of a crew is twenty ops.

Letter to his mother, to be opened in the event of his death, written by 22-year-old Pilot Officer Cyril Joe Barton on 578 Squadron.

On the night of 30/31 March 1944 at the preplanning conference at High Wycombe, Commander-in-Chief 'Bomber' Harris announced that 795 RAF heavy bomber and 38 Mosquito crews were to be employed on a 'maximum effort' on Nuremberg. The force would comprise ten bomber squadrons in 1 Group, eight squadrons from 3 Group, seven squadrons from 4 Group, twelve from 5 Group, nine from 6 Group RCAF and twelve from 8 Group (Path Finder Force). On a huge wall map a line of red tape wheeling around marking pins traced the route that the bombers were to follow to and from their target. The planned route flew in the face of everything that had gone before with the tape streaking in a south-easterly direction to cross the Belgian coast near Bruges and with no change of course, then went on to just short of Charleroi in Belgium, dangerously close to three known radio beacons which were used as gathering and waiting points for the night-fighters. From there it stretched in a straight line that represented nearly 265 miles to the final turning point at Fulda, north-east of Frankfurt, where the force would swing onto a south-easterly heading for the bomb-run on Nuremberg. But for two slight changes the return route the bombers were to follow after the raid was just about as direct as the outward course.

With the weather worsening with a threat of snow and sleet the feeling was that the raid would eventually be scrubbed. Some thought that it might even be cancelled before the navigation briefing, which always preceded the main crew briefing, but there was no such doubt in 'Bomber' Harris's mind. The raid would go ahead.

At 1830 at RAF Snaith, Yorkshire, in 4 Group seventeen Halifax crews on 51 Squadron entered the briefing room with armed SPs standing guard at the entrance doors and took their seats like expectant patrons at a cinema who had queued waiting to see the 'big picture'. At least two new crews were going to fly their first operation. Australian Flight Sergeant Geoffrey Graham Brougham, 21, would be taking LW544 MH-QZ. The other neophyte crew, on MH-L, was skippered by 29-year-old Flight Lieutenant Joe Pawell, a cigar-chewing American from Philadelphia who had joined the RCAF with the intention of becoming a 'Yank' in Canadian clothing in Bomber Command. Surrey-born Flight Sergeant William Albert Stenning, the married wireless operator on the otherwise all-British crew, was a former motorcycle salesman. They had arrived at Snaith on 27 March from forty-eight hours leave after having completed a conversion course from Whitleys to Halifaxes at 1652 Heavy Conversion Unit, Marston Moor, where Group Captain Leonard Cheshire VC had instilled crew discipline in the air and on the ground. 'We were straight away on a familiarization flight,' Stenning recalls. 'We were also detailed for ops that night but the squadron was stood down due to weather. Next day the weather was again dicey but we were given a five-hour cross-country and then, hardly having had time to think much or look around, 30 March was with us and ops were on again. About 150 of us were present and the big map board was covered. We knew overload tanks had been fitted but this, at that stage, didn't mean much to me. Group Captain N.H. Fresson DFC the station commander entered and our commanding officer Wing Commander Ling opened the proceedings. I remember the cover coming off the briefing map and looking at this long, long red tape which seemed to stretch a hell of a long way into Germany. It must have also impressed the others, judging by the remarks I overheard.

The wing commander informed us that we would be the second wave of a heavy attack on Nuremberg and warned new crews, including us, about keeping in the Main Force bomber stream. Weather seemed good and apart from a long trip carrying mainly 500 lb HE bombs and incendiaries it all sounded fairly straightforward. We were to go out over the east coast and cross the enemy coast somewhere below the Frisian Islands. There was to be a feint attack on Berlin while we maintained a course to Nuremberg. Intelligence spoke of expected night-fighter opposition, flak areas on the way back and the fact that Nuremberg was a city with many old timbered buildings. There was a separate signals briefing which I attended and, as a newcomer, was duly detailed to go around the dispersals and check huge quantities of 'window' parcels for each of the aircraft.

We met in the sergeants' mess for the ops meal at about 2000. Take-off was scheduled for 2130. By 2100 we were on the crew bus and soon out at the aircraft, checking and rechecking. Wilf Matthews looked like a commando with his two knives, a Colt .45 and a police truncheon.

At 1500 sixteen Halifax crews on 640 Squadron and sixteen on 466 Squadron RAAF attended the main briefing at Leconfield. Wing Commander Dudley Thomas Forsyth DFC RAAF, the 28-year-old commanding officer of 466 Squadron, was on the Battle Order on 'J-Jig'. His DFC citation said that he 'always displayed the greatest determination to make every sortie a success'. When crews learned that they would be attacking Nuremberg with the second wave of the main bomber stream Forsyth thought that this was the first Bomber Command operation of any size and depth of penetration carried out in the 'moon periods'.

Sergeant Donald Stewart RAFVR, a 20-year-old wireless operator on 424 'Tiger' Squadron RCAF, which shared Skipton-on-Swale with the 'Porcupine' Squadron, had an extra special reason for wanting to return from the raid on Nuremberg. Two weeks earlier he had married his fiancée, Joan, of Finsbury Park, Middlesex, and had been promised leave for a honeymoon if he volunteered as a replacement on 'A-Apple' (LV879) skippered by 31-year-old Flying Officer John Doig RCAF who was short of a WOp/AG. Stuart discovered that he would be the only married man on the crew, who were on only their second operation.

In all, twelve crews on 433 'Porcupine' Squadron and another dozen on 424 'Tiger' Squadron attended the briefing. A squally March wind spattered the windows and rattled the roof as the Met man took the stage. The briefing was remarkable only in that the met officer was 'a bit vague' about what the weather would be like over the target. Just one more trip and Pilot Officer Jens Paul Christian Nielsen DFC RCAF and crew on *Nielson's Nuthouse* (HX272) on 433 Squadron could say goodbye to the 'Porcupine' Squadron. Screened from operations after surviving a full tour, they would be sent home as instructors. Warrant Officer2 John Gilchrist 'Moe' McLauchlan, the rear gunner, was uneasy; he could not really believe that their luck would last. Observing ground crews fitting overload fuel tanks to the Halifaxes, he hoped that the long-distance target was not Nuremberg. The crew had been there twice before; a long, dreary, eight-hour trip. The last time, McLauchlan had shot down a Dornier 217 night fighter which had attacked and damaged *Nielsen's Nuthouse*. Nielsen, or the 'Mad Dane' as he was known, was born in Denmark and enlisted in Toronto in August 1942. Nielsen would have with him a new pilot on the squadron who was making his 'second dickey' trip to gain operational experience before taking his own crew on their first operation.

At Leeming in North Yorkshire sixteen crews on 427 'Lion' Squadron RCAF and thirteen on 429 'Bison' Squadron RCAF were on the Battle Order. Twenty-nine-year-old Squadron Leader George Johnstone 'Turkey' Laird DFC RCAF would fly 'W-Willie' (LV923) and 23-year-old Squadron Leader Jack Montgomery Bissett DFM RCAF, 'D-Donald' (LV898). Now on his second tour of ops, he had volunteered to carry on rather than return to Canada on leave, as was his privilege on completion of his first tour. His crew were on their fourth operation of their second tour. Laird took off from Leeming for Nuremberg at 2200 and was followed five minutes later by 'E-Easy' (LW618) captained by 23-year-old Flying Officer Walter Norval McPhee of Vancouver, whose crew were on their first operation. Squadron Leader Jack Bissett took 'D-Donald' off at 2220.

At Melbourne there had been the usual air of tense expectancy until the 10 Squadron commander, Wing Commander Dudley Spencer Radford DFC AFC, uncovered the big wall map to reveal the big, blood-red button – Nuremberg – was in position. Warrant Officer 'Paddy' Clarke's experienced Halifax crew looked at each other. They had mixed feelings. The last time they had attacked the city on the night of 27/28 August 1943 they had been caught in the cold blue glare of a radar-controlled master searchlight on the way past Frankfurt-am-Main and had been coned by a concentration of 'slave' searchlights for seventeen minutes while their skipper had taken violent and seemingly endless evasive action. They had escaped without being shot down but had lost their bomb aimer, a victim of the ferocity of the Frankfurt defences and Clarke had to belly-land the Halifax at Manston in Kent where the North Foreland stands guard over the confluence of the Straits of Dover and the wide and windy approaches to the Thames Estuary. Now they were going to Nuremberg again. Admittedly there would be a night fighter's moon but there would also be nine-tenths cloud cover for most of the eight-hour flight. Flying Officer Denis Eyre Girardau, the rear gunner and the only Australian on the crew, was glad to hear it. This attack would be the last of their tour of operations.

Australian Flying Officer Fredrick Robert Stuart, formerly the mid-upper gunner on his crew, should not have been on the battle-order. They had already completed their tour of operations and were 'screened' from operational flying, but Stuart did not relish the prospect of returning to a training unit to fly as a tour-expired gunnery instructor and had remained on operational flying on the squadron. Reporting to the gunnery leader was Squadron Leader George Lowe DFC – better known to the air gunners on the Squadron as 'Jarge' – who had already completed one tour of operations. This cheerfully cynical type had grinned when Stuart asked him if there was anything doing because if there wasn't he intended dodging off to his quarters for a recuperative sleep after his London leave and the long trip in the slow, crowded train back to Yorkshire. Lowe had sat back in his chair, closed one eye in a conspiratorial wink and said, 'I think you'd like to be on this one. It's a DP.' Stuart now discovered that he was on the battle-order to fly this deep-penetration attack with a new, all-RAF crew on 'M-Mike'. In view of his operational experience he would be flying in the mid-upper turret as fire controller.

After final checks, Warrant Officer Clarke's crew was ready and at 2000 they were taxiing out onto the perimeter track. By 2005 ZA-L was rumbling down the flare-path on take-off. The weather was 'very fine' with what seemed to Denis Girardau to be almost a full moon. Crossing the French coast at 22, 000 feet he could see no sign of the cloud cover that the meteorologists had promised: there was no cloud in sight at all. The weather over Belgium and eastern France was 0/10ths to 4/10ths thin cloud while Holland and the Ruhr were cloudless. At Nuremberg there was 10/10ths cloud at 1,600 to 12,000 feet but the cloud veiled at 16,000 feet with generally good altitude visibility.

At Snaith, where press correspondents and photographers watched seventeen Halifaxes on 51 Squadron take off, 'Joe' Pawell in a Halifax about half-way in the line-up was chewing his usual Phillies cigar which he never lit but always rolled around until it was oxygen time. During engine run-up he and Alf Barnard the flight engineer had some trouble on the port inner motor with some unexpected magneto drop which had not been there during the morning's run-up. The ground crew gave the all-clear after some minutes and all seemed OK on restarting the motor. Airborne, Pawell circled base keeping a lookout for Halifax aircraft coming up from Burn a few miles away, climbed to about 5,000 feet, set course for The Wash and climbed to about 12,000 feet over the North Sea.

Bill Stenning saw a huge burst in the sky ahead over the enemy coast and on the intercom someone said, 'They've had it.' I went back down into the nose and spoke to 'Bob' Clarke the navigator who had been quiet and matter-of-fact. He wasn't at all surprised that we were well and truly in the bomber stream.

At a quarter to one, the leading bombers reached the end of the Long Leg at Fulda and started to turn south to Nuremberg. The first Nachtjäger reported making contact close to Liège, which was the start of a running battle that lasted ninety minutes until 0130 hours. The 220 miles from Liège to the last turning-point was by now clearly marked by the blazing remains of forty-one Lancasters and eighteen Halifaxes. It is unlikely that a single hour, before or since, has seen a greater rate of aerial destruction. By the time the Main Force reached the target area they would be missing 79 aircraft, a figure exceeding the Leipzig total of six weeks earlier.

No word had been received from Pilot Officer Chris Nielsen's crew on Halifax HX272 'N-Nan'. With the bomb doors open for the run-in to the aiming point at the target and with the intercom silent except for the voice of the bomb aimer giving Nielsen corrections on the bombing run, the Halifax was intercepted just before the bombing run south of Bamberg by Leutnant Wilhelm Seuss piloting a Bf 110 who had got under the Halifax unseen. His 'Schräge Musik' guns were out of ammunition and Obergefreiter Bruno Zakrzewski, his bordfunker (radio operator), had to change the drum before his pilot could fire them. *Nielsen's Nuthouse* dived to one side, flew through the burst of cannon fire and began to burn immediately.

Seuss recalled: 'We must have hit an important point in the fuselage. The aircraft threatened to drop down upon us so I went into a steep dive. It was with great difficulty that I managed to regain control.'

Nielsen's Nuthouse was the German's fourth and final victim of the night. McLauchlan, Chris Nielsen, 'The Mad Dane' and Warrant Officer Harry Cooper the Canadian wireless air gunner who were blown through the side of the aircraft when it exploded at around 15,000 feet were taken prisoner. The four others, including the 'second dickey' and 19-year-old flight engineer Sergeant 'Chris' Panton who had wanted one day to become a pilot, were killed.

The first and second of four Abschüsse claims on 30/31 March by Leutnant Hans Raum of 9./NJG3 flying a Bf 110G-4 were Lancasters, followed by a Halifax and a '4-mot', which were claimed in quick succession. His third victim was probably Halifax III LW537 on 51 Squadron flown by 21-year-old Flying Officer Malcolm Mason Stembridge whose crew was on its sixth operation. Stembridge and the rear gunner were killed. The five other crew bailed out safely and were taken prisoner. Shortly after, Raum was shot down and injured by a Mosquito intruder near Roth an der Sieg. He survived and would finish the war as Staffelkapitän of 9./NJG3 with between fourteen and seventeen kills.

Thirty-six year-old Hauptmann Ernst-Wilhelm Modrow of 1./NJG1, who had been ordered to intercept the bombers on their homeward flight, picked up an SN-2 contact over France. It was the Halifax III on 640 Squadron flown by Warrant Officer2 David Warnock Burke RCAF who was heading home to Leconfield at the end of what was their fifth operation. The Canadian, who was from London, Ontario, never made it. Modrow hit the bomber in the starboard wing with a burst of his six wing and nose cannon and it exploded. Momentarily blinded by the glare he banked into a steep starboard turn and right into the sights of the rear gunner of the Halifax. Most of the return fire was deflected by the Owl's strong undercarriage and he watched as the bomber went down and crashed near Abbeville. Burke and the crew – one Scotsman, one Irishman and four Englishmen – perished. Modrow's next victim was another Halifax, 'B-Bertie' (HX322) on 158 Squadron at Lissett flown by Flight Sergeant Albert Brice. This time Modrow's kill was quick and the bomber crashed in flames at Caumont north of Dieppe. Sergeant Kenneth Dobbs the wireless operator was the only survivor. Modrow continued his search but finding no further victims he eventually turned on course for Venlo.

Oberleutnant 'Dieter' Schmidt, Staffelkapitän, 8./NJG1, claimed a Halifax, which returned fire before crashing to its doom north-west of Würzburg for his eighteenth Abschuss (and 16th confirmed victory) of the war. As the stricken Halifax pulled away Schmidt could see the cockade and the recognition marking 'NP' (158 Squadron) on the fuselage. Then he was behind to the left, diving down. When Schmidt examined his Bf 110 after landing at Langendiebach he found to his horror some human hair and flesh stuck to the port propeller boss of the aircraft.

Hauptmann Fritz Rudusch of 6./NJG6 flying a Bf 110, who shot down a Lancaster shortly before midnight for his first victory, scored his second Abschuss just over an hour later when he successfully attacked Halifax HX241 EX-P on 78 Squadron flown by Flight Lieutenant Harry Hudson from end to front. The Halifax was already burning as it approached a village from the west, circled once and broke in half before crashing with a full load of bombs on the premises of a chemical factory. 'Scouse' Nugent was the only man to bail out before the bomber crashed and was soon taken prisoner: 'I realized the plane was doomed and in all probability the rest of the crew were already dead. I was on my knees becoming weaker and weaker without oxygen and started to feel for the escape hatch situated mid-way between my own turret and the rear turret. Next thing I knew was that I was hard up against the rear turret. I had no control over my actions but something guided me back and unwittingly my hand felt the door handle. One twist and I was out, spinning through the air like a top. I didn't need to jump – the air rushing past plucked me out like a mammoth vacuum cleaner picking up a fragment of dust.'

Almost all the confirmed Abschüsse on the outward route were achieved by twin-engined 'Tame Boars'. Many a 'Zahme Sau' crew achieved multiple victories: Leutnant Hans Schäfer of 7./NJG2 and his regular crew who had taken off from Twente in their Ju 88 at 2321 hours in search of their first Abschuss destroyed two Lancasters and a Halifax before landing back at Twente at 0149 hours. Schäfer's third Abschuss was possibly Halifax ME624 'X-X-ray' on 166 Squadron flown by Flight Sergeant Roy Barton Fennell whose crew were on their 13th operation. The bomb aimer was the only survivor. Schäfer noted in his Flugbuch that his first two adversaries put up a very weak defence, but that he was subjected to 'very strong defensive fire' from his third victim.

Oberleutnant Günther Lomberg of 1./NJG6, flying a Bf 110, who had one victory, added his second and third Abschüsse, claiming a 'Lanki' between Klofeld and Bockeroth at 0021 and a Halifax, possibly 'S for Sugar' (LW724) on 158 Squadron, which crashed at Herbon-Seelbach. The skipper 27-year-old Flight Sergeant Eric Ronald Fergus MacLeod RAAF and five of his crew were killed. Flying Officer Anthony Shanahan, the Australian bomb aimer who was flying his first operation, managed to escape by parachute: 'We were attacked at 20,000 feet and a fire broke out. The order to bail out was given and I was just about to leave when I felt a violent blow to my head,' he wrote. 'The events of the next few days are somewhat hazy, but I fear the rest of the crew are dead.' Sadly, Shanahan's head injuries led to his death after the war.

'J-Johnny' (LW628) skippered by Flight Lieutenant R.J. Bolt, which limped home with the starboard inner engine out of action and fuel disappearing fast from a broken fuel pipe, had no hope of making it back to Holme-on-Spalding-Moor. Pilot Officer Fred P.G. Hall DFC, the navigator, had never seen so many aircraft attacked, on fire and falling, or so many attacks by fighters so early in a trip. Hall had lost his original crew in a tragic air test crash in November 1943. 'I felt sure that my 26th trip was going to be my last,' he said. 'I had made my first trip of eight hours to Nuremberg on 27 August 1943. My 26th was rather more spectacular. We were in the last wave and fighters were seen to be up in strength as we crossed the Rhine. Aircraft were continually falling out of the sky on fire and I gave up logging them. One minute after leaving the target we were shattered as cannon fire suddenly hit us from underneath putting the starboard inner engine out of action. The navigation table was covered in debris, the wireless set hit, the starboard wing, bomb bay and fuselage on fire. The pilot dived twice to put out flames and we all tackled the fires with extinguishers, eventually successfully. As if this was not enough, twelve minutes later we were approached by a fighter from dead astern, but we took evasive action and he passed fifty yards over the tail receiving full blasts from both gunners.

'We made straight for the nearest part of the French coast. We crossed the Channel safely and headed for Ford, but this airfield was full of circling aircraft so we continued on to Tangmere. The engineer had to take an axe to the undercarriage up lock housing to manually release the jammed starboard leg. We landed, but swung off the runway as the tyres were burst. A fuel check after landing showed that we had only five minutes fuel remaining. The squadron engineer flew down from Holme-on-Spalding-Moor the following morning to confirm that the aircraft was beyond repair; indeed, he couldn't understand why the starboard wing had not folded. But our only injury was when the wireless operator discovered his cigarette case had been flattened by a cannon shell and he had a bruise on his right hip!' Hall and Bolt were awarded DFCs. 'J-Johnny' was written off.

424 'Tiger' Squadron lost two Halifaxes and one aircraft damaged. On the outward journey 'A-Apple' (LV879) captained by Flying Officer John Doig was attacked by a night-fighter and crashed six kilometres north-east of the centre of Giessen with only one survivor who was taken prisoner. Twenty-year-old Donald Stewart – who it will be remembered had been promised honeymoon leave if he returned – and the others were interred at Hanover War Cemetery.

'D-Dog' (LV944) flown by Squadron Leader Harry Warren Metzler RCAF was brought down possibly by flak near Schweinfurt while running towards the target. All seven crew were killed. Flying Officer Frank Fletcher Hamilton DFM RCAF remembered Nuremberg as the worst of his career – a 'horror trip'. An indication of the remarkably clear conditions was the fact that a night fighter attacked his Halifax head-on. 'All I could see was white tracer getting nearer and then Bang! It all happened in one or two seconds. The attack set one engine on fire and I knew we probably had about ten seconds to get out. A small panic developed among the boys trying to get the hatch open but there always seemed to be at least one guy standing on it. We were hit again from above and behind.' This second burst shot the burning engine completely out of the wing. It tumbled away, taking the fire with it. To his surprise, Hamilton found the Halifax responded to the controls, despite the huge hole in the wing, so he ordered, 'Hold everything,' and no one jumped. 'We were hit a third time and had lost a lot of height. We jettisoned the incendiaries and continued on our happy way with the main stream across Nuremberg. The aircraft would only fly at just above the stalling speed and so we rapidly fell behind. We were sharpened up by flak several times and only by the grace of God reached England, landing at West Malling.'

Out of his little port window Bill Stenning could see flak coming up. 'It seemed very light with all the flares around us. I was now studying "Fishpond" very closely and imagining all sorts of blips coming but they were probably interference at that stage.' Several of the bombers had been installed with this radar set which was operated by the wireless operator and was capable of locating enemy aircraft with a five-mile radius.

'Soon there were reports from the flight engineer and the gunners of activity above and below. They hadn't seen any fighters yet but it was obvious that they were about. I saw a lot of flak ahead and to port followed by two very big explosions in the air. I could see an aircraft falling away in pieces. This was the first I had ever seen shot down but the feeling I had was that it just couldn't happen to us. We were heading towards the target on time with regular broadcasts coming in on W/T at fifteen minutes and forty-five minutes past the hour when a signal came through warning all aircraft to listen out on the 'Tinsel' frequency. I tuned in and heard German controllers saying 'Victor, Victor' or something similar.

'Soon after this I could hear 'Nobby' Clark the navigator telling Joe Pawell to turn starboard towards the target. We were now at about 18,000 feet and I could see some fires on the ground, to port. Night-fighter activity was increasing with tracer appearing in the bomber stream. About 0100 I went around with coffee for the crew and checked that the photoflash flare was OK and ready to go as we bombed.

'So far, it had been a fairly quiet night and I settled down and, as briefed, began dropping 'Window'.'

From the nose Bob Burgett the prone bomb aimer reported sighting the target. Bill Stenning went onto 'Master Bomber' frequency. The area was well alight and he could see the pattern of streets and roads. Joe Pawell had a cine camera going. He had used this on a trip to Schweinfurt but Stenning had never seen the films. They were soon going in and Stenning went back down to the flare chute and plugged into the intercom to listen to the bomb aimer. Bombs were away and the photo-flash bomb and 'L-London' was away too, turning to starboard and losing height in a dive. Stenning went back to his position in the nose and looking out saw a Lancaster diving steeply followed by what looked like an Me 110. The Lancaster caught fire. The flak was 'fairly bad' leaving the target area and the crew felt some of the closer bursts. Joe Pawell headed around onto the homeward course towards France and Belgium with the aircraft just riding the cloud tops. They had barely settled down on the new heading, with the target safely behind them, when the rear gunner, Sergeant 'Jock' Baxter, reported an aircraft closing in astern, slightly below and partly in cloud. 'I got it on "Fishpond" and it was certainly moving in but not fast,' said Stenning. 'I also reported to the pilot and he started to corkscrew. As the contact was now visual and Alf Barnard the flight engineer could also see it, Jock was all set to fire from the rear turret but something made him hold off. We lost the aircraft in cloud and some argument arose as to whether it was an Me 110 or a Lancaster as their twin tail fin arrangements were rather similar. We never did find out as the aircraft finally disappeared for good.'

Thirty-nine bombers were shot clown on the final approach and over the target area. The force had by now lost 79 aircraft, exceeding the Leipzig total of six weeks earlier. Of all the aircraft shot down on the outward flight, there was only one from which the entire crew survived; from one crew in every three there were no survivors at all.

Pilot Officer Cotter flew a Halifax that night on his 30th op; his navigator was only on his first or second trip: 'With the heavy fighter attacks, the navigator could not have had a more unfortunate introduction and eventually he was unsure of his position. Before we were due at Nuremberg, we saw Path Finder markers going down just off our track. We had not been briefed on any diversionary target here and I just thought we were lucky that we'd got to Nuremberg and so we bombed. Not one of us queried the target.'

Flight Lieutenant Geoffrey Graham Brougham, a Halifax pilot from Sydney reported, 'There was cloud over the city but it was broken. Through the gaps we saw fires getting a firm hold. The Path Finders had marked out the area with sky and ground markers and though there had been scores of fighters along the route, there were not enough of them over the target to interfere seriously with the bombing.'

The navigator on 'M-Mother' on 78 Squadron, one of sixteen Halifaxes that had taken off from Breighton (soon reduced to twelve following early aborts), had given up logging bombers that had been shot down. 'M-Mother's' pilot was Squadron Leader Cooper DFC who was on his second tour of operations. Flight Sergeant Ramsden the wireless operator was a veteran of the Berlin raids and during the early part of these operations was usually completely absorbed by crossword puzzles in the *Daily Mirror*, but though Nuremberg meant relatively little to him as a target, for once he found it too unnerving to concentrate. Then he picked up two blips on his 'Fishpond', a second H_2S cathode ray tube indicator, which showed the other aircraft as spots of light. A night-fighter was obviously circling a

Halifax crewmembers in the cockpit.

B.Mk.VII NP763 on 346 'Guyenne' Squadron at Elvington.

Free French crews at RAF Elvington.

Free French crew on *Zuopinette* at Elvington.

Capitaine Marchal on 346 'Guyenne' Squadron and crew being debriefed by Flying Officer Ginette Plunkett of the Deuxième Bureau (Military Intelligence) at Elvington following a bombing raid on the Ruhr in 1944.

Unmarked B.Mk.III taking off in 1944 before delivery to a squadron.

Halifax bombing a target in France during the daylight offensive in 1944.

A Halifax radio operator.

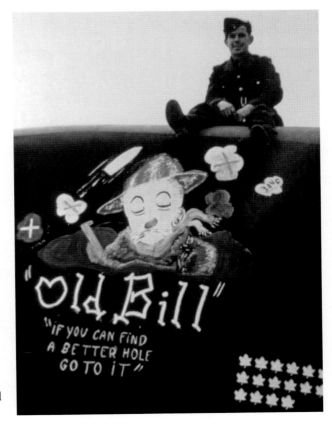

B.Mk.III MZ674 *Old Bill* on 429 'Bison' Squadron RCAF in 1944, which was later transferred to 425 Squadron and re-christened *Honey*.

B.Mk.III *Honey Chile* on 426 'Thunderbird' Squadron RCAF at Dishforth in 1944/5.

B.Mk.VII NP715 in flight in 1944.

Russell McKay's crew sitting on Halifax Mk.III KB732 VR-X *X-Terminator* on 419 'Moose' Squadron RCAF at RAF Middleton St. George in April 1944. The Xs on the side of the aircraft are crossed bones, each bone representing one operation, and the aircraft had completed forty-nine operations when this photo was taken. McKay is 2nd from right. Of the Canadian-built Lancasters, KB-732 was arguably the greatest of them all, completing more operational flights against the enemy than any other, flying its 84th operation on 25 April 1945 on the raid on Wangerooge, the coastal batteries on the Frisian Islands that were controlling the approaches to the ports of Bremen and Wilhelmshaven.

Halifax II Series Ia JP113 NA-A *Git up them stairs* (Guts) with Pegasus artwork on the nose on 428 'Ghost' Squadron which was attacked by a night fighter and set on fire on 20/21 April 1944 on Lens. The pilot, Flight Lieutenant 'Chuck' Charles George Ford DFC RCAF, 22, ordered the crew to bail out, and within moments three of the crew did so (one evading capture and the other two being taken prisoner), but then the fire went out. Ford got the Halifax back to England and crashed into a forest near Attlebridge airfield in Norfolk. All four remaining crew, badly injured, were taken to the Norfolk & Norwich Hospital.

On the night of 2/3 October 1943 the crew on Halifax V LK640 *Q-Queenie* on 431 Squadron took off on a mine laying flight during which the navigation equipment became unserviceable and one of the engines suffered damage from fire from a flak ship, but the crew managed to make a safe return to Tholthorpe on the three good engines and landed safely. *Q-Queenie* was quickly repaired and was being flown by the same pilot within a week operationally again. This was the crew's first operational flight on 431 Squadron. *Q-Queenie* was lost on Mannheim on 18/19 November 1943 when it crashed into the sea with no survivors from Flying Officer Garnet Oliver Carefoot RCAF's crew.

Halifax II HR868/MH-B of 51 Squadron was attacked by a night-fighter en route to Frankfurt on the night of 20/21 December 1943. The bomb aimer was killed and a fire started in the bomb bay, which blew itself out. Unable to jettison the bombs, the crew were forced to bring them back to Snaith. Despite the extensive damage, HR868 was repaired and flew again; eventually going on to serve with 1656 HCU. It was one of the few Halifaxes delivered during this period that survived the war. Note the aerial for the Monica tail warning radar below the rear turret.

Flight Lieutenant Joe Pawell, a cigar-chewing American from Philadelphia, at the controls of a Hudson.

Flight Lieutenant Joe Pawell and crew on 51 Squadron at RAF Snaith.

Crew on B.Mk.III LW724 NP-S on 158 Squadron, which was lost on Nuremberg on 30/31 March 1944. Standing, left to right: Sergeant L.J. Craven, flight engineer, of Harrogate, Yorks; Flying Officer Anthony Shanahan, bomb aimer, of Mascot NSW; Flight Sergeant James Arthur Nicholson, rear gunner, 22, of Ainslie, ACT. Left to right, sitting: Flight Sergeant Leonard Gower Paxman, wireless operator, 26, of Naremburn NSW; Warrant Officer Eric Ronald Fergus MacLeod, pilot, 27, of Townsville, Queensland; Flight Sergeant Ernest Roy Moore, navigator, 22, of Braddon ACT; Flight Sergeant Douglas Fitzgerald Bickford, mid-gunner, 22, of Gordon, NSW. Shanahan bailed out and was taken prisoner. The rest of the crew were killed.

Halifax *Sir Roger de Coverley* on 76 Squadron flown by Flight Lieutenant Henry Denys Coverley who took the CO's Halifax to Nuremburg on the night of 30/31 March 1944 – his fortieth trip, the tenth of his second tour – because *Sir Roger* had gone unserviceable.

Joe Barton VC.

The story goes that 158 Squadron at Lissett lost seven Halifaxes coded 'F-Fox' in succession within a year. B.Mk.III LV907, the eighth to bear this code, arrived on the station on 10 March, but fate had other ideas. It returned safely from Nuremburg on the night of 30/31 March when it was flown by Flight Sergeant 'Joe' Hitchman and his crew after his flight commander Squadron Leader Samuel Davis Jones DFC had taken Joe's regular aircraft, 'G-George', which was shot down. When LV907 was inherited by Pilot Officer Cliff Smith and his crew 'Smithy' characteristically decided to give the 'unlucky' Halifax its new title, *Friday the 13th*, and painted on it the Grim Reaper, upside down horseshoe motifs, and an open ladder above the crew entry hatch, but this was considered taking things too far and its removal was ordered. Incredibly, *Friday the 13th* reached twenty-one operations, distinguished by a key with a swastika, the 70th with a blockbuster trailing a spiral and the 100th with a larger than usual bomb lying in an open box or coffin. *Friday the 13th* ended the war with 128 operations; more than any other Halifax.

The *Friday the 13th* crew. Back row, left to right: Pilot Officer Cliff R.R. Smith, from London; Harold King, navigator, and Keith Smith, bomb aimer, both from New Zealand; Flight Lieutenant Eric King, WOp/AG, from Ipswich; Rod Neary, flight engineer, from Enfield; Ron Clarkson, mid upper gunner, from Australia, and Stan Hardacre, rear gunner, from Bradford, Yorkshire, who was replaced after four ops by Jack Goff from Romford, Essex.

Crews on 433 'Porcupine' Squadron RCAF.

Halifax crewmembers placing oranges in their kitbags before an 'op'.

'Thumbs up' as a Halifax on 420 'Snowy Owl' Squadron RCAF taxies out at RAF Tholthorpe.

Halifax III HX318 *Oscar* (formerly *Guthrie's Gut Bucket*) on 424 'Tiger' Squadron RCAF at Skipton-on-Swale, which was lost with Pilot Officer William P. Hugli's crew on 24/25 April 1944 on Karlsruhe when it was hit by flak at 20,000 feet. Hugli and four of his crew were killed. Two crew survived when the aircraft exploded, sending them clear of the machine; they were taken prisoner.

Halifax B.Mk.VII NP780 EQ-C *Chesty*, suitably adorned with a buxom female figure and a Scotty dog as nose art on 408 'Goose' Squadron RCAF at Linton-On-Ouse, survived the war and was sold for scrap in December 1949.

Flying Officer Humphrey Watts' RCAF crew on B.Mk.VII NP793 on 426 'Thunderbird' Squadron RCAF at Linton-on-Ouse. All seven crew were killed on 5 March 1945 while outbound for Chemnitz when Watts tried to get above freezing fog after take-off. This attempt failed and the aircraft came down after control had been lost and it crashed at Hutton-le-Hole, Kirkbymoorside. There were no survivors.

Halifax B.Mk.III LV937/MH-E *Expensive Babe* on 51 Squadron which recorded its 100th op on the Osnabrück raid on 25 March 1945. Group Captain B.D. Sellick DFC, the station commander at Snaith, was there to greet Flight Lieutenant R. Kemp's crew on their return. LV937 had started out with 578 Squadron in March 1944, with which it served for only a month. The swastika symbol is for a Ju 88 claim.

An RAF Halifax crew pictured at the end of their tour.

'Scotty' Young.

bomber. Then the blips disappeared from the radar screen. Flight Lieutenant F. Taylor, the squadron gunnery leader who had replaced the regular tail gunner who had reported sick, confirmed that he had just seen a bomber going down in flames four miles to their port quarter. A little later Ramsden picked up a suspicious contact almost dead astern and it was closing rapidly from a range of half a mile. Ramsden warned the rear-gunner and Taylor fired his four Brownings at the angle given to him by the wireless operator. 'He's on fire! Going down to port!' Taylor shouted. Ramsden jerked back his blackout curtain and peered through the porthole to see an FW 190 as it hurtled under their wing tip in a mass of flames. Ramsden wrote later that 'another five seconds on that course and we could have thrown cream-puffs at him.'

Sergeant Taylor the rear gunner on 'H-Harry' (LV795) on 78 Squadron first observed an FW 190 dead astern and well below at a range of 900 yards. Before sighting enemy aircraft, he had notified the pilot that the intercom was cutting out when the turret was turned to port and when Taylor tried to give combat manoeuvre, the pilot was unable to hear the instructions. By the time the rear gunner was able to get through on the intercom and warn the pilot, the enemy aircraft had closed to within 600 yards. At 500 yards the Halifax pilot did a diving turn to port and Taylor opened fire with a long burst. Hits were observed to enter the enemy aircraft which climbed vertically and Taylor was able to fire a long burst underside of the FW 190 which immediately burst into flames and dived straight down. Three members of the crew witnessed the fighter go down and explode when it hit the ground.

Twelve aircraft on 427 Squadron successfully bombed the target and returned safely home. Flight Lieutenant A. McAuley, a veteran of twenty-four trips, made his first turn back due to engine trouble. Leaving the target, 'V for Victor' piloted by Warrant Officer Alexander E. 'Rex' Clibbery DFM RCAF turned sharply onto a leg to starboard. He then began to lose altitude rapidly to get the cover of the ground against possible fighter attacks as quickly as possible. 'Once out of the target area and down at a lower level I manipulated the fuel system controls, draining the nearly empty tanks and reserving fuel in four main tanks, one for each engine, for landing. I only remember one incident. We were up at about two to five thousand feet and ahead we saw some tracer exchanged. A little while later we passed very close to an aircraft burning on the deck. One could see some sort of building and trees in the glow of the fire.' Near Cologne Clibbery suddenly put the nose very sharply down into a dive. He shouted, 'Didn't anybody see that boy?' and an FW 190 went from nose to tail over the top of them and carried straight on. The crew were then fully alert.'

The enemy coast was recrossed without trouble and Clibbery made his way north across England to Yorkshire only to be diverted, because of fog, to Stratford. On their eventual return to Leeming it seemed, by the empty dispersal pens and the familiar faces missing from debriefing, that many other crews had also been diverted because of the fog which had cloaked Yorkshire.

Three of the Halifaxes on 427 'Lion' Squadron, including LW618 captained by 23-year-old Flying Officer Walter McPhee, were posted missing. Outbound and south of track, LW618 was hit by cannon fire from a night-fighter and crashed with no survivors. Pilot Officer John Moffat, Squadron Leader 'Turkey' Laird's rear gunner, who had counted twenty-two aircraft going down in as many minutes on the outbound trip, watched a solitary Halifax over the target. Suddenly a Bf 109 'Wild Boar' dived down to attack. The pilot was either wounded or he miscalculated. The fighter flew straight into the bomber, hitting it in the rear of the fuselage, tearing off the entire tail unit. Moffat saw the Halifax fall in a curious flat spin, its shattered tail end down and on the inside of the spin. It vanished from view. Twenty-four year-old Pilot Officer Joe Corbally got his bombs away and Laird turned for home, the crew relieved to get away from Nuremberg. But twenty minutes later, after the navigator ordered a forty-five degree turn to port over the south-east corner of Belgium, Lancaster ND776 flown by Flight Sergeant Eric Pickin on 622 Squadron emerged out of the darkness on a collision course. In an instant the Halifax and the Lancaster smashed into one another. Jim Moffat was the only survivor from the two crews and was doubly lucky because by the time he pulled himself out of his turret and crawled forward and jumped, the Halifax was down to 1,000 feet. Moffat evaded capture and after many close shaves and fighting with the Resistance, met up with the American advance and was flown to England in September.

'D-Dog' (LV898) skippered by Squadron Leader Jack Bissett was shot down south-west of Cologne by Oberleutnant Martin 'Tino' Becker, Staffelkapitän and his Bordfunker Unteroffizier Karl-Ludwig Johanssen of 2./NJG6. There were no survivors. Almost immediately Becker saw the silhouette of another Halifax about 400 metres away and LV857 MH-H2 on 51 Squadron flown by 21-year-old Sergeant Jack Percival George Binder became the next victim. The Halifax hit the ground at 0023. As they looked down at the burning wreckage Becker and Johanssen saw six other bombers fall within seconds of each other. All of Binder's crew, who were on their third operation, were killed.

After disposing of two Lancasters, Becker's fifth victory of the night was LV822 MH-Z2 on 51 Squadron, which was being flown by

Flight Sergeant Edward Wilkins, a 20-year-old Australian. Becker gave the Halifax a five-second burst and the wing wheeled up and tilted over. All the crew, who were on their sixth operation, died. Although Becker now had little fuel remaining Johanssen picked up a blip on his radar screen almost at once and quickly guided Becker to the Viermot (German for 4-motor bomber or 4-Mot) ten kilometres north-west of Alsfeld. It was another 51 Squadron Halifax and it was MH-QZ, flown by Flight Sergeant Graham G. Brougham RAAF. Becker framed LW544 in his sights and gave the Halifax a five-second burst before it keeled over and crashed. Brougham and four crew were killed. The Australian bomb aimer and the flight engineer survived to be taken prisoner.

After returning to base to refuel and rearm, Becker and Johanssen destroyed 'P-Peter' (LW634), a Halifax III on 158 Squadron, which crashed seventeen kilometres WNW of Luxembourg. Sergeant S. Hughes the pilot and four of his crew were taken prisoner. The navigator and the rear gunner evaded capture. To the victor the spoils: next day, 'Tino' Becker received news that he had been awarded the Ritterkreuz. 'There were such a lot of British bombers around that we could have knocked them down with a fly-trap,' he said. He was decorated personally by the Führer at Hitler's HQ in East Prussia.

Returning crews reported numerous night fighters that were aided by the bright moon although there was no moon on the way out to the coast from Nuremberg. On 427 Squadron 'N-Nuts' piloted by Flying Officer W.J. Weicker was attacked by a fighter. 'The mid-upper gunner first sighted an exchange of tracers from two unidentified aircraft on the port beam. The enemy aircraft apparently saw this aircraft when he broke away from the other bomber and therefore opened fire from 600 yards or more. The mid-upper gunner saw this trace coming from the port quarter down and instructed his pilot to corkscrew to port. This was done and the enemy aircraft was not seen after resume course was given. Neither gunners opened fire and no damage was sustained to the aircraft. A number of the pilots actually saw the night fighters shooting down our aircraft and tracers filled the air.'

429 'Bison' Squadron RCAF lost two of its thirteen aircraft that had departed Leeming. 'N-Nan' (LK800) skippered by 22-year-old Pilot Officer Keith Hamilton Bowly RAAF was shot down by Oberleutnant Wilhelm Engel of 3./NJG6 at 0238 hours for his second victory of the night. The crew who were on their 17th operation bailed out. Bowly evaded capture for a time but was later apprehended and sent to Stalag Luft I. The flight engineer, navigator, bomb aimer and the mid upper gunner were ultimately taken prisoner while the wireless operator and the rear gunner evaded. 'Q-Queenie'

(LK804) piloted by 21-year-old Flying Officer James Henry Wilson RCAF, which had been attacked and badly damaged near Stuttgart, on return ditched in the English Channel. It was only the presence of Sergeant H.J. Robinson of Montreal in the newly installed belly-gun position and immediate evasive action by the pilot that saved the aircraft from complete destruction. Robinson had previously served in the Merchant Navy in 1940 before transferring to the RCAF. Sergeant Harry 'Hank' Glass, the flight engineer, put out a fire by chopping a hole in the side of the fuselage and kicking out two blazing magnesium flares kept there in case of a landing in the sea. After a complicated rescue operation involving Spitfire, Tempest Sea Otter and Walrus aircraft, the six men were picked up that afternoon twenty-five miles off the Normandy coast by two RAF launches from Newhaven. 'Hank' Glass was killed on 8 August just before he was due to receive, from HM King George VI, the DFM for dealing with the blazing flares.

The trip to the target was uneventful for Warrant Officer 'Paddy' Clarke's experienced crew on 'L-London' on 10 Squadron. Denis Girardau, the rear gunner, recalled. 'However, on numerous occasions I reported to the skipper that there were many flares in the sky behind us, much more so than on previous trips and I suggested that the Germans were using many "scarecrows" this night.' Later he was to realize that the 'scarecrows' were actually bombers exploding. His crew arrived on time at the target with the first wave. The bombing run, Girardau remembers, was normal – until Flying Officer Geoff Fenton, the bomb aimer, had dropped his bombs. 'At that moment I called for a corkscrew to starboard having sighted a Ju 88 on the starboard quarter. I opened fire and as he broke away the mid-upper gunner also opened fire. A few seconds later we observed him to be on fire and losing height rapidly. Cloud obscured him quickly.' Within minutes Girardau was glad to hear that his pilot was back on the homeward course. On the way out of Germany there were a number of occasions when Girardau saw other aircraft being attacked although the cloud had built up as had been expected some hours earlier. But neither he nor the Canadian mid-upper gunner, Pilot Officer Don Johnson, had to use their guns again that night.

'Paddy' Clarke's crew were third to land at Melbourne. 'We received a hearty welcome from the ground crew,' recalled Denis Girardau, who had spent 7.55 hours airborne in the rear turret. 'De-briefing was carried out and we explained how Met had boobed for the trip to the target. It was a big shock to learn that overall ninety-four aeroplanes had been reported missing. My own view of this great loss was that it was due to cloud missing on the half-moon trip and the Germans must have known about the operation as we took off. After some hours sleep and return to the flights we learned that six out of our squadron's twelve aircraft had failed to return.' But only 'Y-Yorker' (LV881), flown by 21-year-old Pilot Officer Walter Thomas Andrew Regan of Barnsley, Yorkshire, whose crew were on their fifth operation, had been lost. It was possibly the aircraft claimed shot down by Oberleutnant Fritz Brandt of 3./NJGr.10 flying a Bf 110. 'It was easy to approach bombers unseen as we nearly always came in from below, where it was dark. Bombers did attempt to evade us by weaving and corkscrewing but we fighters stayed on their tails and flew in the same manner. It was possible to plot their course to the target by the number of wrecked aircraft, which we could see next day. They ran in a smouldering line across half Germany.' Regan, his 21-year-old Australian flight engineer, the mid-upper gunner and the wireless operator were killed. The Canadian navigator, the bomb aimer and the rear gunner were taken prisoner. The other missing aircraft must have landed in emergency at other airfields.

Flight Sergeant Roger Callaway, the Canadian rear gunner on Halifax 'N-Nan' on 426 'Thunderbird' Squadron RCAF, recalled that 'things were fairly quiet until Nuremberg when all hell broke loose. Although we were not attacked I witnessed many aircraft going down and Jerry seemed all around us and it was sure cold... Withdrawal from the contested target area was a quiet affair subsequently complicated only by the urgent need for Flight Lieutenant Shedd to visit the Elsan – literally the can – at the rear of the aircraft. During this embarrassing manoeuvre with the controls of the Halifax in the hands of the flight engineer, 'Nan' got slightly off course over France and flak opened up as we flew over a Luftwaffe airfield. The runway lights were then switched on and I surmised that more night fighters were taking off. After this incident I saw several more aircraft shot down. Other than for this it had only seemed like just another long trip, but we were naturally saddened by the number of missing faces at beer call. Our squadron used to buy beer for our missing friends then lean their chairs back against the table and God help anyone who tried to sit in the places of those missing.'

Sergeant David George Davidson the Scottish flight engineer on Halifax 'A-Able', an old Mark III on 78 Squadron at Breighton piloted by Flight Sergeant Paul Eric Christiansen RCAF, noted that the target came into sight at 0018. The crew, on only their second op, still did not have their own aircraft. Davidson, who was from Inverness and a former taxi driver, recalled 'Very bright over the target. I could make out the shapes of some streets with the fires and explosions. Here and there a few Lancs and Halifaxes were in sight. Sergeant J. Liston RCAF, the bomb aimer, announced 'Bombs away' at 0123 and we started turning off to starboard. Height: 20,500 feet. Air temperature; -32° Centigrade. I saw a Halifax going down in a vertical dive towards the target at 0124 with three Ju 88s on its tail. Smoke or haze over parts of target area. The Halifax was diving head-first for this. We turned to starboard and completely lost sight of the diving Halifax and Ju 88 fighters. We were on course for the French coast and holding to 20,000 feet at 0126. A Lancaster, going in the opposite direction, went over the top of us; very close. Too close! A bit of nattering on intercom. We were late on target but that Lanc was even later, heading for the target at this time of morning, 0130. Christ! There was the target coming up again, in front. Quick call to the navigator to check the "off target" course. The skipper went to set the checked course on the gyro compass and found that the gyro had toppled on our first turn away from the target.

'At last the contrails had stopped. It seemed much darker now, away from the target. The wireless operator, Sergeant A. Hale, started passing winds received from Group. They gave 90 mph but the navigator did not agree. He made the wind nearer 120 mph. Things were fairly quiet now and we seemed all alone over Germany. Red TIs were seen on the ground as we passed well to the south of Aachen at 0300. On and on to the coast. Would we ever get there? There was a very bright star dead ahead. It could be Venus. 0430: the French coast was ahead, all black and gold. We were getting lower and lower but there was nothing to worry about. The navigator said that our ground speed against the head winds was 64 mph. We could taxi faster. Coffee and biscuits would never taste so good before or since with the English Channel below. We began to relax now. It had been so quiet for the last hour.'

The crew's relaxation was premature for at this point the Halifax suddenly began to shudder and shake. Checking his panel, coffee forgotten, the flight engineer pin-pointed the trouble: the port inner engine was losing oil pressure and the engine rpms were surging. At 0450 he stopped the motor and feathered the airscrew. Christiansen immediately asked the navigator for a course to the nearest airfield. Luckily it turned out to be Ford, an emergency field on the south coast. He was cleared to make a straight-in approach as by this time the Halifax was down to about 500 feet above the sea. Joining the Ford circuit pattern Christiansen wasted no time getting down and landed eight minutes later. Ford was crowded with returning Lancasters and Halifaxes which had made emergency landings there. The crew reported to flying control for debriefing and Christiansen tried to telephone Breighton but the connection was poor so he made arrangements for news of his emergency landing to be passed on to 78 Squadron. 'All we wanted was food and sleep,' Davidson concluded. 'Sleep, mostly. I felt as if I had been gutted. There was nothing inside me. Dirty and sweaty we went over to the mess. Lord, I thought all Bomber Command was here. And the cigarette smoke! An LAC took us to our billet, moaning all the way about making hundreds of beds and lighting fires. "What a bloody air force," he said. We didn't care: "Where are the beds?" we asked.'

Like everyone else, Pilot Officer Frank Collis, pilot of 'V-Victor' on 207 Squadron, was surprised to learn the following day of the high losses. He wondered if there might have been a leak in security. He had recrossed the French coast near Dieppe at 15,000 feet by 0400 and continued descending to 10,000 feet over the English Channel. Navigation lights were switched on again as he crossed the English coast to the west of Beachy Head. After that it was Reading and Peterborough and then finally, at 0517, Collis landed at Spilsby at 0525 after 7.25 hours in the air.

At Tholthorpe a dozen Halifaxes on 425 'Alouette' Squadron and fourteen Halifaxes on 420 'Snowy Owl' Squadron had been dispatched. Flight Sergeant Bob Furneaux, a 425 'Alouette' Squadron air gunner, saw about a dozen aircraft shot down. 'R-Robert' on 420 'Snowy Owl' Squadron had returned early due to hydraulics. 'U-Uncle' was an early return due to oxygen supply malfunction. On return, aircraft were diverted to Tangmere, Thorney Island and Ford. Lost in thick cloud with his petrol almost exhausted, Flight Sergeant Jack Ward, a former 'Mountie', crashed 'C-Charlie' (LW683) into a small farm building after a wheels-up landing in open country three miles from RAF Cranwell. Incredibly, there were no casualties. Squadron Leader Arthur G. Plummer RCAF on 420 Squadron recalled, 'Soon after starting the long leg eastward we began to see plenty of activity abeam of us. We knew that some of what we saw was certainly our bombers going down in flames and hitting the ground. I distinctly remember saying to the crew: "They sure knew we were coming."'

Some squadrons returned relatively unscathed. At Elsham Wolds sixteen Halifaxes on 576 Squadron had taken off and only one had been lost. Flight Lieutenant T.R. Donaldson RAAF piloting 'P-Peter' said: 'There were fighters all the way and they were making the most of the bright moon. I watched tracer flashing across the sky as bomber after bomber fought its way to the target. The Germans were doing their damnedest to beat us off. Searchlights...flak and fighters...'

Crouched over his chart table for eight hours and fifteen minutes of navigation in the cramped tunnel on 'P-Peter', Flight Sergeant John Gordon Earl RAAF recalled only that 'the volume of attacks was considerably greater than we had experienced on any other trip and there was ten-tenths cloud over the target.' It was the crew's seventh operation.

578 Squadron at Burn had dispatched eleven Halifaxes and one was among those aircraft, low on fuel or badly damaged by enemy action or both, that struggled into Silverstone airfield home to 17 OTU, four miles south of Towcester in Northamptonshire. Crews that had already landed watched 'S-Sugar' (LW478) piloted by 26-year-old Squadron Leader Maurice McCreanor coming in on three engines at the end of what was their fifteenth op, but the visibility was poor and he could not line up with the runway. The control tower heard McCreanor say *I'll try to come round again. I'll try to* but he failed to see the masts of the Assisted Safe Landing equipment. By inches he missed the main hangar, clipped the trees, went straight through main stores and tumbled and exploded across some playing fields beyond for 200 yards. McCreanor, the 'second dickey' and five crew were either killed outright or died later.

Meanwhile, there had been no word from MZ508 flown by Flight Sergeant Albert Edward Pinks. All of Pinks' crew, who were on their first operation, were dead. They had been on the squadron just five days. Sergeant R.C. Corker, a Halifax flight engineer on the squadron, was another who experienced a fighter attack: 'Without any warning at all, we were attacked from underneath; there was an enormous bang as a cannon shell exploded in the starboard-inner and four or five pieces caught me in the fleshy part of the bottom. The fighter shot across our nose and attacked another Halifax about 11 o'clock high from us. It blew up. He had made the two attacks in about twenty seconds.'

For those crews that made it back safely the feelings of relief can only be put into words by someone who experienced it time and again. When Sergeant Mitchell the flight engineer on Halifax 'D-Dog' on 640 Squadron reported a fuel shortage, his skipper, Flight Sergeant Johnson, decided to land at Tangmere instead of pressing on north to Leconfield in Yorkshire as it was suspected that a fuel tank had been holed during one of the night-fighter attacks. On landing, cannon-shell strikes were found in the wings, the fuselage and in both fins and rudders. The Halifax had been airborne for 7.45 hours. After a brief sleep in strange surroundings instead of at their own familiar base, the crew flew thoughtfully home to Leconfield with the sun in their faces and the slipstream whistling through the jagged cannon-shell holes.

'L-London' on 51 Squadron, having survived its brush with an unidentified aircraft, Bill Stenning reckoned that they must have been somewhere near Stuttgart when they ran into searchlights and heavy flak. Stenning poured out 'Window' and they had a hectic ten minutes. This was about 0200.

'Soon afterwards,' recalled Stenning, 'Alf Barnard called me and asked me to help him with Joe Pawell who seemed half asleep and drugged. We could not think he was wounded. Over the intercom he mumbled *I'm OK. I'm OK. Get the wheels up.* They were down we discovered – and so were we. Without realizing it we were down to only about 5,000 feet instead of 20,000 feet. Something had gone wrong somewhere as fuel was very low on one tank and Alf had to do some quick calculating. We couldn't get the undercarriage up but the pilot seemed to be better and we were getting well over France. I got the trailing aerial out and tuned into 500 kilocycles just in case and we headed for Tangmere, one of the emergency airfields in the south of England.'

Approaching the English coast Pawell's crew of could see a lot of activity with searchlights homing incoming bombers. By about 0345 the Halifax was over Tangmere where there appeared to be some confusion with Lancasters and Halifaxes milling about, flares going off and urgent Mayday calls crowding the air as bombers, diverted from their fog-bound airfields further north, were stacked over Tangmere. In the middle of it all they were diverted to Wing near Silverstone. Stenning immediately began working Wing HF/DF radio and got a bearing, which he passed to Bob Clark the navigator. 'About twenty minutes after leaving Tangmere,' said Stenning, 'the mid-upper gunner shouted that there were trees just below us and, sure enough, we were only a few hundred feet up. Great panic! Joe Pawell was in a stupor again and would not respond quickly. We managed to get on a bit more boost and gained height again. All engines were OK but the wheels were still dragging. I later learned that we had flown over Hindhead only eight miles from my home and its height above sea level had nearly finished us. By now it was half-light and very misty. At about 0400 we were approaching Wing airfield and got them on R/T. Visibility was bad but they were putting out goose-neck flares on the runway. We joined the circuit and made two attempts to get in. I went up by Joe Pawell with Alf Barnard, but our help wasn't much good as each time he was sure he could do it but each time we overshot. Third time lucky and we were down – right on the goose-neck flares. I looked back from the astrodome and it looked like 'FIDO' where we had knocked over some of the flares and the spilled paraffin had caught light, burning all over the runway. The wheels had locked down OK.'

Several other crews diverted to Wing reported worse trips than Pawell's crew had experienced but Bill Stenning and the rest of the crew were 'thunderstruck' when they heard on the BBC news at breakfast next morning that ninety-six aircraft were missing. 'Joe Pawell was still very ill and obviously not fit to fly but when we reported to flying control we were told that we must leave for Snaith immediately. Joe telephoned the base and was informed that our squadron had had no aircraft back at all from Nuremberg and that we might be required for operations again that night. As luck would have it our own aircraft was unserviceable with a hydraulic line cut by flak and a fuel tank split open.

When they finally arrived at Snaith, Flight Lieutenant Joe Pawell's crew discovered that of the seventeen Halifaxes on 51 Squadron that had left the airfield that night, four had been shot down by night-fighters and one – LV777 MH-FZ piloted by Squadron Leader Frederick Peter Hill DFC – was shot down probably by flak at Stuttgart and crashed at Neckar with the loss of all seven crew; one had crashed and one was damaged. Everyone on Halifax III LW579 'V-Victor' flown by Pilot Officer James Brooks, who was trying to find RAF Benson for an emergency landing, were killed when the aircraft crashed at Stokenchurch in Oxfordshire. In all, forty-two men were missing, seven of them prisoners in Germany.

The press correspondents and photographers that had watched the Halifaxes take off the previous evening had watched and waited 'so considerately' but they too became aware that were some losses and the notebooks and cameras were put away and they left, obviously not wishing to intrude.

Joe Pawell's crew was sent on leave for four days but none too happily as it had been established that their pilot had burst a duodenal ulcer while flying home from Nuremberg and had lost a lot of blood which explained his lapses into semi-consciousness at the controls. 'That finished his RAF career,' said Stenning. 'We were heart-broken. He was a most experienced pilot. He had been flying since he was sixteen in America and had nearly 10,000 hours. He later returned to Philadelphia. We re-crewed with an Australian, Flying Officer Danny King MiD who had previously broken his back after colliding with the spire of Selby Abbey, but for medical reasons he never completed his tour with us.' With his crew, Stenning went on to complete a tour of thirty-two operations on 51 Squadron.

At Lissett four of the sixteen Halifaxes on 158 Squadron were missing and one returned damaged. Wing Commander 'Jock' Calder later drove down to S-Sugar's dispersal, inspected the Halifax and put the pilot in for a DFC. He found only two bullet holes in the tiny wireless hatch and reflected gravely that a nod of the operator's head might have meant the difference between him living and dying. 'F-Fox' flown by Flight Sergeant

Joe Hitchman had returned at 0534 having 'never been so tired in all his life'. 'We were logging combats almost all the way to the target and back. I was weaving all the way and corkscrewing as the gunners saw fighters. We saw so many aircraft shot down the navigator logged about twenty until eventually I said "For Christ's sake, lads, don't report kites shot down, just keep your eyes open for fighters," so we didn't log any more. Because we had used so much fuel in corkscrewing we couldn't get back to base and had to land at Odiham. We'd been in the air seven hours and thirty minutes. We didn't go to bed and got back to Lissett at about 10 or 11 am. The flight commander asked me before we went to debriefing what it had been like and I said I thought at least fifty had been shot down. He told me off and said I shouldn't be claiming as many missing as that. Then someone else landed and he asked that pilot what it had been like. "Piece of cake," he said. "I didn't see a thing." He thought he had just seen spoof flares. I told him that if he hadn't realised they were aircraft going down in flames he wouldn't be here in a fortnight and he wasn't.'

Later, 'F-Fox' was allocated to the crew skippered by Pilot Officer Cliff R.R. Smith, a Londoner. 'Smithy' branded the superstition 'stuff and nonsense' and named the aircraft *Friday the 13th*. He also painted a scythe on the side, a skull and crossbones and an upside down horseshoe to break the curse. Smith even painted an open ladder above the crew hatch so they would have to walk under it as they climbed on board and painted over the parachute escape hatch on the belly of the aircraft, but these details were later removed. Unlike its predecessors, the bomber racked up an impressive number of operations, the 21st operation distinguished by a key with a Hakenkreuz (Swastika), the 70th with a blockbuster trailing a spiral and the 100th with a larger than usual bomb lying in an open box or coffin. *Friday the 13th* ended the war with 128 operations; more than any other Halifax aircraft.

On return to Breighton, Sergeant David Davidson, Flight Sergeant Christiansen's Scottish flight engineer, found that three of 78 Squadron's aircraft – 'Z-Zebra', 'P-Peter' and 'Q-Queenie' – were missing. 'Christ,' thought Davidson, 'we went out to dispersal in the same crew bus.' He remembered talking with the rear gunner [Sergeant F.R. Wilson] on 'Z-Zebra'. Two years later Davidson was drinking a pint of beer in the sergeants' mess at Catterick when he found himself talking to Wilson. It transpired that the air gunner's Halifax had been attacked and set on fire just after crossing the French coast at 2334, only minutes ahead of Davidson's aircraft and that Davidson had witnessed the action. Spirited return fire from the Halifax had scored strikes on the twin-engined German fighter which then broke off the attack and vanished. Getting no replies when he called on the intercom, the gunner climbed out of his turret and went forward to the nose of the Halifax. It was very draughty in the fuselage, with no member of the crew in sight. He found the cockpit empty and the forward escape hatch open. The crew had bailed out. While there was still time to do so the gunner made his lonely way back to the rear turret and did likewise.

Flight Sergeant Christiansen's crew finally tumbled into their beds at Breighton at 0650. They had spent 7.20 hours in the air, 5.16 hours of it at 20,000 feet in temperatures of minus 33 degrees Centigrade and had breathed oxygen for 6.50 hours. They had taken off with 2,046 gallons of fuel and landed with 86 gallons left, sufficient for little more than fifteen minutes flying. When Christiansen's crew returned to their battered Halifax seven hours later Sergeant David Davidson the Scottish flight engineer found a civilian ground engineer looking it over. Inexplicably, the Halifax's port inner motor checked out satisfactorily on run-up. The previous night's malfunction was diagnosed as being due to coring up of the oil cooler on descent.

When the civilian asked Davidson where the crew had been the night before, Davidson said, 'Nuremberg'.

'You lost ninety-six,' said the civilian who had been listening to the BBC.

Davidson stared at him, astounded. 'You must be kidding,' he said. 'It didn't look that bad to us.'

In fact it was worse. The losses had come through a few hours earlier to the Intelligence Rooms and the number was 104, but that included the known 'ditchings' in the North Sea. The aircraft which had crashed in the sea after sending out 'Mayday' signals would not be included in the number. Command knew where they were and knowing reasoned they were not 'missing'. Christiansen's crew were one of many that had slept through the lunchtime news bulletin and the messes on the bases were unusually quiet as the doom-laden one o'clock news came over the wireless sets.

'Paddy' Clarke's experienced crew on Halifax 'L-London' were third to land at Melbourne. 'We received a hearty welcome from the ground crew,' recalled Denis Girardau, who had spent 7.55 hours airborne in the rear turret. 'De-briefing was carried out and we explained how Met had boobed for the trip to the target. It was a big shock to learn that over all ninety-four aeroplanes had been reported missing. My own view of this great loss was that it was due to cloud missing on the half-moon trip and the Germans must have known about the operation as we took off. After some hours sleep and return to the flights we learned that six out of our squadron's twelve aircraft had failed to return.'

'M-Mike' with Flying Officer Fredrick Robert Stuart and the otherwise all-new RAF crew was one of the luckier ones. Stuart flew home to Melbourne with the freezing slipstream howling through the hole punched in his turret perspex by a cannon shell from an Me 109 over the target and nearing home base they were not happy to hear 'Milkpail', the call sign for Melbourne, warning that there were 'bandits' in the area and that they were to disperse. 'However,' recalled Stuart, 'we were shortly afterwards recalled and, thank goodness, were able to land at our home base.'

At Holme-on-Spalding-Moor, where fourteen Halifaxes had been dispatched by 76 Squadron, the clock in the big briefing room ticked on. On the ops board in the column headed 'Time Down' there were three blank spaces. One of the missing was 'P-Peter' (LK795), Wing Commander Douglas 'Hank' Iveson DSO DFC the squadron commander's aircraft which Flight Lieutenant Henry Denys Coverley took on this, his fortieth trip, the tenth of his second tour because his usual aircraft, *Sir Roger De Coverley*, had gone unserviceable. The Intelligence Officer looked at his watch and checked it with the clock. Hopefully 'P-Peter' or *The Blue Barge* as it was better known – and 'W-William' and 'X-X-ray' – had made emergency landings at dromes on the south-east coast; the telephone at his elbow would ring in a moment confirming it. The room was crowded and there was acute expectancy in the air. Crews who were down were hanging about, deliberately taking their time over mugs of tea, forgetting the hot flying suppers waiting for them in the messes. As the minutes ticked by, many considered the chances of the three crews bailing out and spending the rest of the war as a PoW or lobbing down somewhere in the drink off the coast. It was the best that they could hope for.

As he flew down the 'long leg', Henry Coverley was humming the popular song *Paper Doll* to himself. 'It was a clear night – the weather report was wrong because the Met Officer had told us it would be overcast and the fighters wouldn't be able to get up. But there was no cloud – there wasn't a bloody cloud in the sky! However there was nothing much you could do. I did notice a hell of a lot of aircraft going down all around us and at the time thought it was special shells... "Scarecrows!" We thought the Germans were putting those up to make it look like it was an aircraft going down. They were going down quite fast.'

Suddenly *The Blue Barge* was hit by flak near Hamm. The 6,000 lb load of incendiary bombs exploded causing a massive fire. 'We were about the thirtieth casualty on the way out,' said Coverley. Listening out for a Group broadcast on his wireless set, 20-year-old Sergeant Peter Wilmshurst, on his thirteenth operation, failed to hear the order to bail out and realised all was not well when he saw Sergeant George Edwin Motts the 20-year-old flight engineer heading for the nose escape hatch with his parachute clipped on, closely followed by the pilot, who was last to leave. 'The rest of the crew went out first,' said Coverley. Flight Sergeant W.A. 'Archie' Blake the bomb aimer, the navigator, mid-upper gunner and the rear-gunner got out safely before *The Blue Barge* crashed. George Motts died when he evacuated the Halifax with his parachute on fire. His body was found three days later suspended in a tree, the burnt remains of his parachute canopy draped around him. When the Halifax had gone into a steep dive, Peter Wilmshurst had great difficulty trying to reach his parachute in its stowage and clip it on. Having succeeded in this he found that he was then unable to leave his seat: 'For some unknown reason the dive became more shallow,' he recalled. 'This allowed me to get out of my seat and make my way forward to the escape hatch.' As soon as he jumped he realised that he must have been low to the ground by this time so he pulled the ripcord. After two or three swings under his parachute he hit the ground with an almighty thump, breaking his leg.

Coverley could not leave: two engines had gone on one side. 'I was fighting the controls and the thing was on fire. The only way I could get out was to leave the controls, take a couple of footsteps to the other side of the aircraft and go down a couple of steps to the escape hatch in the front. By that time the aircraft was upside down, doing God knows what. There was no question of just opening a door and jumping out. I'd never carried a parachute. We had ones you slipped on and I put this thing on, but I put it on wrong. I can't remember getting out of the aircraft and I couldn't find the handle to pull the ripcord. But we were at 24,000 feet, so I had plenty of time to think about it. The other thing was the standard harness I had was not my size and we'd ban anyone who took his own. I didn't think it would be any use anyway; and the strap that should have been across was in front of my nose. I was awfully sick on the way down; I landed in some trees. I couldn't see anything – something had hit me in the face before I'd jumped out and I couldn't see very well. I was suspended from these trees and I didn't know how far I was from the ground. Eventually after swaying around in this tree for a while I thought I'd better get myself out and my feet were about six inches from the ground! So then I started walking. I was lucky.'

Coverley walked for thirty miles and evaded capture for four days before being caught crossing a bridge over the Rhine. Peter Wilmshurst too was apprehended. In the ambulance that picked him up he was most surprised to find 'Archie' Blake on a stretcher next to him. He had spent several hours dangling on his parachute which had become entangled in a tall pine tree. Unable to reach the trunk of the tree and starting to suffer from frostbite he had turned the quick-release buckle on his parachute harness and fallen about thirty feet to the ground. Consequently he was suffering from a fractured pelvis. The injured pair were hospitalised. Nineteen weeks after they had been shot down both men arrived at Stalag Luft VII (Bankau).

'W-William' (LW647) was skippered by Flying Officer Gordon Charles George Greenacre who was on his second tour on the squadron. His was possibly one of three Viermots shot down by 23-year-old Oberfeldwebel Rudolf Frank of 3./NJG3 flying a Bf 110G-4 on his 176th night sortie. Frank had taken off from Vechta with his bordfunker Oberfeldwebel Hans-Georg Schierholz but minus his usual air-gunner, Feldwebel Heinz Schneider, who had been replaced by a young pilot fresh from training to gain combat experience. Using his oblique guns Frank shot down his first victim, which he identified as a Lancaster, with one burst which set the Halifax bomber's fuel tanks ablaze and sent it crashing down at 0001 hours. Two men bailed out and were taken prisoner. On 1 April Gordon Greenacre's crew were laid to rest at Nieder Moos, since when their bodies have been reinterred at Durnbach War Cemetery in Bavaria.

Seventeen minutes after 'W-William' went down, a Lancaster fell to Oberfeldwebel Frank's guns in the same manner as the Halifax, in the region north of Fulda. Thirty-four minutes later Schierholz picked up a new contact. It was a Halifax. They were instructed to fly for about five minutes with the bomber to determine its course and altitude before receiving instructions to attack. Frank employed the same tactics as before and the Halifax crashed in flames in the region of the Rhön. His 41st to 43rd kills earned him the Ritterkreuz with Eichenlaub but like many others his career was short-lived. Having scored two more Abschüsse to take his score to forty-five night victories, Frank was killed on 26/27 April when he crashed after being hit by debris from a 12 Squadron Lancaster which was falling to the ground near Eindhoven. He was posthumously promoted to Leutnant at the end of April on Hitler's birthday.

Halifax 'X-X-ray' (LW696) flown by Squadron Leader Kenneth Arthur Clack DFM was sent down in flames twelve kilometres north-west of Wetzlar by a Bf 110 using 'Schräge Musik'. Kenny Clack had gained his DFM for bringing his crippled Halifax home from a raid on Trondheim on 27 April 1942 during his first tour on 76 Squadron. He had recently taken command of 'C' Flight. All of the crew except for Sergeant Guy L. Edwards, the mid-upper gunner, were killed. The crew were on their fourth operation of their second tour.

Hauptmann Fritz Lau, a 32-year-old Bf 110G-4 pilot and Staffelkapitän of 4./NJG1 and a former Lufthansa pilot who had flown Ju 52 transports in the Polish campaign before transferring to night fighters, had finally taken off from Laon-Athies with his bordfunker and bordschütze at 2354 hours. They flew for about thirty minutes when they saw an aircraft going down on fire. When they reached about 5,500 metres his bordfunker saw a contact on his radar set. Lau flew towards it and recognised it as a Viermot, whose pilot was weaving in 'crocodile line' at 20,000 feet. It was a Halifax; probably 'Z-Zebra' (LK762) on 78 Squadron flown by Sergeant Ronald Arthur Horton. Lau considered that the crew may have seen him but more likely the enemy pilot was weaving to fly through the many 'burn-ups' in the sky. Lau tried to get into an attack position but each time he thought he had got the Viermot in his sights he moved out of them. At one moment he was 150 metres away, the next 200 metres. This continued for about two minutes. The Halifax weaved. Lau weaved. Gradually the German pilot came to the conclusion that he would lose him unless he did something quickly. He decided that the next time he got into a reasonably close position he would attack. The moment came when the Halifax, which was somewhat higher than the Bf 110, went into a gradual right-hand turn and Lau turned with him. The distance between them was now about 100 to 150 metres. Lau pulled in the stick, lifted the 110's nose and fired. Flames shot from the bomber and he went into a steep dive. Lau flew over the Viermot and saw three of the crew bailing out before the aircraft crashed near Herbon-Seelbach south-west of Bonn. The flight engineer, bomb aimer and the rear gunner were taken prisoner. Before hitting the ground the Halifax broke into two parts, of which one, the larger, again broke on impact so that in the end three parts of it were burning below. The others were laid to rest in Rheinberg War Cemetery.

All told, 76 and 78 Squadrons each lost three Halifaxes, plus 76 Squadron would have one return damaged and another would be written off. Thirty men were killed and thirteen were taken into captivity.

Unteroffizier Otto Kutzner of 5./NJG3, piloting a Bf 110G-4, returned with claims for three Lancasters destroyed. However, the second of these victories was probably 'C-Charlie' (MZ504) on 432 'Leaside' Squadron RCAF at East Moor seven miles north of York skippered by Flying Officer Earle Kerr Reid of Milford Station, a small village in southern Nova Scotia.

'C-Charlie' was shot down at 0040 hours, five minutes after Kutzner had claimed his first victim seven kilometres north of Mengerskirchen. The Halifax crashed in a cornfield astride a railway line three kilometres south of Friedberg. Reid remained at the controls until other crewmembers jumped clear but by then it was too late for him to follow. The flight engineer was unable to escape; his parachute had opened inside the burning aircraft. The mid upper gunner was the last to bail out but he landed on high-tension wires not far from the downed aircraft and was electrocuted. The rest of the crew survived and were taken prisoner. Otto Kutzner's third Abschuss fell south of Nuremberg at 0133 hours.[34]

The 'Leaside' Squadron lost a second aircraft when 'Z-Zebra' (LW687) was shot down by a night-fighter. Even though their attacker was spotted by both the mid-upper gunner 19-year-old Pilot Officer Robert William Rathwell and the tail gunner, 22-year-old Pilot Officer Samuel Saprunoff, the Halifax was hit broadside before Pilot Officer Chester Russell Narum could take evasive action. Narum, his two gunners and Sergeant Robert Thomson the Scottish flight engineer who came from Glasgow were killed. The three other Canadians on the crew survived and were taken into captivity. The crew was on their fifth operation.

Oberleutnant Helmuth Schulte of 4./NJG5, a Bf 110 pilot at Parchim, shot down two Lancasters, after which Unteroffizier Georg Sandvoss, his bordfunker, picked up a contact thirty kilometres south-west of Eisenach. It was the Halifax III on 640 Squadron at Leconfield flown by 20-year-old Flying Officer James Dutton Laidlaw RCAF. Schulte blasted the Viermot with his oblique guns, which were now working again. Laidlaw received terrible wounds to his legs and just had time to order his crew to bail out before he died. The flight engineer was either killed outright or mortally wounded. The navigator, also badly injured, fell across the forward escape hatch and prevented others using it. The wireless operator and the two gunners who left by the rear hatch were taken prisoner. The bomb aimer refused to leave the injured navigator. Although he had time to escape he was last seen by the side of his dying comrade. The Halifax crashed and exploded on the west bank of the Ochse just south of Vacha.

---

34 His twelfth and last victory was a Halifax on 7 March 1945. On this night he was attempting to land his Ju 88 at Göttingen which had a short runway when he hit the second of two trains. He cart-wheeled and was thrown clear but the other crewmembers were killed. He lost his left leg and was hospitalized from 7 March to May 1947.

All told, 640 Squadron lost three of its sixteen Halifaxes dispatched and three were damaged, with the loss of eighteen men killed and three taken prisoner. Apart from LW500 captained by Warrant Officer David Burke already mentioned, 'L for London' (LW555) skippered by Flying Officer Charles Edward O'Brien RCAF was shot down, probably by Leutnant Hans Zettel of 12./NJG6 who claimed his victory as a 'Stirling' at Montabaur at 0035 hours. The skipper and his crew who were on their fourth operation were killed.[35]

Eleven Halifaxes on 578 Squadron had taken off from Burn. One of them was Halifax LK-E in 'A' Flight skippered by 22-year-old Pilot Officer Cyril Joe Barton who had lifted off at about 2200 hours on his nineteenth operation. Barton was born at Elveden, Suffolk, on 5 June 1921, the son of Ethel (1896-1958) and Frederick (1892-1963) and was brought up in New Malden, Surrey, where he had attended Beverley Boys School and Kingston College. At 16 years of age he was apprenticed as an engineer at the Parnall Aircraft Factory works in Tolworth and was a part-time student of engineering at Kingston Technical College in Surrey. On 16 April 1941, when he was 19, Barton left his reserved occupation apprenticeship at the Parnall Aircraft Factory and volunteered for the Royal Air Force Volunteer Reserve. His father, who was a veteran of the trenches, reluctantly gave parental permission. In a letter to his son he wrote: 'Stick to your principles and faith (this will be very hard in the RAF) and I am confident that you will win... May God bless you and help you in the days that lie ahead.' Cyril volunteered for aircrew duties and joined the RAFVR on 16 April 1941. He entered pilot training in the USA under the Arnold Scheme in late 1941 having set sail from Gourock, Scotland, to Halifax, Canada, aboard the transport ship *Pasteur*. After acclimatization at Maxwell Field, Montgomery, Alabama, he received his Primary Training at Darr Aero Tech, Albany, Georgia, and was one of a relative minority who were allowed to complete their training, having been 'held back' by illness or accidents, finally qualifying as a sergeant pilot on 10 November 1942. He then trained at 1663 Heavy Conversion Unit at Rufforth in Yorkshire.

On 5 September 1943 Barton and his crew joined 78 Squadron and the skipper was commissioned as a pilot officer three weeks later. The crew consisted of Pilot Officer Wally Crate RCAF, bomb aimer; Sergeant Maurice E. Trousdale, flight engineer; Sergeant Jack Kay, wireless air gunner;

---

35 Zettel was killed in a crash on 24/25 April 1944 when he hit trees on landing at Halle-Nietleben airfield.

Sergeant Harry 'Timber' Woods, mid-upper gunner; Sergeant Fred Brice, rear gunner; and Sergeant John Leonard Lambert from Newcastle upon Tyne, navigator, who was unaware that he had been commissioned since 21 March, nine days earlier. Deeply religious, Cyril was afraid that the vigour of his prayer had suffered because he was worried about offending or upsetting his two roommates at Burn by ostentatious shows of faith. On Sunday evening, 26 March, Barton got back from church to the quarters that he shared with Jack Kay and Wally Crate, the two other officers on his crew. On 28 March, two days before the Nuremberg raid, he said that he would be off the 'intercom' for ten minutes and knelt by his bed. Jack Kay had been listening to the wireless, but 'very reverently' turned down his favourite wireless programme out of respect to his skipper and 'an awkward hush settled on the room'. Kay forgot to turn it off when he went to bed, which perhaps showed how shaken he was by Cyril's behaviour.

Undertaking their first operational sortie against Montluçon, Barton and his crew completed nine sorties on 78 Squadron and then, on 15 January 1944, they were posted to 578 Squadron. The crew's second sortie on the new squadron was to Stuttgart in Halifax LK797. Barton was promoted to Flying Officer on 26 March. By 30 March, he had completed four attacks on Berlin and fourteen other operations including six sorties in LK797 – which the crew had named *Excalibur*. On one of these, two members of his crew were wounded during a determined effort to locate the target despite appalling weather conditions.

When Cyril Barton approached the run in to Nuremberg, in accordance with the crew drill John Lambert folded up his navigational gear as he sat directly over the forward escape hatch. Over the target, navigation was from notes on his knee-pad taken from callings by Wally Crate. 'I think we had the bomb-doors open when there was a shout from the rear gunner,' Lambert said. 'His sentence was unfinished as the aircraft shuddered from a rain of cannon shells and the intercom was destroyed. The Halifax was on fire and being thrown around the sky by the pilot. A signal over the emergency light flashers was misunderstood by me, the wireless air gunner and the bomb aimer and I donned my parachute pack. In removing the escape hatch door which had jammed I caught the rip-cord inadvertently on some part of the aircraft interior. The parachute opened in the aircraft and in a flash it was sucked out of the half-open hatch and I was whipped out after it. I was amazed to find myself dangling in mid-air with a torn parachute canopy flapping above me. It was still moonlight but all seemed very quiet and there was no sign of the target. It was bitterly cold. My hands were unprotected and I must have been ejected from the aircraft at a considerable height. Because of the damaged parachute canopy I descended rapidly and hit the middle of a very hard, frozen field.'

Lambert landed without injury on the hard, frozen, German earth. Disposing of his parachute canopy and harness and flying gear, he walked all that night through heavily wooded country and hid all the following day. The countryside was sparsely populated but, after a second night's marching, he was captured trying to steal food from a farmhouse near Hassfurt on the railway line between Bamberg and Stassfurt, about fifty miles north-west of Nuremberg. After being taken to a Luftwaffe camp at Schweinfurt, Lambert duly arrived at Dulag Luft at Oberursel outside Frankfurt where he saw Wally Crate and Jack Kay. At Stalag Luft VI Heydekrug in East Prussia, Lambert was to learn that his pilot had succeeded in navigating and flying the severely damaged Halifax back to England with Maurice Trousdale, 'Timber' Woods and Fred Brice aboard but had been killed while attempting a forced landing near Ryhope Colliery on the Durham coast south of Sunderland. George Dodds Heads (58), a local miner, on his way to work was killed also.

On 27 June it was announced in the *London Gazette* that Pilot Officer Cyril Barton had received the posthumous award of the Victoria Cross. 'My parents never wanted him to fly but he was determined,' recalled his sister Joyce. 'My mother never really got over it.' Joyce remembers a despatch rider at the door soon afterwards. 'Dad opened this big brown envelope and said: 'Cyril's been awarded the Victoria Cross.' All Mum said was: It won't bring him back. But she carried that letter with her until the day she died.'

In a last letter to his younger brother shortly before his death, Barton wrote: *All I can say about this is that I am quite prepared to die. It holds no terror for me. I know I shall survive the Judgement because I have trusted Christ as my own Saviour. I've done nothing to merit glory, but because He died for me it's God's free gift. At times I've wondered whether I've been right in believing in what I do. Just recently I've doubted the veracity of the Bible, but in the little time I've had to sort out intellectual problems, I've been left with a bias in favour of the Bible. Apart from this I have the inner conviction, as I write, of a force outside myself and my brain, that I have not trusted in vain. All I am anxious about is that you and the rest of the family come to know Him. Ken, I know, already does. I commend my Saviour to you.*

Barton's body was buried with full military honours in April 1944 in a registered war grave at the south-west corner of Kingston-upon-Thames Cemetery. Barton Green in New Malden, Surrey, where he had attended school, was named in his honour in the early 1950s. Barton Road at the

Yorkshire Air Museum in Elvington was named in his honour in the year 2000 on the 56th anniversary of his death in action. A housing estate in Ryhope, Barton Park, was also named after him and a nearby street was named Halifax Place, after the bomber-type that he flew in the exploit. Coombe Boys' School (formerly Beverley Boys) in New Malden, Surrey, named a new building after him in 2009. Kingston College, where Barton was a student when the war broke out, offers an annual prize for the pupil of the year, which is named after him. A portrait painting of him hangs in his memory in the 'Wheatsheaf Inn' at Burn, North Yorkshire, where Barton's squadron, 578 Squadron, was based at the time of his last operational sortie. His Victoria Cross is on display at the Royal Air Force Museum at Hendon.

Wing Commander Dudley Forsyth, the Commanding Officer of 466 Squadron RAAF and the crew on 'J-Jig' returned safely to Leconfield after a flight lasting eight and a quarter hours. It had been 'absolutely free of trouble or incident' and he could recall no real damage to any aircraft. He believed that the force's troubles began when quite a number of aircraft bombed the wrong target. After some time on the southerly leg of the course down to Nuremberg, he commented to his crew that he could see the target with an attack developing 30° to starboard. Warrant Officer Wooton, his navigator, was quick to reply that this could not be Nuremberg. He was certain of his position, the aircraft was right on track and there were some minutes to go before reaching the target. As Forsyth flew on south it was obvious that 'a not inconsiderable number' of aircraft were involved in attacking the wrong target. 'The effect was that the aircraft immediately turned onto a westerly heading for home,' he said. 'Thus the force was spread over a very wide area of Germany thus reducing considerably its strength and safety. The offending aircraft also doubtless flew over heavily defended areas instead of along the planned 'safe' track home.'

In all the Luftwaffe claimed 107 bombers for the loss of just five night fighters. The Air Ministry's 39-word communiqué broadcast by the BBC said, *Last night, aircraft of Bomber Command were over Germany in very great strength. The main objective was Nuremberg. Other aircraft attacked targets in western Germany and mines were laid in enemy waters. Ninety-six of our aircraft are missing.* In a subsequent communiqué the Air Ministry amended the number of missing aircraft to 94 but this took no account of the bombers that came down in the sea on the homeward flight or crashed in England. Sixty-four Lancasters and thirty-one Halifaxes (11.9% of the force dispatched) were lost. It took the German night-fighter arm's total for March to 269 RAF bombers destroyed. Fourteen more bombers crashed in England.

Chapter 8

Pride of the Porcupines

The evening was one of those that make you feel it's great to be alive.
Flying Officer John Harvie, navigator, Halifax 'W-Willie',
433 'Porcupine' Squadron, 4/5 July 1944.

In July 1944 Flying Officer William Gordon 'Gordie' Baird RCAF, a 20-year-old fair-haired and slender Canadian from Calgary, Alberta, with a mischievous smile, was a skipper on 433 'Porcupine' Squadron at Skipton-on-Swale, about four miles west of Thirsk on the east bank of the River Swale in North Yorkshire. The squadron had been adopted by the Porcupine District of Northern Ontario. Its motto was *Qui s'y frotte s'y pique* ('Who opposes it gets hurt' or 'Whoever rubs himself there will be pricked there'). Not expecting to fly on the night of Tuesday 4/5 July with one of the crew in sick quarters, Flying Officer John Dalton Harvie, the 20-year-old navigator, took the opportunity to visit the station dentist after lunch and have a tooth filled. However, late in the afternoon Baird's crew learned that they *were* scheduled to fly the operation. Briefing was set for after supper and take-off for 2215 hours at the end of a long summer day. When the crew checked in at the general briefing Harvie discovered that the squadron senior bomb aimer, Pilot Officer Donald Frederick Wilson (23), would be filling in for Hugh Fraser, the regular bomb aimer who had been suffering from a strep throat for several days and was grounded by the station medical officer. Wilson needed only one more trip to complete his tour of thirty operations. Crews were never happy about a 'stranger' in their midst for it might mean bad luck. 'However,' wrote Harvie, 'we did not have much time to worry as we were soon fully occupied absorbing and digesting all the details of the forthcoming operation.'[36] The other members of the crew were the RAF flight engineer Sergeant James Henry Marler

---

36 *Missing In Action: A RCAF Navigator's Story* by John D. Harvie (McGill-Queen's University Press 1995).

(32); wireless operator, Warrant Officer1 Robert Thomas William 'Bill' Longley (22, of Winnipeg, Manitoba); and the two gunners, Sergeants William Henry Winder of Quesnel, British Columbia and Thomas Corson Jenkins, of Esquimalt, British Columbia, both 21.

When Harvie looked at the large map at the front of the briefing room he saw that the target for 282 Lancasters and five Mosquitoes of 1, 6 and 8 Groups was the railway yards at Villeneuve-Ste-Georges near Paris again, despite the continued risk of casualties to French civilians. On Easter Sunday, 9/10 April, when more than a hundred 6 Group RCAF aircraft accompanied 118 bombers from RAF groups in an attack on Villeneuve, considerable damage was done to the yards but 400 houses were damaged or destroyed, 93 French citizens were killed and 167 were injured. At Lille over 230 bombers, mostly Halifaxes, got their bombs away but the yards were hit by just 49 bombs, which destroyed 2,124 of the 2,959 goods wagons in the yards, the rest falling outside the railway area killing 456 French civilians. In the suburb of Lomme more than 5,000 houses were destroyed or damaged.[37] According to the Bomber Command Operational Research Section, 875 of the 3,335 bombs dropped had fallen into the designated target area and that it was the 'best centred of all the marshalling yard attacks to date'. It was an inescapable fact that over 2,000 bombs had fallen into mostly urban areas.

Amid protests from the Vichy regime, raids on marshalling yards continued unabated. Villeneuve was attacked again on 26/27 April, with good results this time. The Canadian Group suffered no losses. But things would be different on 4/5 July when thirty-eight Lancasters on 408 'Goose' Squadron at Linton-on-Ouse, 419 'Moose' and 428 'Ghost' Squadrons at Middleton St. George and sixty-four Halifaxes on 424 'Tiger' Squadron, 433 'Porcupine' Squadron at Skipton-on-Swale, 427 'Lion' and 429 'Bison' Squadrons at Leeming, were scheduled for the latest attack on the rail yards. As a navigator, Flying Officer Harvie had to know the route intimately. The route to the target was reasonably direct but the route home seemed to have them flying over occupied France for an unusually long time. After leaving the target they had to head south and then past Chartres, before finally turning north of home past Rouen. Total flying time was estimated at six hours. The route into and out of enemy territory was planned with frequent changes of course to avoid known concentrations of German anti-aircraft guns and at the same time make it difficult for the enemy to predict

---

37   Middlebrook and Everitt.

their target. Unfortunately. The weather forecast for 4/5 July was for a full moon over France, with no clouds. The best form of defence was always total darkness and clouds that hid them from enemy fighters. They were informed that only Lancasters and Halifaxes would be taking part on the night raid. Path Finders in Lancaster bombers would mark the target with ground flares five minutes in advance of the main bomber force.

Gordon Baird's crew had not completed enough ops to be assigned the same bomber each trip. It was the belief of the junior crews that they were always assigned the 'leftovers', the older and temperamental aircraft. Tonight they were assigned 'W-Willie'; an 'old crock' that had taken them safely to Paris and back on 7 June. 'The evening,' wrote John Harvie, 'was one of those that make you feel it's great to be alive.'

'Standing beside 'W-Willie', I looked beyond the ugly dark bombers scattered around the perimeter of the base and saw the English countryside at its summer best. The sun setting in the west behind our dispersal area gave a mellow glow to everything. As yet, no harsh roar of airplane engines disturbed the peace of the perfect evening. It was hard to believe that men were at war and that many of those standing around their bombers, engaged in idle chit-chat and smoking a last cigarette before embarking, would never return.'[38]

The crews were over the target at between 9,000 and 13,000 feet, releasing 791,000 lbs of high explosives. According to reports, the target was accurately bombed with severe damage to the rail yards, but the Canadian Group encountered German night-fighters near Rouen and nine 6 Group aircraft, or 8.8 per cent of the force, went down. Pilot Officer H.A. Kirkby on 424 'Tiger' Squadron was attacked by an FW 190 and a Bf 109. The Messerschmitt was claimed damaged and the FW 190 was claimed destroyed by Flight Sergeant E.A. Snider, the rear gunner. Flying Officer W. Palidwar and crew flying 'S for Sugar' on 424 'Tiger' Squadron was fired upon by a corkscrewing Halifax but there was no damage. Flying Officer J. Keys and crew flying 'E for Edward' were attacked by an unidentified single engine aircraft which was attacking a Fortress at the time. There was no claim or damage. Flying Officer D. Brown and crew flying 'U-Uncle' were attacked by an Me 210 just after it shot down a nearby Lancaster. There was no claim or damage. Flying Officer D. McNaughton and crew on 'F for Freddie' on 429 'Bison' Squadron were attacked three times by Ju 88s. One was shot down in flames by Sergeant P.F. Hunt, the rear gunner. Wing Commander A.F. Avant and crew on 'B-Baker' were attacked by a

---

38   *Missing In Action,* Harvie.

twin engined enemy aircraft. There was no claim or damage. At 21, the youngest wing commander in Bomber Command, Avant was injured in an air test crash on 13 July and spent the rest of his tour in a body cast. Pilot Officer L. Mitchell and crew flying 'U for Uncle' were attacked by an FW 190; there was no claim or damage. Flying Officer M. Sloski and crew flying 'O-Oboe' were attacked by a Me 410. Strikes were seen and it was claimed 'damaged'. Pilot Officer K. Carter on 428 'Ghost' Squadron returned on the Master Bomber's orders without bombing.

Among the German victors this night was Obergefreiter Johannes Strassner of 2./NJG2 who claimed two Halifaxes near Chartres for his second and third Abschüsse of the war. Hauptmann Fritz Söthe (29), born at Lohfeld in Minden, flying a Ju 88 in 4./NJG4, claimed a Halifax shot down for his 17th Abschuss; possibly 'S for Sugar' on 427 'Lion' Squadron flown by Flying Officer Claude Alexander 'Bud' Moss RCAF, which crashed fifteen minutes after 'bombs away'.[39] Moss and his flight engineer were killed; the navigator and air bomber evaded and two others were taken into captivity. Flight Sergeant Harold Atkin RCAF successfully evaded until betrayed by the Mayor of Artenay and was imprisoned in Fresnes and Buchenwald before being recovered by the Luftwaffe and delivered to Stalag Luft III.

Flight Lieutenant H. Woodruff and crew on 427 'Lion' Squadron flying Halifax III 'E-Edward' were attacked by a Ju 88. There was no damage, but some strikes were seen on the Ju 88. Flying Officer R. Penrose and crew flying 'L for Leather' were attacked by an Me 210 and a Ju 88. The Me 210 was claimed as 'damaged' as many strikes were seen. They were also hit by the Ju 88 which put holes in the nose and port side of the fuselage. Pilot Officer A. Sovran and crew flying 'K-King' were attacked twice by Ju 88s. Some strikes were seen on one Ju 88. Flying Officer A. Stein on 433 'Porcupine' Squadron landed at Rufforth on return. Flying Officer J. Nixon and crew flying 'A-Apple' were attacked by an unidentified single engine aircraft and a Ju 88. There was no claim but their starboard wing was damaged. Flying Officer Leonard Taylor Sykes RCAF, the American pilot and his crew flying 'T for Tommy', were killed, the Halifax crashing seven kilometres southwest of Arpajon. In all, five Halifaxes – three on 433 'Porcupine' Squadron (as well as six Lancasters) – were lost on Villeneuve. Flight Lieutenant Bernard Yunker RCAF, 26, of Balgonie, Saskatchewan,

---

39 Söthe's other claim, a Lancaster, occurred near Artenay for his eighteenth and final Abschüsse. Söthe was killed in action on 28/29 September during aerial combat with a Mosquito.

and crew flying 'E-Edward' were shot down by a night-fighter. Yunker and Sergeant 'Bill' Gracie the rear gunner was hit in both legs and died of his wounds. For a time Sergeant G.N. Watmough, the RAF flight engineer, Flying Officer S.G. Hetherington, bomb aimer, Pilot Officer P. Scullion, wireless operator, and Flight Sergeant L.T. Grenon, the mid-upper gunner, evaded capture. Only the navigator, Flying Officer M. Wiome escaped. American born Pilot Officer G.A. Wolstencroft RCAF and crew flying 'X-X-ray' were on their way home when they were attacked by a fighter and shot down. Flight Engineer Sergeant S.J. Chambers RAF came forward with two parachute packs, but they were useless, having been damaged in the attack. He tossed them overboard. By this time the aircraft was full of smoke and fires were burning fiercely. Wolstencroft had no choice but to attempt a crash landing. He later reported: 'I kept the aircraft level and flew into the ground at 130 mph, landing in a soft field with no damage to either of us.' The wireless operator, Flight Sergeant Hedley Royden Brewer (23), might have survived had he stayed with the aircraft but he chose to jump with a burning parachute and plunged to his death. He was the only casualty from this crew. Sergeant Laird MacLean, the 18-year-old rear gunner, was so keen to join up that he forged his older brother's birth certificate to show that he had reached the minimum required age of 18. He was sworn in at the recruiting office at Sydney, Cape Breton, on 12 November 1942, eleven days short of his 17th birthday! Laird MacLean and Sergeant S.J. Chambers the flight engineer arrived at Stalag Luft VII three weeks later. Wolstencroft was captured and sent to Stalag Luft I.

As Flying Officer Gordon Baird's crew on 'W for Willie' headed deeper into enemy territory, John Harvie noted 'a feeling of tenseness begin to pervade the confines of their Halifax. In expectation of a sudden fighter attack we were each at the ready. Tom, in the rear turret, was straining his eyes to the rear as he scanned the sky above and below. Bill, from the upper turret with its more limited field of vision, searched above and alongside while paying added attention to the rear. These two would be the first to spot a fighter attacking from astern, the area from which, an attack would most likely come. Tom Marler in the astrodome checked all the area above the aircraft, again with extra attention to the rear. It was unlikely that an attack would come from head-on, but as 'Gordie' flew the plane he kept a watch forward. He had to be ready to bank or dive instantly on a shouted warning. Bob, in his wireless cabin, had the job of throwing out bundles of 'Window' which interfered with the operation of enemy ground and airborne radar. Don, beside me, kept passing me position fixes obtained from the H_2S set, with which I plotted our progress. At any sign that we were straying off course and away from the safety of the bomber swarm, I would give a course alteration to Gordie. Periodically, a crewmember would call out the position of a new searchlight battery, flak battery or an aircraft going down in flames and I would enter it in my log.

'Everything had been going well when, shortly before we were due to make our last turn to the east for the run in on target, 'Gordie' called me. He thought that his gyro compass was slightly out of adjustment and asked me to make another position check. The possibility that we might have wandered away from the main bomber stream was an ugly thought as we all knew that the German night fighters picked off the stragglers first. My fix showed that we had angled off by a matter of ten to twenty miles to the west. I quickly calculated a course alteration that would bring us over the target only three minutes behind schedule... not too serious a matter. When we were only a few minutes away from our target, Don prepared his bombs for release. I updated our ground speed, the latest wind velocity and direction and gave them to him to set in his sight. He rose from the table and I turned off the lights in our navigation compartment as he parted the blackout curtains to move forward to his bomb sight in the Perspex nose.

'My navigation skills were hardly needed as the bursting anti-aircraft shells and searchlight concentrations indicated the direction of our target. As we came closer, the green blobs of the Target Indicators glowed on the ground. These markers had been dropped by the Path Finders who had arrived a few minutes ahead of the Main Force and were now circling to one side to guide the bombers onto the target and to replace the markers if they should go out. I kept the blackout curtains closed so that I would not be distracted by the flak, searchlights and aircraft going down in flames. Besides, I had to have my new courses ready for when we flew away from the target. On our intercom we could hear the Master of Ceremonies [the 35 Squadron CO, 24-year-old Squadron Leader Alec Cranswick DSO DFC, a veteran of 106 bomber operations] calling to the approaching bombers, "Main Force ... this is 'Barn Door." The TIs are slightly short of target. Aim your bombs about 150 yards beyond them.'

'My God,' I thought to myself; 'he is a cool one, circling around over the target, exposing himself to flak and fighters as he calmly directs the attack until the last bomb is dropped and he can head home.'[40]

---

40   Shortly after Squadron Leader Alec Cranswick's aircraft was shot down.

'In the isolation of the Perspex nose Don had a full view of the action as we headed for the target. He needed several minutes to feed the latest data into his bomb sight, adjust all the switches on his control panel to the proper settings and open the bomb doors. Only then was he ready to hunch over the sight with the release tit in his hand and guide Gordie towards the green TIs... "Left, left, steady, right, steady, steady," he called over the intercom. At the instant when the illuminated yellow cross-hairs on his sight coincided with the aiming point he pressed the release button and, as the 16,000 lbs of high explosives hurtled downward, called out "Bombs Away!" Gordie held the aircraft straight and steady for a few moments more so that our automatic cameras could take photographs of our strikes. None of the bombs had hung up on the racks so the doors to the bays were closed. We had survived the agonizing run over the target during which we had to fly straight and level, making us vulnerable to the curtains of flak bursting over the target.

'East of the target we turned south on the first leg of the trip home. We also started descending from 12,000 to 8,000 feet as part of the raid strategy. Now we were well within the range of light flak with several hours of flying over territory still left. However, 'W-Willie' was now lighter by eight tons of high explosives which made the aircraft more manoeuvrable and increased its speed to 200 mph.

'Forty miles south of Paris we banked 90 degrees to the right and headed due west. I was getting good position fixes and consequently was able to give Gordie courses which kept us right on track. Not only had we regained the time lost before we came over the target but we had not been hit by flak nor seen any fighters. We were all beginning to breathe a little easier. On the H_2S set we saw Chartres off to the right. I called out to Gordie the new heading to the north and the time to swing onto it. Soon I felt us banking onto the last leg for home. It was just before 2 o'clock in the morning and in less than an hour we would be back over England and nearing our base. Beside me Don kept getting me fixes as I monitored our flight. Except for the roar of the engines, all was quiet and peaceful as we concentrated on getting home safely.

'Twenty-five miles from our last turn, Tom Jenkins in the rear turret suddenly yelled over the intercom "Fighter ... Starboard Go!" and the peace was broken. This was the dreaded warning that we were in the gun sights of an enemy fighter which had dived in unnoticed from the rear starboard side. Gordie commenced evasive action. He dipped our starboard wing violently as he turned 'W-Willie' sharply into the fighter and dived away.

If we were lucky the small fighter diving at high speed would be travelling too fast to make a tight turn and follow us. Then we would corkscrew in the opposite direction.

'Don and I clung to the edge of the navigation table with our stomachs churning from the abrupt change from straight and level flight. I waited for the cannon shells to tear into me and wondered if I would feel anything. The aircraft shuddered several times, which could be caused either by our guns firing or by the enemy cannon fire striking us. In the navigation compartment we could not see what was happening towards the rear. I waited for my stomach to drop to my knees as Gordie pulled the plane out of the dive and corkscrewed to port. But nothing happened. We continued diving. Then Tom from the rear turret called over the intercom, 'Gordie, Gordie!' but there was no answer from our pilot. Instead Tom Marler, who was standing in the astrodome directly behind Gordie, replied: 'We have been hit ... we had better get out!' Normally the order to abandon ship came from the pilot but Tom must have seen that Gordie was dead or unable to use the intercom. In any case neither Don nor I questioned the decision, for we knew there was very little time left before we would hit the ground. Without a word we quickly unplugged our intercoms, stood up and folded away our seat. The space above the main escape hatch was now clear. Don hurried forward to the nose to retrieve his parachute pack. In a matter of seconds I had picked up mine and snapped it onto my harness. A few more seconds and I had twisted the handle of the escape hatch. The hatch came open easily thank God and I threw it out the opening to leave the way clear for the crew members who would soon be crowding forward to jump.

'Don was still up front getting his chute ready. I sat down with my back to the front of the aircraft so that when I eased myself into the opening I would go out cleanly without hitting the back of the hatchway. My intention was to sit with my legs partly through the hole and wait to see how the others were making out. However, I forgot about the pull from the slipstream as we headed for the ground. First my left flying boot was pulled off my foot and then I was sucked out effortlessly. As I was dragged out I remember seeing our wireless operator's blackout curtain billowing towards me in a strong draft. With it was something large and white which I think was his parachute. Bob must have accidentally pulled the rip cord when he picked it up to put it on. As I slid out into the night, I couldn't see any other crew members coming forward to bail out.'[41]

---

41 *Missing In Action,* Harvie.

'W-Willie' crashed near Laons, fifteen kilometres WSW of Dreux in the Eure-et-Loir. Their adversary was probably Leutnant Lothar Jarsch of 6./NJG2 who claimed a 'Viermot' (four-engined bomber) in the Dreux area for his fourth of ten Abschüsse in the war. 'Gordie' Baird, Tom Marler, Don Wilson, 'Bill' Longley, 'Bill' Winder and Tom Jenkins were killed. After hiding for several days at a French farmhouse, John Harvie started back to England with the help of the Picourt Network established by Raymond Alfred Edouard Picourt, born 21 October 1900 at Le Tréport, an ex-French Army officer and chemist in Chartres since 1934, who since 1940 had been instructed in passing information of value to Allied Intelligence by means of radio. Not only was Picourt wanted by the Gestapo, but Jean-Jacques Desoubrie, a double-agent who had been working for the Gestapo since 1941, was also now operating in the Chartres area. Desoubrie, a short, stocky man with piercing grey eyes set behind a pair of thick-lensed spectacles, the illegitimate son of a Belgian doctor, was assisted in his treachery by Madame Orsini, 'an unpleasant-looking woman with copper-coloured hair and spectacles' and wife of the manager of the buffet at Chartres railway station.[42] She also had a Paris apartment. In Paris John Harvie was betrayed by Desoubrie. Harvie spent a month in solitary confinement on charges of treason and then on 15 August was transported by boxcar to Buchenwald where he and his fellow prisoners endured appalling conditions, indignities and extreme hardship. Later he was transferred to Stalag Luft III where, with food from the Red Cross and the comradeship of fellow prisoners, his body and spirit were restored. As the Russian army advanced into Germany, Harvie and the other prisoners undertook the long march from eastern Germany to a camp near Bremen and then to Lübeck near the Danish border, where he remained until Allied forces broke through and he was liberated by the British army.

---

42 See *RAF Evaders; The Comprehensive Story of Thousands of Escapers and their Escape Lines, Western Europe, 1940-1945* by Oliver Clutton-Brock (Grub Street, 2009). Desoubrie infiltrated several Resistance groups and was responsible for the arrest of over 150 Résistants and the capture of 168 airmen. He was arrested after being denounced by his ex-mistress and executed as a collaborationist in December 1949.

Chapter 9

The Tour

Eric Tansley was born in St. Albans on 6 March 1921. 'At the end of schooling I went to a business college and studied bookkeeping and other business studies for a year and a half. In 1937 I got a job as an audit clerk with a small firm of Accountants. After a time I was persuaded to take up work with the True Form Boot Company in footwear factory management. When war commenced in 1939 I particularly remember the effort that was required to make the factory satisfactorily 'blacked out.' Many curtains for windows and ceiling drapes for skylights were made. Also we had to set up lookouts on the roof for when air raid alerts were sounded and organise night watch teams for the hours of darkness. I hoped that the war would be of short duration and be over by the time I would be due for call-up in 1941. By December 1940 there was no sign of an end to the War so I decided to volunteer to avoid conscription in the Army. The Navy was out as I hated the sea as a result of a near drowning when I was young. So I volunteered for RAF aircrew.

'By early January 1942 I was called to undergo medicals; I think in Edgware. Next, a call to go to RAF Uxbridge. There with dozens of other volunteers came an examination in the form of a long question paper. This was a new type of exam for me as each question was supplied with about four possible answers. It was just a question of deciding which was the true answer and I soon seemed to work out what the examiner had been intending with the questions. At the end came a statement that I was required to write 200 words on the topic "The significance of Gibraltar in the conduct of the war in the Mediterranean." I had some difficulty deciding exactly where Gibraltar was but finally managed about 207 words. We waited around to hear the result of our exam efforts. Then I realised that "Mr. Tansley" was being called out on the Tannoy. I had to go to a headquarters office. I was shown into an office and soon two apparently high ranking officers came in. I was as yet unaware of RAF ranks. One of them was waving a sheet of paper and said to me that

he was going to have it framed and hung on his office wall. I began to think I was in a madhouse. He said, "Of all the thousands of these exams that have been taken, this is the first one with every question answered correctly." I had even stronger doubts about someone's sanity. They then questioned me closely about my reasons for volunteering for pilot training. I quickly said I had always been interested in flying, making models etc. This was somewhat of an untruth, but felt I had to say something as it seemed they were trying to prevent me flying. After more questioning as to my true intentions, they suddenly said, "We are prepared to offer you an immediate Commission in the Intelligence Branch. But you will need to start straight away." I immediately turned this down as I was already aware that flying recruits were having several months of deferred service – and I was not hankering after military service. This always mystified me over the years until a year or two ago when I learned that at that time they were recruiting people to work on Enigma.

'About July time I had to report to Aircrew recruiting Wing at Babbacombe. After some weeks of square bashing there I was posted with two or three others to Regent's Park for Eye Training. Apparently at some stage my eye depth perception was not up to standard. At Regent's Park there were no facilities for Eye Training and we were just dogsbodies for doing all the cleaning of blocks of flats for the new Air Crew Receiving Centre that was being set up. We saw many intakes of new recruits come and go and finally we revolted when we found they had misplaced our pay records and Kings Regulations were read to us. Eventually equipment was found from some hospital and we started our Eye training. After some time I was posted back to Babbacombe which was now No. 1 ITW. At this Initial Training Wing we had instruction in various subjects including navigation. A highlight of this was to go out in RAF launches in Torbay and do Navigation at boat speed.

'The next move was a blacked out train journey of some hours to a station, which of course had no name signs in wartime. A somewhat long journey in an RAF lorry finished up in the muddiest place I was ever to know in the RAF – it was Clyffe Pypard which seemed to be somewhere in the downs above Marlborough. We flew for just a few hours in Tiger Moths before going to Heaton Park, Manchester. Here I was issued with my third set of flying clothes. After a few days we boarded a train in darkness, with no clue as to where we were bound. It chugged on through the night and in the morning light we were near to water. Off the train and on to a ferry boat and we were taken out to SS Banfora *sitting in the middle*

of the Clyde at Gourock. This was a 6,000 ton Spanish coaster which had been captured and converted to troop carrying. There were 1,500 RAF people on board! Holds had had decking put in and there were rows of closely spaced hammocks, with mess tables underneath. We were to be accompanied by a P and O liner SS Rangitiki *which towered over our steamer but in fact could only manage 8 knots as its engines were broken down. It carried about 150 German PoWs. We still did not know our destination but after passing land which we decided was Northern Ireland it seemed we were heading for an Atlantic crossing. About the fifth or sixth night we looked out in the morning to find the* Rangitiki *missing. We then circled in mid-Atlantic for 24 hours but did not get attacked by U-boats, but we never saw the* Rangitiki *again.*

'After nineteen days we finally reached Halifax, Nova Scotia. We boarded trains which took us to Moncton, New Brunswick. At Moncton, a large personnel camp, we finally learned our destinations. Back in England I had been told at one place "Your code word is Fisher - remember it." I found that there were several code words distributed amongst my companions. Eventually as "Fisher" I was gathered together with a group of other Fishers and we finally learned that we were destined for training with the American Army Air Force. Then came a train journey across Canada to cross the great lakes to Detroit. There we boarded a quite luxurious train which set off south. Two days later we arrived at Albany, Georgia. We were now on a similar latitude to Cairo and the climate was much warmer. We had about three weeks of acclimatisation and were then posted to various training schools.

'I was to go to Darr Aero Tech which was just the other side of Albany – it had been a civilian flying school and still had the civilian instructors. My instructor was a Mr. Hawkins and with him I learned to fly Stearman PT-17 training planes – I soloed in seven hours. The course lasted nine weeks and then I was posted to Macon, Georgia, where I was to learn to fly Vultee Valiants, basic trainers. I soloed on these in about four or five hours. Again it was a nine weeks course. I had always wanted to be a fighter pilot right from joining up, but at the end of Basic I was posted to a training unit at Valdosta which had twin engine planes.

'These I could take off and fly in the air, but on the ground could not control them – so off the course and posted to Trenton, Ontario. I travelled with another fellow and our train chugged northwards all the way from the Florida border. We halted at Cincinnati but did not think much of it. We stopped at Detroit and at that time it was so pro-German

that our RAF caps were drawing abuse – so we got back to kill time on the train. Shortly after that, crossing into Canada was like a breath of fresh air. After a year of seeing the Stars and Stripes raised and lowered each night and morning, here was a Union Jack flying and people that understood English.

'After remustering as an Air Bomber I set off with another companion to get to Dafoe in Northern Saskatchewan. We were given ten days to get there. We stopped in Toronto for two days. While there we managed to get to the top of the Bank of Commerce building, then the tallest building in the British Empire at 33 stories. I thought I would go to an Ice Hockey match as I had never seen the game before. I wrote afterwards and told my Father and he replied that he had, surprisingly, decided to listen to the same match broadcast on the BBC!

'The train chugged on over the prairies at about 40 mph. We had two or three days in Winnipeg, then it was another 550 miles to Watson. We were now further from the East Coast of Canada than we had been in Scotland. Here a lorry took us the 28 miles to Dafoe. There was about a metre deep of snow everywhere and only a fortnight or so before I had been in near tropical Florida. At Dafoe we flew in Ansons and with pilots who seemed to be mostly of East European descent – they had very little English language. In February I was posted to 5 AOS at Winnipeg. One night there over a metre of snow fell in the night. We had to dig our way out of the hut in the morning. Nearby Winnipeg managed to get all its transport flowing again within two days. On 2 April 1943 I graduated as an Air Bomber and was given a commission. Then back to Moncton, New Brunswick, another three day train ride, to wait for transport across the Atlantic.

'Sometime in June we were suddenly told to be ready for transport and were told we could only take what we were wearing and two suitcases. We boarded a train expecting to go to Halifax, but the next day the train was rolling through New England in the US. We arrived in New York and were whisked at high speed in coaches past Times Square and Broadway and then down 49th Street. In the distance loomed a huge grey shape, we got closer and found it was the liner Queen Mary. *We hurried up a gangplank and our group of 55 officers were shown into what had been two single first class cabins. The whole space was taken up with bunks five high. When I got into a lower bunk my nose was only about two inches from the bunk above. I volunteered for night watch duty on the bridge. and only went back to the cabin for an hour or two's sleep in the day. The liner had a complete*

American Division on board. In fact the ship was carrying in total 22,500 people, the greatest number that had ever been carried in a boat. One third of the Americans were sleeping on the open deck and they rotated each day.

'The liner was zigzagging all the way across the Atlantic, making about a 600 alteration of course every four or five minutes. As it was steaming at full speed the tilt on the turns was alarming. We arrived in Gourock five days later. We were boarded by a Customs officer who got our group together. He said that he knew we had all bought lots of presents in America which would be dutiable and he would be all day if he went through our cases. So he suggested we each pay duty on a dozen pairs of nylons and he would be satisfied. My two cases were worth at least $800 and I had over forty pairs of nylons so I quickly agreed to that arrangement! We were lectured about the importance of not revealing to anyone which ship we had come home on, as the Germans did not know the liners were being used.

'When I saw my Father two days later, his first question was "Did you come over on the Queen Mary?*"*

'I was staggered. He said that he had given a lift to a seaman who had immediately said "I've just arrived on the Queen Mary *from the US." So much for security.*

'After leave I was posted to Wales to do Bombing and Gunnery. Then in September I was posted to Abingdon. Here we were to form up into crews and fly Whitleys. I joined with an Australian navigator and together we chose an Australian pilot – Doug Bancroft. Then we got the other members of the crew who were to join us. In November 1943 we went to Rufforth near York which was an Operational Training Unit. We flew in four engined Mk. II Halifaxes until February when we were posted to 158 Squadron at Lissett near Bridlington, not far from the Yorkshire coast. In a surprisingly short time the pilot had learned to fly the Mark III Halifaxes which were completely different to the Mk IIs we had been flying.

Flying Officer Eric Tansley, bomb aimer, 158 Squadron.

Bruce Douglas Bancroft – better known as Doug – was born in Rochdale, New South Wales, Australia, on 29 October 1916. He enlisted in the Royal Australian Air Force on 28 February 1942, gaining his 'Wings' as sergeant pilot in Canada in March 1943 and arrived in the United Kingdom the following month. He was eventually posted to an Operational Training Unit at Abingdon, Berkshire, on Armstrong-Whitworth Whitley aircraft and it was here that he teamed up with his first crew members: Pilot Officer Eric A.

Tansley, bomb-aimer; Sergeant Alwyn F.C. Fripp RAAF, navigator; Sergeant David 'Jock' R. Arundel, rear gunner; and a sergeant wireless operator who was transferred to 101 Special Duties Squadron after a few weeks and replaced by 23-year-old Sergeant Leonard S. Dwan. From Abingdon, Doug Bancroft and crew flew on one 'Nickel' (propaganda leaflet dropping raid) over France.

'My crew and myself were posted on 8 November to Driffield airfield (which was non-operational at that time, having been rendered unserviceable by enemy attack in 1943) to undergo a commando-type battle course. We were placed under the instruction of a section of the King's Own Yorkshire Light Infantry (KOYLIs) and advised by the NCO in charge of our group that all rank was to be disregarded for the duration of the course. This action was willingly accepted by all, but imagine our feelings, as aircrew, when we received an issue each of rifle, bayonet, webbing, backpack, ammunition, boots, etc and were advised that one must always move at the double and that, in any case, the marching rate was 140 to the minute. The weather was exceedingly cold with snow and ice in abundance as we ran miles and miles around the countryside. We climbed over high brick walls and back again, over barricades by ropes, jumped great ditches full of icy water and mud, crawled on our bellies under low bridges through streams which were about to freeze up, scaled rope ladders, ran across fallen trees, fixed bayonets and charged madly at straw dummies and screamed like banshees and then ran the several miles back to camp at Driffield in pouring rain where the hot showers were always most welcome to soothe the aching, bruised bodies and thaw out our veritably frozen bloodstreams. At the conclusion of several weeks of this training we had learnt what would be required if we were involved in a joint exercise such as a combined effort to secure an airfield, etc and we were all certainly more fit than when we arrived at Driffield.

'At the end of November we were posted from Driffield to 1663 Heavy Conversion Unit at Rufforth, Yorkshire, and here we were joined by Sergeant Kenneth L.G. Le Heup, mid-upper gunner, and Sergeant Robert Stacey, flight engineer. Rufforth had been the base for 158 Squadron from 6 November 1942 to 28 February 1943. The weather was still holding very cold, wet and foggy. Rufforth Conversion Unit was equipped mainly with ex-operational Halifax II aircraft fitted with Rolls-Royce Merlin XX motors, many of which had done a considerable number of flying hours and the ground crews were kept very busy maintaining a degree of serviceability under the prevailing difficult weather conditions. Although the morale of my crew was of a very high standard, as was the case with all of the aircrews, the frustration grew as the weather continued to stop flying operations for long periods and personnel moved about in the rain, the mud and the snow day after day.

'My crew did get one break when a lone rabbit was seen near our Nissen hut. There was a long chase across the muddy fields, over ditches and through hedges until it was eventually caught and triumphantly brought back to the hut where it was beheaded with a fire-axe, skinned and nicely baked in front of the coke fire. Of course, the drying out and cleaning of clothes and boots was rather a lengthy process, but all enjoyed the tasty meal.

'A good friend of mine Flight Sergeant M. 'Mick' Cowan and I were advised during the morning of 21 January that, following our mid-day meal, we were to be transported to 10 Squadron at Melbourne, Yorkshire, to each act as 2nd pilots (2nd 'Dickies' as they were known) with two crews from that squadron on an operation to take place that night for our operational acclimatization. We were duly taken to Melbourne at about 1400 hours and each of us reported to separate flight commanders for allocation to a crew. Passengers such as 2nd 'Dickies' were not really welcomed by the crews they were to join and I can well understand that kind of reasoning in the minds of a trained and experienced operational crew. The pilot with whom I was to fly just shook my hand and said that he would see me at the main briefing a little later in the afternoon. Mick Cowan was similarly greeted and in fact when having the 'flying meal' together we agreed that we would rather be attached to another squadron when we became operational ourselves as the whole atmosphere at Melbourne appeared on the 'damp' side.

'The operation consisted of 749 aircraft on Magdeburg. For the take-off I took up a crash position at the main spar while the bomb aimer retained his usual position in the second pilot's seat; a situation that I could well understand. At about 1,000 feet altitude, when the crew took up their usual positions in the aircraft, I sat in the second pilot's seat for the remainder of the flight. The crew acted most efficiently all through the flight with very little conversation between them except to pass essential information or instructions and I, of course, was not included in these matters other than to be told to keep my eyes searching for other aircraft in the vicinity. I did gather that the met wind forecast was not reliable and that the course required correction several times as a result of this, but I was most interested in noticing how clear was the sky and how brightly shone the stars on this very cold night. It was brought to my attention, also, that enemy night fighters were extremely active just after crossing the enemy coast, as I had seen several of the bombing force going down in flames and blowing up and some exchanges of tracer fire.

'Our flight to the target was incident-free however and a successful run-up was effected on a target which had been set burning well by the time we arrived. There was not a great amount of anti-aircraft gun-fire but the enemy night fighter force was very active and had many successes in the target area.

'Looking down at Magdeburg at the time it seemed to me to be of quite an unusual lay-out, especially for an old city, as the fires were burning in a quite rectangular pattern, seemingly about eight miles long by three miles wide, with fires in straight lines in two directions at right angles to each other as though along the length of straight roads. It did strike me as being rather odd.[43]

'Having disposed of our bomb load of mainly incendiaries we turned for the flight home which again was incident-free except for suddenly being caught by a radar-predicted searchlight near Wilhelmshaven but which was fortunately almost immediately lost by diving into a patch of cloud.

'On returning to base and in the debriefing process I learnt that Mick Cowan and the crew he was with were missing and later all were posted as killed in action. Although we actually had a quite easy and uneventful flight to and from the target, losses were heavy for the Command (55 failed to return) and bombing appeared very scattered and inaccurate and the attack was somewhat ineffective as a result.

'I returned to my unit at Rufforth during the morning of 22 January to a warm welcome from my crew and also to talk to Mick Cowan's crew members who were deeply saddened and shocked at the loss of their pilot, while I could not help but ponder on the fortunes of such operations, as it was like a mere 'toss of a coin' as to whether it would be Mick or I who went with that missing crew.

'On 7 February we were detailed for three-engine daylight landing exercises, using Lissett as the airfield with Halifax V EB195 from our unit at Rufforth. Following several successful three-engine landings, we [Flying Officer J.R. McCormack RNZAF was the captain of the aircraft, which had nine members on board[44]] were making another left-hand circuit with the starboard outer engine shut down. In the final turn to the landing approach at 600 feet altitude with undercarriage down and flaps at 30-40 degrees down, there was a violent explosion in the starboard inner engine which

---

43 Quoted in *To Shatter The Sky: Bomber Airfield at War* by Bruce Barrymore Halpenny (PSL 1984).

44 *Bomber Command Losses, Vol.7 OTUs 1940-1947* by W.R. Chorley (Midland 2002).

sent pieces of engine cowling and carburettor air-intake flying into the air. The engine stopped, leaving only the two port engines running. The aircraft swung to starboard in a diving turn and as there was insufficient power available in the port engines, all that could be done was to endeavour to fight the controls down to the ground. The aircraft hit the ground in more or less a landing attitude, wiped off the undercarriage in a ditch, cut through several hedgerows, knocked down several circuit light poles and came to rest about thirty yards from the back door of a farmhouse [Harpham Farm]. The farmer rushed out from the farmhouse and called out, "Is anyone hurt?" On being advised that the crew were shaken up but unharmed, his next words were "What about my bloody turnips? Seven of you bastards in the last week!" And sure enough, when I looked over his fields, there were six more aircraft scattered about, either with their tails in the air or on their bellies with broken backs, as was ours. A few weeks later, when we were posted to 158 Squadron, Lissett, our sleeping quarters were just outside this farmer's entrance gateway but he would always drive past us on his way to the mess area for his pig scraps and leave us to walk the mile or so – rain, snow, or sunshine.

'As the cold, bleak days and weeks passed, we were gradually able to build up sufficient hours of experience on the Halifax II and we were able to do a few hours on night landings during the odd nights which were free of fog. On the night of 16 February we were detailed for night circuits and landings in Halifax DKI73 and after completing several such exercises we made a landing approach and touch-down. As the wheels touched the runway the aircraft began to sway from side to side and no amount of rudder or braking control or even engine power seemed to be able to control the erratic swaying. As the aircraft's speed dropped off, the swinging about became worse and although my early thoughts had been of a blown-out starboard tyre, I erased this thought because of the violence of the side-to-side swaying motion and the failure of the aircraft to answer to applied controls. Eventually the aircraft dropped to the runway on the starboard side, the starboard wing hit the ground and the aircraft swung violently in a semi-circle and came to a halt. On a full investigation the following morning it was found that the main holding shaft attaching the starboard undercarriage to the wing had simply fallen out of the old aircraft in the circuit area and left that undercarriage to be loosely held only by auxiliary attachments such as hydraulic lines and struts. It was found that the aircraft was not economically repairable and it was written off.

'A few days after this incident, Sergeant Robert Stacey, flight engineer, received a posting to another unit and Sergeant Leonard 'Spike' Cottrell joined the crew as flight engineer. Cottrell, incidentally, had such a crop of fuzzy hair that he had permission to carry his field-service cap tucked into his tunic belt as it was impossible to keep it on his head. He had also been with us as a passenger when we crashed at Lissett on 7 February.

'We were posted to 158 Squadron, Lissett, on 29 February and on 1 March I was detailed to fly as a second pilot with one of the squadron crews captained by Flying Officer Doug Cameron (I think) in LV792/'E-Easy' to attack Stuttgart. The attack was carried out without incident and I and my crew were to attack that same target twice more during our tour with 158 Squadron. While I was on this detail, the remainder of my crew was called out of bed at about 2 am to assist in the clearing of snow from the runway and the spreading of salt to prevent icing up of the surface in preparation for the landing of the returning aircraft early in the morning.

'158 Squadron had just recently been re-equipped with the Halifax III, having commenced using this aircraft on operations on 20 January 1944. As my navigator, Flight Sergeant Fripp, had been trained in the use of H_2S we were detailed to use various squadron aircraft as available fitted with this equipment until, after several weeks on the squadron, we were allocated 'E-Easy'. It was my contention that this aircraft had the smoothest running and best engines on the squadron as the previous captain had really 'nursed' them along.

'While many of the aircrew carried what they claimed were lucky charms, possibly the most notable one during our stay at Lissett was that of Pilot Officer (later Flying Officer) C.E. Smith who sported a real Air Force type moustache. He always carried with him when flying a large white toy elephant 18 inches tall, which was known as 'Dumbo'. It was in the cockpit beside Smith at all times and he himself got the nickname of 'Dumbo' Smith. From early April until the beginning of August 1944 his aircraft was LV907NP-F *Friday the 13th*. For myself, I always insisted on having my cap hanging on the emergency hydraulic pump lever – for what reason, I still fail to understand.

'On 6 March 1944,' recalls Eric Tansley ('my 23rd birthday'), 'we were briefed for our first operation. We were very apprehensive as 158 Squadron had been suffering heavy losses. The target was a railway centre in Northern France and turned out to be relatively easy going. At this point with my earlier pilot flying I had flown over 400 hours.'

'As the weather began to improve in March, operations were stepped up, including the last massed bombing attack on Berlin on the night of 24/25 March when 'Bomber' Harris dispatched 811 aircraft to attack the 'Big City'. For the attack 158 Squadron dispatched fifteen aircraft to join the second and third of five waves. Zero hour on the target was set at 2230 on 24 March with each wave being allocated three minutes over the target. Flight Sergeant Bancroft lifted 'C for Charlie' off at 1859.

'We were detailed as a Windfinder crew for the operation and were briefed to attack in wave three between 2236 and 2239. The met report at briefing advised good weather conditions all of the way with little cloud and winds only light and variable. We were detailed to fly below 1,000 feet across the North Sea to keep below the enemy radar screen until Anrum Island – about 100 miles from the enemy coast – at which point we were to begin our climb to our bombing height of 20,000 feet. From previous experience we knew that our aircraft would be struggling to reach 18,500 feet, but that was the least of our worries as it so happened.

'We were on track as verified by fixes taken by the navigator, until over half-way across the North Sea, where we had commenced our climb to bombing altitude. On reaching the Danish coast the navigator advised me that we had drifted fifty odd miles south of our flight-plan track and that he had calculated the wind velocity as 100 mph from the north and that his new ETA target was about 2252 – fifteen minutes late. I instructed him to have the wireless operator, Sergeant Leonard Dwan, immediately advise Group Control of the wind velocity and direction and for him (Fripp) to give me a new course directly to the northern side of the target area in an endeavour to make up some of the time. We would then be able to attack the target on the planned heading. We arrived in the target area still ten minutes late and I could see that the bomber stream was very widely scattered, no doubt because a large number of the crews were adhering to the met forecast winds. Anti-aircraft fire was very concentrated but we were able to make a good bombing run up to the target and get our load of incendiaries and high explosives onto the target. Enemy fighter aircraft were very active in the searchlight area and even in the flak area but as several searchlights converged to form a cone I pushed the control column forward and we dived through the space which they had left clear.

'When we arrived in the target area there was about 9/10ths cloud cover. We were able to get glimpses of the ground area from time to time and were actually able to bomb visually onto the aiming point. The PFF marking was very scattered and so was the bombing generally.

Some markers and bombs were as much as ten miles off target and a number of crews bombed as much as fifteen miles short of the area in their haste to set course for their home bases. I witnessed several mid-air collisions, no doubt caused by aircraft which had gone wide of or to the south of the target area turning back directly into the main stream which was entering the area from the NNE. Anti-aircraft gunfire was very concentrated (I am advised that there were some 1,500 guns protecting the city) and masses of searchlights ringed the city. In addition, groups of night fighter aircraft began their attacks well before the target area was reached and these were also very active, even amongst the flak. We were able to make a good bombing run up to the target and drop our load of incendiaries and high explosives right in the target area from our height of 18,000 feet without being attacked by a night fighter at that crucial stage or being hit by the mass of anti-aircraft shells exploding around us, although we were bounced about considerably by the force of these explosions.

'Once the bombing photograph was taken it became a matter of getting out of the heavily defended area as quickly as possible and trying to avoid being caught in the beam of the searchlights, especially a blue-coloured radar-controlled master light. I put the nose of the aircraft down and increased power on the motors to gain mote speed and, when several lights converged to form two cones in the sky, we were able to dive through the space between the cones and then to head for our turning point for the route back to base. Still using the wind velocity and direction as calculated by Flight Sergeant Fripp, we were able to maintain the original flight-plan tracks for the whole of the homeward flight without incident, although while north of Osnabrück we could see well to the south, over the Ruhr Valley area, that many aircraft had drifted down there and were caught in the heavy defences of that area and many were being shot down there. Of the 73 aircraft from the Command which failed to return from this operation, 158 Squadron lost two.[45]

---

45 LW718 NP-T flown by Pilot Officer Keith Shambler Simpson RAAF returned early with engine trouble and ditched in the sea just off Winterton-on-Sea on the Norfolk coast but the aircraft exploded as it hit a mine. All the crew perished. LW721 NP-S piloted by Warrant Officer2 Allan Ross Van Slyke RCAF was shot down and crashed at Pausin. Van Slyke and two other crewmembers were killed. The four others were taken into captivity. HX334 NP-C was lost with Flight Sergeant J.H. Evans and crew on 12/13 May 1944 on Hassett, the aircraft crashing at Monastry Bokrijk. Evans and four others evaded. Two crew members were taken into captivity.

'Essen was our next target for 26/27 March and we attacked above 10/10ths cloud using H$_2$S. Before crossing the Dutch coast on the homeward leg, the starboard inner engine main drive shaft snapped. This allowed oil from the constant speed propeller control to escape, which feathered the propeller blades. The engine was shut down and a smooth homeward run and landing were completed.[46]

'Attacking the marshalling yards at Villeneuve-Ste-Georges near Paris on the night of 9/10 April, close bursts of heavy predicted flak jammed the bomb-bay doors in the closed position and we were unable to open the doors to release our bomb load onto the target although we made seven runs over the target, each time endeavouring to get the bombs away. Eventually, I decided to leave the area and try to jettison the load over the sea. The bomb-bay doors were opened by emergency procedures over the English Channel and the bomb load safely jettisoned, although an amount of damage was done to the fuselage bomb-bay doors in the effort. We landed back at Lissett some considerable time after all the other aircraft.[47]

'During March, April and May,' adds Eric Tansley, 'we flew on about nineteen operations of which six were to German targets. The rest were French and Belgian railway and military targets. Approaching June it became obvious that the expected Invasion of Europe would soon take place, but we had no idea where that would be. Several of the railway targets were on lines that headed towards the Normandy coastline.'

'In spring 1944, as the Allied 'D-Day' invasion of occupied Europe drew near,' continues 'Doug' Bancroft (now Pilot Officer), 'Bomber Command was required to strike consistently at targets such as railway marshalling yards, road centres, canals, etc in order to deny supplies of men and materials to the coastal areas of Normandy and regions nearby. Towards this end, on the night of 2/3 June the Command despatched 128 heavy bombers to attack the large railway marshalling yards at Trappes, approximately fifteen miles south-west of the centre of Paris.'

'This was the same target we had been to in March,' says Eric Tansley. 'Up until now all our operations had been carried out at near the maximum altitude we could reach over 20,000 feet. For this trip we were told that because of a layer of cloud over the target at 8,000 feet we were to fly at 6,000

---

46 705 aircraft (476 Lancasters, 207 Halifaxes and 22 'Oboe' Mosquitoes, which marked the target well) carried out a successful attack. Nine Lancasters and three Halifaxes FTR.
47 225 aircraft (166 Lancasters, 49 Halifaxes and ten Mosquitoes of all groups) attacked without loss.

feet. This seemed dangerously close to the anti-aircraft guns on the ground and did not give much altitude for diving away from enemy fighter attack.'

'For the attack,' continues Doug Bancroft, '158 Squadron contributed twenty-three aircraft and my crew was one of those detailed for this action using our regular squadron aircraft, 'E-Easy'. Zero hour on the target was 0050 hours and we were logged airborne at 22.16 hours into a clear, cloudless sky lighted by an almost full moon.'

'When we got to the French coast,' continues Eric Tansley, 'there was a layer of cloud at 6,000 feet and a bright full moon. Above the cloud we threw a large black shadow and below the cloud it was like flying below an illuminated ceiling. It was a small operation with only seventy planes taking part. Soon after crossing the coast we saw a nearby plane burst into flames and dive to the ground. We could see no anti-aircraft fire or fighter tracer bullets. Then before reaching the target we had seen fourteen planes blown out of the sky.'

'A trouble-free flight was made to the target,' says Doug Bancroft, 'and we released our load of high explosive bombs from 7,500 feet and were able visually to see the bombs hitting right in the middle of the railway yards and to witness the destruction of the tracks and rolling stock.'

Eric Tansley had just released his bombs at the target when a bomber just ahead of them burst into flames and went down. 'We were now very apprehensive!' says Tansley. 'The pilot ordered us all to keep a lookout all round the plane. I lay over my bombsight with my face against the glass bombing panel trying to look back under the plane. We were over Evreux when I saw a flash come up from under the plane. Then there was a tremendous concussion, which thumped the bombsight into my chest. I thought I had been hit and was dead. This was brought about by the sudden silence in my headphones and a great quietness in the plane. We had been hit by about seven large shells, which had blown a large hole in the side of the plane just beyond my feet. An engine had been blown up and was on fire. All electrics and radios were knocked out. There was an eight foot long hole in the fuselage. Two members of the crew had bailed out through this hole. The bomb bay doors were blown open and were on fire. A hole about two feet across was blown through the wing and the main petrol tank. This stopped another engine.'

'As the bomber stream left the target area,' continues Doug Bancroft, 'which was only lightly defended by anti-aircraft gun-fire, attacks began by enemy night fighter aircraft in substantial numbers and there were many combats in the bright moonlight. Twenty-five miles to the south of Rouen and near Evreux at a position logged by the navigator, Pilot Officer Alwyn Fripp, at 0117 hours and on the way to the French coast, our aircraft was attacked from below by a Ju 88 night fighter apparently using the recently German-devised form of attack known as 'Schräge Musik'. The attacking aircraft flew at a lower altitude and directly beneath our bomber and was therefore unseen against the darker background below. Our 'Fishpond' warning system at our tail did not operate anywhere near ninety degrees downwards.

'The enemy's cannon and machine gun fire ripped into our aircraft from tail to nose of the fuselage and also into the wings and started fierce fires in the bomb bay, inside the fuselage forward of the rear bulkhead and oil from fractured hydraulic lines also caught fire. A fire also started in the starboard inner engine. A hole about three feet wide was made across the width of the fuselage forward of the rear bulkhead where the radome and scanner had been blasted away and another hole some eighteen inches in diameter was blown in the port side of the fuselage alongside the wireless operator's position above the port wing root. Both wings and flaps and ailerons were severely damaged and a fuel tank in the port wing was holed and fuel from that tank left a white vapour trail as it was blown backwards.

'Shells and bullets punctured many holes in the aircraft, including the cockpit where the instrument panel was pitted by shrapnel and I saw several tracer missiles as shells came up between my legs and close to the front edge of my seat and blew out the perspex of the cockpit covering immediately above my head. The radio set and intercommunication system were completely destroyed as were the navigational aids of H_2S and 'Gee' and several oxygen bottles were hit and exploded. As the hydraulic system had been severely damaged and broken in several places, both the mid-upper and rear gun turrets were inoperable, the wing flaps dropped to about forty-five degrees and the bomb bay doors partly opened. Much of the turret gun ammunition exploded in the transporter racks on the port side and the bullets pierced the starboard side of the fuselage. I feathered the propeller and switched off the starboard inner engine, pressed the switch to activate the fire extinguisher in that engine and saw the Ju 88 on the starboard bow breaking away from the engagement at a distance of about 30 yards. I immediately put our aircraft into a steep diving turn to starboard. I could clearly see the face of the enemy pilot as he looked back at us from his cockpit. Evidently seeing the fires burning and the aircraft in a diving turn he must have been quite satisfied with his work and, fortunately for us, he did not return.

'The engine fire was extinguished and Alwyn Fripp and Eric Tansley came up from their forward positions in the nose with their parachutes attached and I handed them the nearest fire extinguisher (which was by my seat) and told them to immediately begin to fight the fires within the aircraft with all available extinguishers and fire axes as I had the aircraft fairly well under control and that, as the wings were not on fire, the fuel tanks were safe for the present time other than the one which had been holed and showed signs of sealing off (being self-sealing tanks).'

'As the engineer had bailed out,' continues Tansley, 'I struggled with the petrol cocks until I managed to get petrol to the engine which had stopped. The wireless operator was wounded when the hole was blown alongside him and he dropped out of the front escape hatch, but was never heard of again.'

Tansley advised Bancroft that the wireless operator, Sergeant Leonard Dwan, evidently had been very seriously wounded and suffering great pain had somehow managed to bail out through the forward escape hatch.

'It was quickly found that the flight engineer 'Spike' Cottrell and the mid-upper gunner [Sergeant Ken Le Heup] were also missing,' recalled Bancroft. 'Jock' Arundel forced his way out of the rear gun turret with the aid of a fire axe and came forward along the starboard side by holding onto the 'stringers' of the fuselage framework in order to cross the hole in the fuselage flooring and to pass the fire which was burning in that area. He said that he came part of the way forward and saw my back and considered that I was in control of the aircraft and he then went back to attack the rear fire with an extinguisher a fire axe and even his gloved hands while Tansley and Fripp were tackling the fires in the bomb bay.'

'We were over the Channel,' continues Eric Tansley, 'thinking we were flying north to England when it was realised that the compass was permanently stuck on north because it had shrapnel damage. The pilot looked around and found the Pole Star and turned towards that. We were sinking gradually lower and lower with the drag of the open bomb bays and the flaps which had dropped almost fully down when the engine blew up.'

Bancroft had kept the aircraft in the diving turn to starboard and levelled out at about 3,000 feet. 'As the P4 magnet compass had been damaged and the D/R compass had tumbled, I turned to a north-westerly course using the North Star (Polaris) as a visual guide and headed for the English Channel and the English coast. As the aircraft was losing height, I decided to re-start the inner engine and was able to do so successfully without any further outbreak of fire and increased all engine revolutions and boost to maximum cruising output in an endeavour to maintain altitude. The aircraft was a bit 'sloppy' on the controls and still slowly continued to descend because of the partly down position of the flaps, the partly opened bomb bay doors and the holes in various parts which all created a great deal of drag and we finally crossed the French coast over Le Havre at about 2,000 feet. In the moonlight the streets and buildings of Le Havre were clearly visible, but although this city was notorious for its heavy concentration of anti-aircraft defences, not a light was seen of a shot fired at us.

'Having crossed the enemy coast and out over the English Channel, I gave some consideration to the likelihood of having to ditch the aircraft in the Channel and decided to keep airborne as long as possible in order to get nearer to the English coast as we did not have a radio with which to send a position signal or 'Mayday' call for assistance. There was a radio for use in the aircraft's dinghy but it seemed obvious that the dinghy, stored in the port wing, would have been badly holed in the attack and we would be solely dependent on our 'Mae West' life jackets for survival. By the time that we were about half way across the Channel, by my approximate calculation, the three crew members had virtually extinguished the fires within the aircraft except for some still smouldering patches in the bomb bay which needed watching.

'Eventually we crossed the English coast at 700 feet and I switched on the navigational lights and instructed the navigator to fire a double red Very signal in case the coastal defences might think that we were 'intruders'. Not far away, on the starboard bow, I saw an airfield lit up for night flying and turned towards it and increased the engine power in order to try to maintain our existing height as we were getting down somewhat low. As we approached the circuit, I had the navigator fire another red Very signal followed by another as we turned onto the down-wind leg of the circuit at under 600 feet as indicated on the altimeter. I instructed Tansley to withdraw the undercarriage uplocks and to take up a crash position with the rear gunner. As I had expected, the undercarriage dropped into landing position and locked under its own weight. I applied full climbing power to the engines in order to overcome the extra drag caused by the undercarriage. I had the navigator stand by with the Very pistol which I told him to fire once more on the downwind leg of the circuit and again on the crosswind leg and finally as we turned to the approach to the runway. Then he took up his crash position. On turning onto the runway approach we thankfully received the green light to make our landing to which we were totally committed in any case either on the runway or on the grass beside it as there was definitely no hope of making another circuit.

'The landing was completed satisfactorily at 0251 hours on 3 June and as the aircraft settled on the runway I realized that we had a blown a our port undercarriage tyre and that there appeared to be some problem with the tail wheel but I was able to maintain control along the runway until the landing run was almost completed and the aircraft swung gently to port and was stopped clear of the runway. The three crew members left the aircraft through the hole in the rear of the fuselage while I switched off the engines and turned off the fuel cocks and left through the missing section of the top of the cockpit and slid down over the port wing. An ambulance and fire tenders were in attendance at the scene but the ambulance was not needed and the fire crews doused a couple of still smouldering spots in the fuselage and bomb bay and we discovered that we had landed at Hurn airfield near Bournemouth, Hampshire.

'While on the downwind leg of the circuit, the airfield lights on the port side disappeared completely from my view for several seconds and I saw a red beacon light thirty feet higher up at an angle of about forty-five degrees on the port side which had me puzzled for some time as I thought a tall hangar or some other structure had blocked my line of vision. In the morning, on investigation, I realized that we had narrowly missed hitting St. Catherine's Hill, approximately 400 feet high, which was in the circuit area and had not been visible in the faded moonlight. The navigator could not have advised me as to our exact position as his maps etc had been blown away through the open front hatch and other items were scattered throughout the aircraft by the incoming airstream.'

'E-Easy' was later visited by the Air Minister and was officially declared to be the most severely damaged aircraft to return to the United Kingdom from an operation. (It was categorized beyond economical repair due to operational damage and finally written off charge on 158 Squadron.) Of the twenty-three aircraft despatched on 158 Squadron for this attack, five failed to return. Of the 128 aircraft of Bomber Command despatched on the operation on Trappes, fifteen Halifaxes and one Lancaster failed to return; 12.5 per cent of the force.

'Doug' Bancroft concludes: 'Leonard Cottrell has since told me that he mistakenly took my action of feathering the starboard inner propeller by raising my right arm with my thumb extended to press the feathering switch as a signal to evacuate the aircraft. He went back accordingly and advised the mid-upper gunner, Kenneth Le Heup, to bail out and both of them, finding that the rear escape hatch was jammed, then went through the flames and out through the hole left by the missing radome and scanner.

Cottrell was picked up within a few hours by a group of 'Maquis' who hid him safely for over three months until the area was secured by Allied troops and he was then moved back to the United Kingdom. Kenneth Le Heup also landed safely by parachute and after wandering about for some time he stepped into some bushes to relieve himself and found that he had walked into an anti-aircraft gun position where he was very quickly apprehended. Sadly, the body of my wireless operator was never found.

'For this action an award of an immediate DFC was made to Flying Officer Tansley, Pilot Officer Fripp and me and an immediate Distinguished Flying Medal to Sergeant Arundel. Unfortunately, after having completed 22 operational missions and one 'Nickel' raid with us 'Jock' Arundel was detailed to fly as replacement air gunner for one attack on Amiens with another crew on 12/13 June. The aircraft was shot down by an enemy night fighter and Jock lost the sight of one eye through being hit by a piece of shrapnel. The crew bailed out and he was assisted by French Resistance forces and later returned to England.[48]

'I formed a new crew with Flying Officer Tansley and Pilot Officer Fripp[49] and four more crew members: Pilot Officer Thompson, rear gunner; Flight Sergeant Proctor, wireless operator; Sergeant W. McLean, mid-upper gunner; and Sergeant Tiltman, flight engineer. We were allocated another H_2S-equipped Halifax, HX356/G *Goofy's Gift* and the ground crew under Sergeant Fitzpatrick, fitter, proudly emblazoned the insignia of the DFC and DFM on the fuselage in our honour. This aircraft carried us through a further 21 operations.

'During the homeward run from Stuttgart on the night of 24/25 July we were attacked on six different occasions by enemy night fighters before crossing the enemy coast and due to the amount of evasive action taken were compelled to land at Hemswell airfield before reaching base in order to refuel.

'On the night of 16/17 August we were detailed to target mark as a backup force to PFF on the dock area of Kiel and were loaded up with target indicators together with 16 x 500 lb bombs. Cloud cover over the target area necessitated bombing blind from 18,000 feet using H_2S and the bombing photographs showed direct hits with bombs and target indicators

---

48   Arundel was a member of Pilot Officer W.C. Reed's crew on Halifax III LV790 NP-L. Two men were taken prisoner. Reed and three others evaded capture.

49   Eric Tansley recalls: 'Six other crews had started with us – 42 aircrew – now we were the only three left!' Flight Sergeant Alan Wesley Giles Fripp RAAF was killed on the raid on Revigny on 18/19 July 1944. Flying Officer Beverley Hudson Gifford's all-Australian crew on 463 Squadron RAAF were killed.

in the target area. Although flak was very concentrated and enemy fighters were very active, the attack was successful.[50] Sadly, though, as we were making our cross-wind leg in the circuit area preparatory to landing I saw 'S-Sugar' (LK839) captained by Flying Officer Rosen RCAF flying parallel on our starboard side suddenly dive to starboard and crash into a field at Foston-on-the-Wolds, Yorkshire. Some of the crew died instantly in the crash and the remainder died a short time later.[51]

'The night of 18/19 August saw us detailed for an attack on Sterkrade, north-west of Essen. The target area was very heavily defended with anti-aircraft gunfire and searchlights with little cloud cover. At the end of the bombing run at 20,000 feet a heavy explosion just under the tail sent *Goofy's Gift* into a vertical dive. I remember for a moment, thinking about being on a parallel line to the searchlight beams. The dive was so steep that I was unable to pull back the control column to get the aircraft flying level again. On glancing at the air speed indicator I noted that it was well above 360 mph and rising fast. Winding back steadily on the elevator-trimming tab control, the nose of the aircraft came up, at first very slowly and then more quickly and old *Goofy's Gift* levelled out at 1,500 feet still doing a high air speed from the impetus of the long dive. Some short time later a voice over the intercom called, "Navigator to skipper! What are we doing down here and at this air speed?" The crew in the nose section had not felt any unusual sensation, apparently. Gradually the air speed reduced from the impetus gained and we flew the remainder of the homeward leg across Holland and the North Sea at 1,500 feet to land at base without further incident.[52]

'We were detailed for several more attacks on various enemy targets, by daylight and night, until reporting as usual to 'A' Flight office on 1 September I was informed by the flight commander that Tansley, Fripp and myself had completed our tour and were screened from further operations. We were also informed by the squadron intelligence officer that our bombing record showed 22 direct hits and nine target area aiming points from a total of 34 operations flown together as a crew, a result which could only have been

---

50   348 aircraft (195 Lancasters, 144 Halifaxes and 9 Mosquitoes) were detailed to attack Kiel. The raid was only partially successful with a large number of bombs falling outside the town. In all, four Halifaxes and one Lancaster were lost.

51   Six crew members died. Flying Officer Walter Bigelow Tower Rosen, who was an American, died of his injuries on 18 August.

52   234 aircraft (210 Halifaxes, 14 Mosquitoes and 10 Lancasters) were detailed to bomb the synthetic oil plant at Sterkrade. One Halifax and a Lancaster FTR. The plant was seriously damaged. Halifax III HX356 NP-G *Goofy's Gift* was lost with Flight Sergeant William Max Freeman RCAF and crew on 8 November 1944 when the aircraft crashed at Gembling, Yorkshire, on a training flight. There were no survivors.

achieved by complete co-operation between each and every crew member, strict discipline and high morale.

'Flying Officer Tansley and I were seconded to the Ministry of Supply for a liaison lecture tour of munitions factories for several months while Flying Officer Fripp was posted to Marston Moor, Yorkshire, as a navigation instructor.[53] After completion of the assignment with the Ministry of Supply, I was posted as an instructor to Lichfield OTU and from there in either January or February 1945 I received a posting to 96 Transport Command Squadron being formed at Leconfield, Yorkshire. There I met again some of my friends from 158 Squadron including my good friend Flying Officer 'Dumbo' Smith, still with his white elephant. As the squadron was forming, our aircraft began to arrive – 25 brand new Halifax VIIs. The ground crews were set to work on these new aircraft, setting them up to carry troops and stretcher cases and polishing the fuselages and wings to a silver colour. We were advised that we would be flying troops and materials to India and bringing wounded personnel back to England, using Cairo as a staging post. Some weeks later we were advised that the squadron would be operating from a base in the south of England and all aircrew were given two weeks' leave. Less than a week after commencing leave we all received telegrams cancelling our leave and recalling us immediately to our unit at Leconfield. Arriving back at the unit we were advised to prepare to fly the aircraft to Cairo where we would be based. On flight testing one of the aircraft, Flying Officer Max Hubbard RAAF was killed together with his crew and several ground crew that were in the aircraft when it crashed into a hill near Leconfield while descending through cloud.

'Within a few days of being detailed to prepare to go to Cairo several crews began to ferry the new aircraft back to the Handley-Page works to be scrapped, much to the complete disgust of the whole squadron. Several of the squadron aircrews, as advance party, were then flown out to Cairo West while the remainder entrained for Gourock on the Clyde and embarked on a troopship for Egypt. Thus ended 96 Squadron's formation and stay at Leconfield.

'With the war now over I was demobilised from the Royal Australian Air Force on 8 February 1946 at Sydney, New South Wales. During my four years of service I was awarded the DFC and George Medal.'

On the night of 12/13 April 1945, Warrant Officer James Harding on Halifax 'F-Freddy' on 296 Squadron at Earls Colne, Essex, piloted by

---

53 At the end of the 21 operations, with the navigator Flying Officer Alwyn Fripp, Tansley went on to do radar navigation instruction. 'I was demobbed in 1946. I had then flown just on 800 hours.'

Flight Lieutenant Watson, flew an SOE op to northern Holland: 'My last tour we flew many operations over the Netherlands flying under Fighter Command for administration. Though they were shorter than our other covert operations (e.g. northern Norway) they were far more hazardous. Our Halifax was loaded with an armed jeep in the bomb bay with the doors removed. We took two SAS drivers and made our take-off at 2240 hours bound for a dropping zone north of the Zuider Zee. Earlier another Stirling took off for the same DZ to drop several SOE and SIS members five to ten minutes before we were due to arrive. They were to immediately take charge of the jeep and supplies and, with the aid of the SAS drivers, complete their mission. We crossed the English coast low enough to avoid detection by German radar but high enough so that German fighters could not splash fire us (firing from above and drawing their bullet splashes in the sea in a line across our plane). We made landfall about the Hook of Holland. Jack, the navigator, gave instructions to the pilot to turn south to cover our objective and he hedge-hopped as much as we could with such an awkward cargo, turning north later on a vector to the DZ.

'As we saw the Zuider Zee in the distance we could see the Stirling on a parallel course well in front and above. We then became aware of two enemy aircraft, which were assumed to be FW 190s, approaching his starboard side. We turned on a course parallel with the lake using our camouflaged fuselage to give us cover against the dark ground. The enemy aircraft broke formation, one circling behind the slow Stirling, the other one flying in front and dropping flares while continuing in a semi-circle from the port side. This made the slow-flying Stirling a perfect silhouette. They both attacked alternately, their tracer looking like a string of beads. Indeed we did hear vaguely a May Day call, as it seemed to disappear somewhere over the Zuider Zee.

'We were still flying low on a diagonal vector keeping strict R/T silence. The enemy aircraft had broken off their contact with the Stirling and were flying in a line, which would bring them nearer to us. We were expecting a recall signal because our operation could not be completed without the other Stirling. As the enemy aircraft came within 800 metres I fired a short burst. It was a mistake, as it appeared to alert them to our presence. For a moment they manoeuvred then flew off westward, probably running out of fuel or ammunition. Our recall came at that moment and we gave a direction for our return. Alas, as we reached the Netherlands coast two more enemy aircraft came into view, obviously alerted. They could easily out-gun and out-fly us. We had already decided to use our intercom as our best defence with the bomb aimer in the nose keeping them to our starboard. Jack in the dome and myself in the tail turret passed the information one to the other. I directed the pilot in the manoeuvres to keep both planes and flares at one side of us when possible and turning directly into any attack after the fighters had been committed and turning when the fighters were momentarily blind to us in the turn. This went on right across the sea to the English coast. We were concerned as we were still carrying the Jeep under our bomb bay and though it helped us in making the fighters overshoot, we still had the problem of landing at our base. No one had ever landed with a jeep hanging underneath. If the fighters followed us we would be a sitting target. To our relief American Mustangs met us. We landed with a slight crosswind. It was an awful landing, possibly due to our nervous tension. It felt as if we had been in the air for hours but the whole operation was only three hours thirty minutes. There was a de-briefing and the usual ham and egg breakfast, then to bed with the sure knowledge that we would not sleep due to the caffeine tablets we had taken to keep us awake and alert. Unfortunately they always lasted longer than needed.'

Chapter 10

Return to Bochum

Jules Roy

Commandant Jules Roy DFC *Légion d'Honneur, born an Algerian on 22 October 1907, was the bomb aimer (and capitaine) of a Halifax crew (pilots in the French Air Force did not captain their crews) on 346 'Groupe Guyenne' Squadron (Motto: 'Surgite nox adest': 'Arise, night is at hand') which was formed at Elvington, Yorkshire, on 16 May 1944 in 4 Group with Free French personnel transferred from North Africa under the command of Lieutenant Colonel Gaston Venot and began operations on 1/2 June. Jules Roy wrote two books on his wartime experiences:* La Vallée Heureuse *(Charlot 1946) or* The Happy Valley *(Victor Gollancz 1952) is a prize-winning account of bombing raids on the Ruhr Valley;* Return From Hell *is a diarised account of his wartime career published by William Kimber in 1954.*

With the 'Tricolore' flying proudly beside the Union flag, life at Elvington was distinctly different for the Frenchmen. For a start, with just one exception (Ginette Plunkett, the French wife of an English intelligence officer, affectionately known as 'Miss Pancake'), there were no women on the base, not even among the catering staff. It had been decided that this would provide too much temptation for *liaisons dangereuses*. Although some romance was inevitable as crews enjoyed their time off, such relationships were to be discouraged wherever possible. Then there was the wine, because, in a tradition begun in Africa, each man was entitled to a glass of 'pinnard', the rough, Algerian red wine, with every meal. After the end of the Battle of France and the armistice with Germany on 25 June 1940, a group of French airmen withdrew to North Africa until the Anglo/American invasion (Operation 'Torch') on 8 November 1942. In September 1943 the re-formed Groupes 2/23 'Guyenne' and 1/25 'Tunisie' were shipped to Liverpool to begin intensive retraining with RAF Bomber Command. The 'Groupe Guyenne' Squadron was declared operational at the beginning of June and flew its only operation on the Mk.V on the night of 1/2 June when a dozen Halifaxes took part in the raid by 101 Halifaxes and eight Path Finder Mosquitoes on a signals station at Ferme-d'Urvill near the coast chosen for the 'D-Day' invasion but cloud and haze prevented accurate bombing. Thereafter, the squadron began to receive Halifax IIIs. On 20 June, when the second unit was formed with French personnel, the Halifax Vs were transferred to 347 'Tunisie' Squadron, commanded by Lieutenant Colonel Marcel Vigouroux. 347 flew their first operation on 27/28 June when eleven Halifaxes bombed a V-weapon site at Mont Candon and another Halifax aborted.

Jules Roy flew the first of his 37 Halifax operations on 12 July when 222 aircraft including 168 Halifaxes of 4 Group bombed a V1 storage dump at Les Hauts-Buissons in the dense La Forêt d'Eu, NNW of Campneuseville near some houses nestling in their orchards. It was almost Roy's first – and last – operation, for on the crew's return at 0210 hours, while flying at 2,000 feet in the circuit at Elvington, their Halifax (NA546) was involved in a collision with NA551 piloted by Capitaine Jean Louis Gaubert. A fire started in NA546's engine and there were strong vibrations which made Roy decide to give the order to bail out. The *navigateur* and the *Mitrailleur-arrière* (rear gunner) landed safely in the potato fields, but Gronier his pilot and Roy stopped the engine and the vibrations ceased so Roy prevented those who had not yet done so from jumping. Gaubert crashed near Dunnington, four miles east of York. There were no survivors from the seven-man crew.

Jules Roy's fourteenth operation was on 9/10 October when the target for 375 Halifaxes, forty Lancasters and twenty Mosquitoes was the small town of Bochum on the eastern side of the central Ruhr, a few miles east of Essen; a highly industrialized and an important transport centre for the entire Ruhr. It was home to the huge Bochumer Verein steelworks, which produced 160,000 tons a month and the Robert Muser benzol plant.

Briefing was at 1500 hours. Fortunately things did not drag. At 1710 hours he looked at the clock on the control panel. They took off. The Halifax was heavy; five and a half tons of bombs, five and a half tanks of fuel. Later they had to climb to 20,000 feet through the pea soup (they had been flying low to escape detection as long as possible). At last they started the climb. The aircraft, still very heavy, gained height painfully. They continued to climb in great anxiety. Eighteen thousand, 19,000... 20,000 feet. Green flares shot from the ground to guide the night fighters onto the bombers.

After bombing, the Halifaxes continued northwards and then made a rapid descent to the west. They came out at 9,000 feet between two layers of cloud. The crew talked a little but not too much. It was not over yet. Course on 232. Climbed to 16,000 feet to hop over the Antwerp defences. They were chased by rockets, their red trails gliding through the night, hanging over them for a moment and then quickly swallowed up in the darkness. The navigation aid signals came on again, so Roy took a bearing. They were three or four miles off the course between Antwerp and Ghent. In the distance the English coast and the searchlights beckoned. Roy decided to switch on the navigation lights. In the darkness behind, other lights went on, but there were still 'maniacs' who passed blindly with all their lights out. A tentative descent in the clouds followed and they flew over five, six, eight airfields, looking for the letters 'EV'. When they finally found it they landed very quickly. The whole crew was exhausted but delighted at being safely back but there was no sign of 'X-X-ray'. Roy wondered if it was his Halifax with two engines on fire over the target or another torch he had seen falling in the darkness. Brohon, piloting 'X', decided not to make for the target but to return after dropping his bombs on Germany and he landed safely on the first airfield he saw near the coast.

On 7/8 August a Halifax on 347 Squadron commanded by the bomb aimer Lieutenant Antoine Louis Marie Balas Chevalier Légion d'Honneur, flown by Adjutant (Warrant Officer) Léonce Norbert Millet was shot down on the raid on Fromental. Jean Henri Charles Meyer and Sergeant Jacques Jules Henri Desrumeaux, one of the gunners, who jumped from the Halifax, were reported to have been captured on landing. They were handed over to Joseph Darnand's *Milice française* (French Militia), a political paramilitary organization created on 30 January 1943 by the Vichy regime (with German aid) to help fight the French Resistance. Desrumeaux was taken back to the wreckage of his Halifax and shot.

At Elvington on the night of 18/19 August it was raining when the Halifaxes on 346 and 347 returned from the raid on Bremen by 288 aircraft. Two crews landed at Woodbridge. Vasseur had an engine cut out over the Dutch coast at 15,000 feet and Lieutenant Albert Trouette's Halifax was machine-gunned over the sea near the Dutch coast by a fighter which attacked from below. He flew in corkscrew turns and flattened out twenty miles out to sea. At that moment the first burst from the fighter raked them. Trouette took violent avoiding action and then a second burst fired from behind tore a three-foot hole in the left wing. The rear gunner was slightly wounded in the shin by the burst.

September began with fine weather on the 2nd and 165 97 Halifaxes of 4 Group and fifteen Mosquitoes and nine Lancasters of 8 Group bombed V2 storage sites at Lumbres and La Pourchinte without loss, but there was torrential rain for most of the night. The raids on six airfields in Southern Holland finally went ahead the following day, 3 September, when raids were carried out by 348 Lancasters, 315 Halifaxes and a dozen Mosquitoes. 346 Squadron was given Venlo on the Dutch-German frontier as their target. Two Halifaxes, one of them on 347 'Tunisie' Squadron piloted by Adjutant Henri René Rouillay and captained by Capitaine P.J.L. Millet, was hit by flak and crashed at Bocholt. Rouillay, a Moroccan, and four of his crew were killed.

On the 9th 346 'Groupe Guyenne' Squadron commenced operations again but the operation on Le Havre aborted when the Master Bomber ordered the raid to be abandoned because the target was covered with cloud. Next day at Elvington at 1300 hours crews climbed into the lorries as another attempt to bomb a concentration of troops north of Le Havre went ahead. In the new 'F for Freddie' (MZ709), the navigator's bed had been re-covered with green leather, apparently arousing jealousy. No aircraft were lost from the 992 bombers dispatched and they attacked eight different German strongpoints each marked separately by the Path Finders and then accurately bombed. NA585 H7-M piloted by the CO, Lieutenant Colonel Gaston Venot, landed at dusk, at 1834. Just as he was taxiing there was a violent explosion, which sent shockwaves reverberating across the airfield.

A 1,000 lb bomb had hung up during the attack on a strongpoint at Octeville and fallen to the ground with the landing impact. Flames quickly enveloped the Halifax. Miraculously, Venot, semi-conscious from the blast, had managed to lift the cockpit canopy and jumped several feet to the ground just as the flames were licking at his face and hands. The rest of the crew, stunned by the explosion, were unable to get out. Venot was picked up thirty yards away from the scene of the explosion. Slightly wounded and burnt, his flaming clothes were torn off by the rescue squad. The rear gunner, little Dominique François Biaggi MM CdeG, recovered consciousness and died screaming, imprisoned in his turret. Immediately in front of the Halifax was another piloted by Capitaine Jean Calmel (later Général Calmel, Vice Chief of the Air Staff of the French Air Force). He and his crew could do nothing. Helplessly, Calmel wept at the loss of Capitaine Louis Robert Guillocheau, Jules Joseph Kipferle, an Algerian, Sergeant Marcel Louis Coupeau, Sergeant Gabriel Lhomond; Wilson Georges Finale and Biaggi. He had loved them like brothers.

A few weeks later Capitaine Calmel was diverted while returning from a night operation to an American B-24 base in East Anglia. He cut the engines and went through the standard 'stop' procedures, one of which was to leave the bomb bay doors open on parking. While he operated the levers with Roux, his *mécanicien* (flight engineer), the American crews watched as the bomb bay doors opened. Calmel heard a sinister sound of crumpling metal followed by a dull thud. He knew instantly that a bomb, like Venot's, had hung up and had now fallen to the ground. Luckily it had fallen quite flat without striking its fuse and it did not explode. Calmel dared to look up and saw 'everyone fleeing in all directions away from the aircraft like sparrows or throwing themselves to the ground behind any available shelter'!

On Monday 11 September, the German garrison at Le Havre surrendered after another bombing raid but the port was not cleared for Allied use until several weeks later. All of the bombers returned safely. Meanwhile another 205 Halifaxes, 154 Lancasters and twenty Mosquitoes escorted by 26 squadrons of fighters – twenty squadrons of Spitfires and three each of Mustangs and Tempests – set out for the Ruhr to bomb three synthetic oil plants – the Castrop-Rauxel refinery and the Bergkamen plant just north of Kamen and Gelsenkirchen (Nordstern). German fighters were noticeable largely by their absence but flak was mainly responsible for the loss of five Halifaxes and four Lancasters. A sixth Halifax made it back on three engines only to crash at base. At Elvington there was no sign of NA606 piloted by Lieutenant Georges Henri Berthet, whose crew on 347 Squadron was captained by the bomb aimer, Capitaine Alain Georges Leopol Hilaire. Both men were Moroccans, as was Adjutant Jean Maurice Madaule. Sous-Capitaine Rodolphe Camille Jenger MM, who was a Tunisian, completed the cosmopolitan nature of the crew. NA606 was hit by flak and crashed in the vicinity of Sterkrade. Lieutenant Pierre Maris Paturle and Sergeant Julien Eyraud were the two other members of the crew who died. Only the rear gunner, Adjutant R.M. Oger, survived and he evaded capture. Hilaire, "shy and sad", wrote Jules Roy, "was very much of a conformist. He was already absorbed with his own death and was perhaps waiting for it. Lac's bomb-aimer [Second Lieutenant Rotet] was mortally wounded in the thigh at the moment he released his bombs. He turned round and looked at his navigator. At the same time the flare cartridges caught fire and filled the Halifax with an acrid smoke which covered the windows with a grey film. The crew returned home flat-out but according to the doctor Rotet had died almost immediately from loss of blood."

During the final week of September 1944, 346 and 347 Squadrons joined others of 4 Group to deliver urgent supplies of petrol to the continent to support the 2nd Army. 347 Squadron delivered more than 84,000 gallons of petrol in 113 sorties to Brussels.

On 6 October Jules Roy flew his first operation since returning from leave. It was a familiar tune: the Ruhr in old 'F for Freddie', one of 254 Halifaxes of 4 Group (including the two French squadrons) which, with forty-six Lancasters and twenty Mosquitoes of 8 Group, were detailed to attack the synthetic oil plants at Sterkrade and Scholven-Buer. Clear conditions were predicted at both targets. Three Halifaxes were lost on Sterkrade and four Halifaxes and two Lancasters failed to return from Scholven-Buer. Two of the bombers collided over Holland and broke up in pieces. NA555, the Halifax flown by Capitaine Hablot on 346 Squadron, was shot down by a German night fighter. Hablot and the two gunners, Sergeants Yvars and Manick, bailed out uninjured. Lieutenant de Saint-Marc, navigator, injured his foot. Lieutenant Willemin, bomb aimer, bailed out unharmed but his parachute was holed during his descent and he suffered a fractured pelvis and a burst bladder on landing. The wireless operator, Adjutant-Chef (Chief Warrant Officer) W.H. Philippe, was wounded in the shoulder. The flight engineer, Sergeant Pons, suffered shrapnel wounds to his chest and a wound to the right eye. All returned to France in May 1945.

On 23 October, 1,055 aircraft – 463 of them Halifaxes – attacked Essen. This was the heaviest raid on the city so far in the war and the number of aircraft dispatched was also the greatest number to any target so far. The bombing was aimed at sky-markers, because the target area was covered by cloud and the attack became scattered, but more buildings were destroyed and more people were killed than in the heavier night attack which had taken place thirty-six hours earlier. A photographic reconnaissance flight after the raid revealed severe damage to the Krupps steelworks and the Borbeck pig-iron plant, which ceased work completely. Production only resumed after the war. Commandant Jean Joseph Simon, a Moroccan, had taken a second pilot along, Sergeant Pierre Fournier, to give him experience. The crew on MZ742, who were on their 23rd operation, are believed to have collided with another aircraft over the North Sea. In all, three Halifaxes and four Lancasters failed to return while five Halifaxes and five other Lancasters crashed or were written off in England as a result of battle damage, collision or loss of power followed by structural failure.

During the afternoon of 2 November Jules Roy and his navigator Ravotti went to York to see a Laurel and Hardy film. A few hours later they were on the Battle Order for that night's raid by the crews of 561 Lancasters, 400 Halifaxes and 31 Mosquitoes which were detailed for a raid on Düsseldorf. The attack fell mainly on the northern half of Düsseldorf. More than 5,000 houses were destroyed or badly damaged, plus seven industrial premises were destroyed and eighteen seriously damaged. This was Bomber Command's last major raid on the city. A Path Finder caught fire and, taking it for a very powerful marker, the Main Force released their cargo of bombs onto it. Lieutenant Henry Condé and crew who were on their first operation failed to return. The *mitrailleur-supérieur* (mid-upper gunner) Sergeant DeBroise and Soury-Lavergne, tail gunner, bailed out. DeBroise was taken prisoner; Soury-Lavergne evaded, walked through a minefield and reached the safety of the American lines; the five others were killed.

On 4 November the Intelligence Officer at Elvington began his usual speech about the evening's raid. He began by saying: 'Tonight there'll be twelve hundred of you attacking Bochum.'[54] Jules Roy and his crew were on the Battle Order on 'B-Beer'. There was an interminable wait for the lorries to take the crews out to their waiting aircraft, until finally they took off at 1750 in the dusk. There was a low ceiling with visibility almost nil but fine weather over the sea. With a strong tail wind the bombers gradually took their places in the route. Roy wrote: 'On the climb one of our gunners felt faint but pulled himself together... No defence over The Hague... Rockets to starboard... In the far distance the objective... All the decoys lit up, but there was no mistaking our target... At least fifty searchlights slowly swept the sky... We were lit up as if in full daylight, but fortunately we avoided them... Extraordinary fires of all colours of the rainbow... The searchlights bowed to our passage like saluting swords... Salute us! Salute us, we who are about to die! It was the most beautiful spectacle I have yet seen on the Ruhr. We were in the fourth wave, a quarter of an hour after the attack opened. Six minutes after crossing the target the mid-upper gunner ordered: "Get ready to manoeuvre to starboard." He fired. He had seen tracers coming

---

54 Bochum was the objective for 749 aircraft (384 Halifaxes, 336 Lancasters and 29 Mosquitoes) of 1, 4, 6 and 8 Groups. Another 174 Lancasters and 2 Mosquitoes of 5 Group went to the Dortmund-Ems Canal; a total of 925 bombers. If the raid on Solingen on 4 November (by 176 Lancasters of 3 Group) is added to this total, it makes 1,099 bombers (or 1,096 if the raid on Solingen on 5 November by 173 Lancasters of 3 Group is added instead). By adding the 156 sorties on Minor Operations flown by 43 Mosquitoes to Hannover and 6 to Herford and 39 RCM sorties and 68 Mosquito patrols in 100 Group, the grand total is 1,255 or 1,252 respectively.

in our direction. I encouraged him and stirred up Gronier. The rear gunner was firing too. In front of us were the searchlights.

"Where shall I go?" asked Gronier.

"Where do you think, old fellow? Straight on."

'The searchlights bowed, seeking foolishly to the right when we were to the left within touching distance, above a bright patch of light which I hurried to pass. At moments a light veil of clouds saved us, but the blue gleam of the searchlights remained in our eyes. We descended slowly along a path striped with tracer bullets. After Brussels, which roared with all its guns (probably against the pursuing fighters), we attacked the descent through the muck which brought us over the base at 2,500 feet in a swarm of aircraft. Order to land at Pocklington. Hideous, hideous... Landed at last after appalling anxieties.'

The post-raid communiqué admitted twenty-five Halifaxes and five Lancasters were missing, most of them due to *Nachtjagd* fighters. 346 'Groupe Guyenne' Squadron had lost five of its sixteen Halifax IIIs. NR181 flown by Capitaine Robert Louis Joseph Baron was shot down by a Bf 109 night fighter near Neuss. Baron; Adjutant Joseph Guy Vigneron the Moroccan bomb aimer; flight engineer, Sergeant Charles Georges Cormier; rear gunner, Sergeant Louis Bourrely; and Lieutenant Colonel Noël André Dagan of the French Air Force HQ in London, who had been attached for operational experience, were killed. Navigator and capitaine Lieutenant Armand Truche; wireless operator Adjutant René Mignot; and mid-upper gunner Sergeant Roger Petitjean were taken prisoner. South of Jülich the remains of NR181 hit the ground with the remains of the five crew members still inside. NA549 flown by Capitaine Joseph Alphonse Béraud Légion d'Honneur was shot down by a night-fighter and crashed onto the roof of the Church of Stommeln, seventeen kilometres north-west of Cologne. Béraud; Lieutenant Pierre Vallette; the bomb aimer Lieutenant Pierre Henri Eugene Raffin; wireless operator Adjutant Jean Cloarec, flight engineer Sergeant-Chef François Imart and the two gunners, Sergeant Andrew Claperon and Adjutant Jacques Manfroy, all left the Halifax, but Béraud, whose parachute was torn, did not survive the descent. Raffin was killed when he fell onto electricity cables.

NA558 flown by Adjutant André Hannedouche and captained by Lieutenant Jean Claude Vlès was intercepted by a night-fighter while clearing the target area and shot down out of control. Hannedouche and the wireless operator, Sergeant Robert Vlaminck, were taken prisoner. Vlès, Algerian Sous-Lieutenant Jean Gustave Adoplhe Lambert the bomb aimer, Sergeant Norbert Léon Beauvoit and the mid-upper gunner Sergeant Roger Lucien Limacher were killed. Sergeant-Chef Henri Léon Olive, a Morrocan, bailed out seriously wounded. He walked in the cold, clear night under the trees of an ancient forest, climbed a hill crowned by a feudal castle and at about 0200 that morning, unable to go on, knocked on the door of an isolated farm at the end of a village. The farmer, Paul Beich, gave him a cup of milk and allowed him to rest in his barn. The next morning, around 0800, Beich led Olive into Unterburg and delivered his prisoner to Willi Amann, an SS party member in charge of the local Volksturm. He removed the cigarette from Olive's fingers and cruelly struck him down on the chin saying, 'This man must be shot in ten minutes. I do not want to see it.' Conrad Beging armed himself with a rifle and, in some woods not far from the house of Frau Marta Kaisin, murdered Olive in cold blood. Later, Amann coldly stated that the parachutist was dead because he had tried to escape and Beging had to shoot him. Olive was buried in Cemetery Burg until the end of the war. In April 1945 when the Allies overran the region, Beging committed suicide. Amman was incarcerated in Remscheid Prison awaiting the death penalty.

The news of the missing crews, which Roy at first refused to believe, was confirmed next morning. *Thirty-five comrades at one go. It is a bitter blow which has left its mark on our faces; it was 346 Squadron which took all these losses.*

Chapter 11

Duisburg

Derek Waterman DFC[55]

The operation on Duisburg on the night of 14/15 October 1944 marked the resumption of the bombing offensive against Hitler's armament production after six months of concentration on transportation networks, supply bases and fuel depots in Northern France, under the direction of the Supreme Commander of Allied Forces in Europe, General Eisenhower. Operation 'Hurricane', as it was called in the Air Ministry directive that Bomber Command had received, was to 'apply within the shortest practical period the maximum effort possible, to demonstrate to the enemy the overwhelming superiority of the Allied Air Forces'. According to the directive issued to Sir Arthur Harris, Hurricane's purpose was, 'In order to demonstrate to the enemy in Germany generally the overwhelming superiority of the Allied Air Forces in this theater... the intention is to apply within the shortest practical period the maximum effort of the RAF Bomber Command and the US 8th Bomber Command against objectives in the densely populated Ruhr.' Escorted by RAF fighters just over 1,000 Lancasters, Halifaxes and Mosquitoes were detailed to raid the city while 1,251 American bombers escorted by 749 fighters hit targets in the Cologne area.

'Transport will pick you up in half an hour, breakfast at 0330.'

The corporal who gently shook me and awakened me from a little more than four hours' sleep delivered these words in a somewhat sympathetic and apologetic tone. It was Saturday morning of 14 October 1944 on a large and dispersed aerodrome a few miles south of Bridlington, Yorkshire. RAF Lissett was the home of 158 Squadron,

---

55 *Have a good time chaps,* a booklet by Derek Waterman, a pilot on 96 and 158 Squadron, reproduced in *Wings on the Whirlwind*, compiled and edited by Anne Grimshaw (North West Essex & East Hertfordshire Branch Aircrew Association 1998). Derek died in 1989.

4 Group, Bomber Command, flying Halifaxes. The intruder had already switched on the electric light that showed the cold interior of a barely furnished wooden hut, shared between Fred (who wasn't one of my crew) and myself. It showed too the disgusted expression on Fred's face at being so politely told to rise at such an early hour on this cold autumn morning.

'Half an hour – well it's no use going to sleep again – just time for a cigarette before our batman brings in some hot water. No need to shave as we'll be back again by mid-day at the latest. Anyway we shall have tonight free,' I said.

Such thoughts were merely a consolation as I puffed at the last of the cigarette. I emerged from the warmth of my bed and hurriedly reached for my clothes draped untidily over a bedside chair. The water was refreshing and enabled me to realise more clearly the reason for being in a vertical attitude so soon after going to bed.

'Wonder where the target is Fred?'

'Happy Valley, I suppose,' said he in his customary matter-of-fact tone between puffs at an ancient briar that constantly decorated his countenance. Did Fred ever feel scared? – this thought often passed through my mind at times such as this. I felt extremely weak at the knees, but Fred might easily have been dressing for a routine morning parade. One couldn't help being fond of him; he was a personable soul and, except for his refusal to hurry at any time, made a pleasant room-mate.

'Hurry up, Fred. Transport outside. I'll carry on. See you later but for God's sake get mobile.'

I left him slowly donning his pants, ventured out into the cold morning air and boarded the American-type bus, which by this time held a dozen or so odd-looking, semiconscious beings. Conversation was limited to hasty 'good mornings'.

At such early hours, tempers are varied. Jack, my mid-upper gunner, usually managed to awake cheerfully and I could hear his cheery voice above the quiet hubbub of the crowd. Some were talking but most wished they had taken the CO's advice and not visited Bridlington the previous evening where liquid refreshment, at most times, ran freely. The latter showed their regret with half-closed eyes and by their obvious disapproval of the comparative gaiety of their brighter-eyed colleagues. After all, the CO had told us that there was the likelihood of an early morning show and advised us to drink with moderation and to get to bed early.

Fortunately I had taken his good advice and was very glad. I felt a little tired but otherwise reasonably fit. An impatient driver soon appeared and asked whether there were any more to come. A quick check by crews' captains found Fred (alas a captain himself) the only one absent.

This discovery brought forth in chorus raucous shouts of 'Come on Fred, pull your finger out' and other impolite requests for him to join the not-so-merry throng, or to ruddy well walk. The mess, being nearly two miles away, was perhaps the only reason why Fred, with pipe smoking furiously, boarded the vehicle with the ease and grace of an early arrival and shouted 'OK' to the driver. This caused a considerable amount of good humoured leg-pulling, which Fred took rather seriously.

'Couldn't find my matches,' he explained, this being a good reason for twenty-four men being ten minutes late for breakfast. The driver started up and turned from our site and onto the main road. This led, with dangerously narrow curves, first to the sergeants' mess, where the NCOs left us, then to the main entrance of the officers' mess where the rest of us alighted hurriedly, anxious for a cup of tea to perform its usual wonders of reviving the half-dead. Bacon and eggs are, I think, a delicious breakfast, but somehow at this unearthly hour they seemed utterly out of place. Surely breakfast was best appreciated between the hours of eight and ten o'clock. However, after a cup of tea I tackled the food and even enjoyed it.

By now most early morning tempers had mellowed and eyes began to open. The one thought and topic was the 'trip'. Where were we going?

'Just hope it's a nice easy French target,' said Wilf, my navigator. Reg, the bomb aimer, exclaimed that he wanted 'an op, not a ruddy joy ride.' Surprisingly, these words were sincere; ex-London policeman Reg was a bomber pilot's dream. He would do all those little jobs you yourself would forget in the rush and panic. He could make a joke of tragedy and above all could effect wonders in keeping a cool and cheery atmosphere amongst the rest of the crew. At 29 he was six years older than the average in our 'team'. A grand type for whom I was extremely grateful on numerous occasions – in fact, every time our wheels left the ground.

There were more cigarettes until it was time to report for briefing. Again we boarded the bus and moved down the hill towards the aerodrome with its huge hangars silhouetted against a sky already showing signs of a typical autumn dawn.

Somehow the crowd had changed; the carefree atmosphere that existed over the breakfast table had now gone. Faces were serious; thoughts of wives, mothers and even young children were only partially concealed. I wondered whether I would do this journey again or enjoy the thrill of catching the train to King's Cross and the fourteen days' leave that would follow. I even thought of telegrams and my mother's dread of such impersonal scraps of paper. Perhaps that was the worst part of all this: the ones at home.

'OK, blokes! Ten to one on Happy Valley!' The would-be turf accountant would have shown good returns had bets been made to the contrary. The bright red tapes pinned at various points on the large-scale map of Europe at the top end of the briefing room came to an abrupt halt at Duisburg. This large inland port in the Ruhr spread its arms of heavy industry and oil refineries to either side of the Rhine.

My knees suddenly weakened. We disliked and feared the Ruhr, known throughout Bomber Command as 'Happy Valley'. Its defences were strong and its gunners accurate and enduring. They would fire until the last aircraft had weaved its way through their dangerous barrage. Ten thousand tons of bombs would not halt their efforts to shoot us from the sky.

Our first job was to empty our pockets of all odds and ends with the exception of identity cards. The rest of our pocket contents were put into a small envelope and labelled with one's name and locked in a safe until our return. We were all then issued with escape kits: silk maps, compasses concealed in buttons or collar studs, concentrated chocolate, Benzedrine tablets and one or two other forms of food and drugs to be used in case of emergency. The WAAF who provided us with these ingenious boxes of tricks smiled as she did so; with that smile seemed to go the hope that the need for using them would not occur.

At briefing we took up our seats at our usual tables and awaited the arrival of the station and squadron commanders. Meanwhile, everyone talked of the target, route, bomb loads and guessed at the approximate time of take-off. As it was now almost five o'clock we presumed the latter would be around seven.

The chatter ceased suddenly when the Group Captain and Wing Commander followed by Officers-in-Charge other sections entered the crowded room. The atmosphere was tense and smoky as we all stood respectfully to attention.

'Good morning, chaps. Sit down, please.' The words came from a tall, heavily-built man sporting a handlebar moustache – the Group Captain, our Station Commander.

Chairs moved noisily as the crews again made themselves comfortable. The Wing Commander, a man in his early thirties, was to my mind the ideal squadron commander. He lived to fly, was liked and highly respected by all and was annoyed because as CO he was allowed to operate only twice a month. When he did fly, he chose the toughest targets; he could so easily have done otherwise. We liked him for this, followed him loyally and were grateful for his sound advice.

'Well, gentlemen, as you see, the target is once again in the "Valley". We are putting up twenty-six aircraft this morning. The main force will be 1,200 strong.'

There were sighs of relief from us all. We preferred to operate in large numbers, the defences would be heavy but we knew they could do much more harm to a smaller force. Besides, it was comforting to think of so many others on the same journey.

'Zero hour is 0930. We are in the first wave and our bombing time is zero plus two [0932]. You are to bomb at 21,000 feet and your run in will be on a heading of 087°. I don't think it is necessary to mention defences as most of you are already acquainted with them in this area.

'Take-off time of first aircraft 0630. Set course over base 0700. Climb to reach the English coast at 14,000 feet. You will be fortunate in having an escort of Spitfires and Mustangs provided by our old and trusted friends, 11 Group. They will rendezvous over Beachy Head where they will join you. Keep in close and give the fighter boys a chance to afford cover to the stream. Pathfinders will be marking the target with red and yellow target indicators from zero minus two onwards. Master Bomber will use the code name "Clever Boy" and your code name as the main force will be "Samson".

'Please remember this, any engine trouble, turn round, jettison your load and return to base. Death-or-glory stunts are unnecessary and will be frowned upon, your job is bomb the target and return your aircraft and crews safely. Have a good run boys and very good luck to you all.'

There followed a brief outline of the weather we were to expect from the Meteorological Officer, a small, thin man who seemed to be able to make a description of a cloud formation sound absurdly humorous. He struck one as being much more suitable for ENSA rather than the chart studying Met Officer. Weather can, of course, make a considerable difference to the success of any bombing mission and can make flying either pleasant or dangerous. We listened intently.

'There's a possibility of early morning mist but this should not interfere to any great extent with take-off. Very little cloud over England – perhaps 3/10ths cirrus at 25,000 feet. Target clear, no icing, winds at bombing height, ten to fifteen miles an hour. On your return the mist will have dispersed. The weather should be the least of your troubles.'

A few words from the Wireless and Gunnery Leaders on radio procedure and defence areas brought general briefing to an end. The Group Captain then took the stand and with his customary words 'Have a good time, chaps', he brushed his handlebar moustache and closed the meeting.

All navigators, meanwhile, had been attending their own special briefing and when I walked into their sanctuary, Wilf was methodically drawing tracks on his chart and making out his flight plan.

'Everything OK?' I asked him.

'Just bang on,' he replied. He gave me a captain's map – a small-scale map of Europe on which he had drawn the tracks representing our route. At each turning point he had inserted the estimated arrival time. Should he have the misfortune to be injured, this important piece of paper would help me navigate the aircraft myself. I then made for the flight commander's office to sign the flight authorisation book that, as its name suggests, authorised the flight and was signed by the flight commander.

Pilots briefing was in ten minutes so I quickly strode over to the crew room where I drew my parachute and donned a Mae West, parachute harness, flying boots, an old brown scarf and gathered up helmet and oxygen mask. Then, together with Jock, our engineer, made for the pilots' briefing room where the Wing Commander discussed with us petrol load, recommended cruising speeds and taxi out times. Our machine, with the identification letter 'F' (named *Friday the 13th*), was to be No.6 to move off in alphabetical order, round the perimeter track into take-off position.

Time was now 0545 and transport was waiting outside. Most crew had already collected flying rations and were sitting waiting in the buses. The squadron padre was making his rounds, wishing good luck to all. Although well-intended, his presence always struck me as being rather morbid. Climbing into the bus could be rather a complex business. One would trip over parachutes or become entangled with oxygen tubes and suchlike and I could never quite understand why navigators' bags were so full and bulky.

Despite the numerous obstacles we somehow all managed to squeeze in. A quick glance round assured me that my six pals were all safely on board. I only hoped they'd remembered everything. It was a damned nuisance if we got out to the aircraft and found someone had left his oxygen mask or something equally important behind.

Our bus carried crews for aircraft 'E', 'F' and 'G' – twenty-one of us. We soon arrived at 'E-Easy' and dropped Tommy, a jovial New Zealander, with his mixed crew of fellow countrymen and Australians, a wild bunch but grand types.

'Have a good trip, Tommy. See you at lunch time!'

My last remark was a superstition. I said it to everyone getting out before us and to everyone left in as we gathered our kit and alighted. I never missed saying those words or something similar. I thought they passed unnoticed until one day Reg pulled my leg about it. I still continued with my silly habit even after that although I felt a little embarrassed and always avoided Reg's smiling eyes.

Six o'clock: ten minutes for a smoke and then the start of another adventure.

I always allowed twenty minutes from boarding the aircraft until taxi-out time. Starting, warming and testing the four engines, checking control movements, cockpit lights, oxygen flow, compass and gyro instruments and other lesser but vitally important details, usually could be managed in fifteen minutes. The margin of five minutes left time to get settled in and to make oneself comfortable and, in the case of minor mechanical faults, gave the ground crew a possible opportunity of putting things right.

Every time everything was 100 per cent perfect and I don't think I could possibly say more to stress the keenness and efficiency of the ground crew: Tom the sergeant and his five underlings. They slaved over and nursed the aircraft as a mother would her child. Already our four-engined friend had made eighty-nine visits to enemy territory without one single mechanical fault not attributable to ack-ack or belligerent fighters. We all proudly boasted this great record.

The last few drags at my cigarette were fully appreciated. I smoked heavily and knew it would be about five hours before I would enjoy another.

'OK, chaps, pile in. It's ten past six.'

Cigarettes were reluctantly thrown away and there were good wishes from Tom and the other lads. Jock, our engineer, had a look at the tyres, flaps and so on. Again, everything was fine. He quickly followed the other five into the machine while I said my usual prayer, followed by a rubbing of my right foot over the ground – another ridiculous superstition. I gained this peculiar idea from an instructor at Heavy Conversion Unit. He had told us of an injury he had received on an operational flight. He had always rubbed his foot into the ground before boarding his aircraft but that night he had forgotten to do so. I made up my mind there and then that when I got to a squadron I would do it before each take-off. It all sounds so very stupid now but it was then a vital part of my routine.

Once inside the aircraft, nervousness seemed to disappear; concentration on starting the motors and having much to think about overcame inner

191

feelings. Already as I climbed into my seat the others had settled in and completed their pre-take-off drills. I began mine by opening the side window and shouting to Tom that I was ready for starting up. Thumbs up from him and the boys showed that all was ready. Port outer, starboard outer, port inner, starboard inner – in turn the powerful motors roared into operation drowning all other sounds. Having allowed them to warm up, I pushed open the throttles fully in turn, both magnetos on each engine checked, propeller pitch operation OK, oil temperatures normal.

'Good old ground crew,' I thought as I set the four throttles to keep the engines running at idling speed but not too slowly to prevent oiling up of plugs.

'A-Able' was now taxiing on to the perimeter track.

'Are we all set?'

'Yes, I think I've remembered and checked everything. Too late now anyhow.'

'OK, Reg, Brian, Wilf?' The latter two – the wireless operator and the navigator – then walked (or climbed) back to the fuselage rest position for take-off to lighten the weight in the nose. Reg followed, took up his seat beside me and helped fasten my safety straps. I fastened my oxygen mask over my mouth and he said over the intercom, 'All set to go.'

'OK.' I waved to ground crew for 'chocks away'. The large wooden blocks were drawn out from their positions in front of the great wheels and we were waved an 'OK'. Tom and the ground crew all stood in line. We knew they were wishing us luck and a safe return.

I opened up the throttles and started the machine rolling. 'B-Baker', 'C-Charlie', 'D-Dog', 'E-Easy': we followed the latter and took up our position in the procession round to the take-off point.

Met had been right: there was a slight ground mist but nothing to worry about. The entire squadron seemed to be there to see us off. I was elated. Fears were hidden.

We followed closely behind 'E-Easy' and halted about twenty yards from his tail as he came to a standstill to await his turn to take off.

Brakes on, throttles fully open to clear engines, propeller pitch set fully fine for take-off, flaps 20° down. We rolled forward and as we received our green light, I released the brakes and swung onto the runway heading east and into a slowly rising sun.

'OK, chaps – here we go.'

Take-off was always a hazardous affair – an engine cutting on becoming airborne would not be a pleasant experience. Some 10,000 lbs of high explosive could make a nasty mess. On take-off with a full load, the Halifax Mark III had a strong swing to the right, so as I rolled forward I applied full left rudder and opened up the starboard motors just slightly ahead of the port. This assured a straight start but once momentum had been gained I neutralised rudders and pushed throttles fully open. So far, so good.

I felt Reg's hand behind mine as I held the throttles at maximum boost as I needed both hands for the actual lift-off. I told Reg to hold them there and lock. As I grasped the wheel with both hands, Reg pulled over a small lever on the side of the throttle quadrant that held the four levers in position and made it impossible for vibration to alter their settings. We rapidly gained speed: 95, 100, 110 miles an hour. Stick slowly back – we were airborne.

'2,400 revs, please, Reg,' I said referring to the propeller speed. He reduced the revs. The roar of the engines was less deafening and became a more evenly synchronised hum. At 400 feet I throttled back and raised the flaps. There was a slight drop in height and an alteration of pressure on the stick. This necessitated a slight change of trim. When properly trimmed, an aircraft should theoretically fly 'hands and feet off', but in practice it didn't quite work like that. Nevertheless, trimming lessened the work of the pilot considerably.

Now we were climbing at 160 mph. Jock informed me that all pressures and temperatures were normal. With his broad Glasgow accent he was sometimes difficult to understand. This plus the inevitable crackling of the intercom always caused trouble. One thousand feet – everything was running smoothly, although I was sweating considerably.

'Switch on the oxygen please Reg and you can all take up your respective positions.' Three weighty individuals taking up their positions in the nose made it again necessary to adjust the trim. I asked Ken the rear gunner and the youngest of our crew whether his oxygen was coming through all right. He said it was and in turn the others told me they were also receiving their supply.

Wilf requested me to climb over Bridlington and out to sea on a course of 092° for seven minutes. This would just bring us back over base at 0700 hours to set course with the other twenty-five aircraft of the squadron. As I peered over the side I saw Bridlington partially enveloped in the morning mist but was able to pick out June's house on the outskirts.

'See you tonight,' I thought hopefully.

Wilf came through and in his usual quiet manner told me to be at 4,000 feet over base and to set course on a heading of 225 degrees. I set this course on the compass grid ring in readiness and steered by the directional gyro indicator that was synchronised with the magnetic compass.

We were now approaching base. The rest of the squadron all appeared miraculously at the same time and we closed in and formed a loose formation. I counted twenty-five aircraft – everyone had got off without mishap. The aerodrome below looked empty and deserted.

As we turned onto our first course Jock told me quite casually that the starboard outer cylinder head temperature was running high.

'OK, Jock, thanks. Keep your eye on it and let me know if she gets any higher, will you?'

On reaching Goole, only a short distance from base and our first turning point, we turned port and headed east towards the coast. I secretly envied the few people below, some walking, others cycling along the winding country roads. They seemed insignificant and appeared as pinheads. The mist was clearing rapidly showing the countryside in its thousand and one colours – so wonderfully peaceful it was difficult to believe that within two hours we should be a target for unfriendly gunners.

Now our twenty-six aircraft, still close together, formed only a small part of a long procession. I didn't attempt to count the black specks that covered the entire sky. Twelve hundred bombers, each with a sting of 10,000 lbs. Surely the German population would collapse soon? In addition to this saturation bombing, our armies were meeting with success in all sectors. The American Air Force was even penetrating the Reich as far as Berlin in daylight. The tired people of the English cities were enjoying long-deserved peace in the absence of German raiders and rockets. Once again my thoughts were interrupted by Jock's voice.

'All temperatures normal now and everything bang on.'

Wilf informed me that we were dead on track and on time over Beachy Head. I could now see numerous squadrons of fighters circling a few thousand feet above us, just small dots in the sky. It gave one a grand sense of security – they were there to protect us – the hazard of enemy fighters would be lessened considerably.

'E-Easy' was now flying thirty yards or so on my port beam. We kept together and climbed on slowly towards the Dutch coast. Slowly gaining altitude made it necessary for me to increase boost periodically as the air became thinner with height; to maintain a steady climb more power was needed.

The Dutch coast gradually became clear and Reg was checking his map carefully to give Wilf a crossing pinpoint. Our route did not take us over any large coastal towns. Experience told us that such places were heavily defended. Naturally it was almost impossible to miss some of the inland towns. One of these was Tilberg and clusters of black puffs were already welcoming the leaders of the stream. From a distance they looked surprisingly harmless, but as we neared the town I realised they could be and were horribly unpleasant. One or two bursts appeared rather too near to be healthy so I made a slight climbing turn to the right to skirt the town.

'E-Easy' remained on course. I couldn't help thinking him rather foolish. It was unnecessary and asking for trouble – trouble that could be avoided. Most of the stream in front of us had crept round to the right of the town's defences just as we had. I watched until he emerged from the cloak of lingering black smoke puffs into the comparative safety of the clear blue sky on the other side of Tilberg.

We slowly turned to port again to regain our track. I couldn't catch 'E-Easy' as he must have been a few hundred yards ahead. He had become lost from view and added to the forerunners of the stream. Other squadron aircraft were now mixed with us as we ambled on towards the German border.

Wilf told me that the slight deviation from track had put us a minute behind schedule and asked me to increase speed. I explained that we were now at 20,000 feet and would climb the remaining 1,000 feet to bombing height, then would increase air speed to 175.

At 21,000 feet I levelled out and trimmed her to fly straight and level. The engines were behaving magnificently and the occasional OK from Jock assured me that all instruments were showing normal readings. Only another fifteen minutes to zero hour. Soon we would reach our destination. My apprehension returned. My clothes were moist with nervous perspiration. My jaws ached through chewing gum from the moment I had entered the aircraft – another habit, but it did serve a dual purpose, of clearing one's ears which occasionally cracked due to changes in pressure and was also a substitute for smoking.

Reg was now giving Wilf frequent pinpoints that he plotted on his chart. The bombsight was ready.

I could see the Rhine winding its way through the large industrial towns of the Ruhr Valley. One of these Reg identified as Duisburg.

'0925,' said Wilf as he instructed me to alter course to 087°. This was our bombing direction and, theoretically, should bring us over the target. The Pathfinders were now being fired at. The sky filled with black bursts. It was difficult to differentiate between the leading aircraft and the lethal puffs, most of which indicated spent 88 millimetre shells.

'There are the first target indicators,' Reg shouted excitedly as I observed massive red cascades of fire bursting on the thickly built-up area forming the target. Brian, the wireless operator, took command of the intercom and asked me to switch on the receiver to Channel 'D', the radio frequency for this mission. As the set warmed up, I was deafened by the atmospherics through the headphones and also the attempts by the Hun at jamming – these were usually unsuccessful for we always managed to receive the Master Bomber's instructions. (Master Bomber was the name given to a few hand-picked Pathfinder pilots and crews who went into the target with the flare-dropping aircraft. They were without exception veterans of numerous operations and their task was to decide the accuracy of the target indicators and to subsequently transmit instructions to the main force.)

We were now in Reg's hands. He could see his target and it was his job to give me the necessary alterations to course to bring us up to it.

'Hello, Samson; hello Samson; this is Clever Boy. Bomb the north side of the red TIs – bomb the north side of the red TIs,' came the instructions referring to the target indicators.

'Bomb doors open,' requested Reg as we ran up with two minutes to go. I could now see stick after stick of bombs falling from the leading aircraft. It was an impressive sight. The town was already covered by thick grey smoke against which brilliant red flares burned marking the target.

'OK Reg. Bomb doors open.'

No longer were voices calm and steady. We now shouted. We were tense and tempers were short.

'Five degrees starboard,' yelled Reg.

'OK, OK, keep her there – left, left, bit more, left, left, steady, steady.'

It was now a struggle to keep the aircraft on an even keel. The slipstream from those in front tossed us about and made it difficult to fly straight and level. The flak was intense and I could smell cordite. Its unpleasantly pungent smell meant that the bursts were dangerously close. There was a loud bang then a noise like hail rattling on a corrugated iron roof. We had been hit, but how badly, I did not know. The aircraft still responded to the controls and that was the main thing.

'Bombs gone - keep her steady, we want a good photo.' A red light flashed in the cockpit which meant that as the bombs were released, the camera had automatically taken a photo of the area over which our bombs were dropping.

Fifteen seconds later a further two flashes of the red light indicated that the photo had been taken. I had to fly as straight and as level as possible to get a good photo. It was important not only for Reg's satisfaction whose job was judged by this, but was also instrumental to intelligence in assessing the damage caused by the massed assault.

'Bomb doors closed.' We were now through the worst of the flak as I dived to port building up speed to 250 mph. We had descended to 17,000 feet as I straightened out and turned onto the course Wilf had given me for our first leg on the homeward journey. I asked Jock to check the bomb bays – by lifting small panels he could see whether all the bombs had released or not.

We were out of the range of the gunfire and could still see the rest of the stream going in amidst a heavy curtain of flak. By now the target was almost completely covered by spirals of smoke that blanketed the whole town. It looked like hell. I saw a Halifax receive a direct hit from a shell and burst into a thousand pieces. No parachutes emerged. I didn't think it was one of our squadron for they should have all bombed by now.

'All bombs have gone,' reported Jock after I had asked Wilf to log the time and position of the aircraft that was hit.

I felt safer now. We were on our way home. I would see June tonight – perhaps go to the pictures. It seemed such a contrast to the hell we had just left in our wake.[56]

We still could not determine where we had been hit but everything seemed OK – probably a few holes in the fuselage. We maintained 17,000 feet; our cruising speed should have been 175 but we flew at 200 miles an hour. Everyone hurried home; to be among the first to land was everyone's aim. This annoyed Flying Control for to have about ten aircraft all requesting landing instructions at the same time was not easy.

'Everyone OK?' I asked. Everyone was – and excited too. 'How about some rations, Jock. Come on, you ruddy foreigner, give the driver some chocolate, I'm hungry.'

Jock duly passed round a bar of chocolate cream which, after unhooking my oxygen mask, I quickly ate. Oxygen always created an awful taste in my mouth and the chocolate was wonderful.

On crossing the Dutch coast, I again put the nose down in a gradual descent, aiming to be at the English Coast at 10,000 feet, at which height we would fly over England. The sun was now shining brightly – a heavenly morning. The sea looked bluer than ever before, the foam of folding waves glistened like sequins on an evening gown.

---

56 At Duisburg 957 RAF heavies dropped 3,574 tons of high explosive and 820 tons of incendiaries for the loss of thirteen Lancasters and a Halifax to flak. American casualties were just five bombers and one fighter.

We were safe now – life was precious. I wondered if any of our squadron had been shot down. We'd had a lucky run lately. This was our thirty-fourth trip – maybe one or two more to do – would we make it OK?

We reached 10,000 feet a little before we got to the English coast so I levelled out and asked Jock for a cup of coffee. Hours-old coffee from a flask tastes like anything but coffee and this was no exception, but now it tasted divine. At 10,000 feet it was safe to discontinue the use of the oxygen so Jock took a cup to each of the crew. I felt refreshed after it and my mind was on Bridlington that evening. Now the fields of England looked more beautiful to me than ever, with the sun tracing its shadows over a green and yellow carpet of English farmland. But I was beginning to feel uncomfortable. I was cramped from sitting in the same position for so long. Hull was a welcome sight – just twenty minutes back to base. I eased forward on the stick and increased slightly the throttle settings that gave us around 220 mph and a descent of 500 feet per minute to bring us in at about 1,000 feet, the height at which we made the airfield circuit. Three or four other aircraft were in front but I couldn't distinguish their markings and so didn't know whether or not they belonged to our squadron. We hadn't done so badly.

'Hello Stepin, Hello Stepin, F-Fox approaching base at 3,000 feet, permission to join circuit please. Over.'

'Hello F-Fox, Hello F-Fox, this is Stepin, you are No.3 to land, landing is to the east, over. Stepin from Fox, Roger, out.'

The flying control WAAF whose voice I heard sounded wonderfully feminine; it could have been a personal welcome.

'OK chaps, climb into the rest position.'

Back came Wilf, a satisfied grin on his face. Yes, he'd navigated us well. His job, for today at least, was finished. Brian passed me next, he too was smiling. He lived, ate and slept radio – he knew his job 100 per cent and we all had the utmost faith in him. If ever we were lost or not sure of our position, by contacting various stations Brian would be able to give Wilf a fix that he could plot and so determine our whereabouts.

'Good trip,' said he as he passed me. Then the seat by my side was clicked home into position and Reg jumped into it to assist me in the landing.

'Stepin from Fox, downwind, wheels, wheels.' This was a safety check to make sure one didn't forget to lower the undercarriage! Many a landing had been made with wheels still in the retracted position.

'Quarter flap please Reg. Fox to Stepin, flaps, flaps, over.'

'Stepin to Fox, Roger, out.'

'B-Baker' was landing as we turned onto the base leg. One more had landed before him so we were third back – not too bad out of twenty-six.

'Stepin to Fox, you are number one to land. Out.' We now turned gently onto the final approach at 800 feet.

'Pitch fully fine and half flap please Reg.'

I slowly eased back the throttle as we approached at 125 mph. I was slightly overshooting so asked Reg for 3/4 flap to give us a quicker rate of descent without having to cut down the power. Heavy aircraft drop like stones if power is reduced too much. We came over the airfield boundary nicely.

'OK Reg, cut throttles.'

This he did while I checked our descent into a very shallow dive and then slowly eased back on the stick to stall the aircraft at about five feet from the ground. She landed with a slight bump but in one piece.

'Stepin to Fox, turn right at intersection.'

'Fox to Stepin. Wilco. Out.'

As we started to lose speed I applied the brakes, taxied to the intersection and made for our dispersal point.

Tom and the ground crew boys were waiting. They were pleased to see us. I swung the aircraft into position at dispersal and before switching off once more checked all engines, magnetos, flap operation and so on. Everything was OK; we couldn't have been hit too badly. It was quiet when the engines stopped and how lovely it was to get out of that seat and stretch my legs. Before I could get out of the cockpit, Tom appeared in the fuselage and asked whether everything was all right. He sounded more serious than usual.

'Yes, Tom, she's fine, but why the harassed look?'

He told me that the aircraft was needed again that night – another twenty-six were needed again that evening. This shook me. Normally at the most we did only one trip a day – usually one every other day. I consoled myself with the thought that another crew would take her tonight. We'd never been asked to do two in a day – one Ruhr trip would last me for two or three days.

Ken and Jack, the gunners, had been the first out and immediately rushed around looking for damage. They found five holes in the fuselage and beamed proudly as they told the rest of us as we jumped out. Wilf was carrying a jagged piece of iron fragment that he found lodged in one of the holes.

'Souvenir!' he said.

'The bus was waiting for us. Two crews already aboard shouted to us to hurry; they were anxious to get their cup of tea and get the job of debriefing over. We bade farewell to Tom and the boys and quickly climbed into the bus. The crews asked us how our trip went and told us that they too had been hit but not seriously. One had sprung an oil leak in an engine but it had functioned well enough to keep running all the way home.

On arriving at the briefing room the words 'All back' written boldly in chalk across the blackboard were a cheerful welcome – our run of good luck was continuing. As we handed in our escape kits and drew out our personal belongings, a WAAF officer handed us cups of tea and biscuits that we took with us to the debriefing.

Flight Lieutenant 'Chalky' White smiled in his usual way as we sat down. He was glad to see us – he seemed to like us all and took a personal interest in every individual on the squadron.

'What was the trip like?' he asked as we took our seats and helped ourselves to the free cigarettes. Perhaps it was because they were free that they tasted so good and I chain-smoked throughout his informal questioning. I told him we'd had a good trip although comparatively uneventful and proceeded to give him details of bombing height and defences encountered. From his log Wilf then gave positions of aircraft shot down.

I had a slight headache and felt even worse when I saw my name included in the list for the night's trip. I could hardly believe it. Tom had been right – there was another show on. And we were participating. My dreams of a quiet evening were dashed. I was even more despondent when I learned that the captain of the crew that should have taken our aircraft had gone sick.

Having changed my flying kit and deposited Mae West and parachute, I ran over to the Flight Commander's office to sign the flight authorisation book, indicating a completed trip. I looked up at the record of sorties. Our crew had two more to do to complete one tour, after which we would enjoy at least six months' rest. The only consoling thought at the time was the fact that another trip tonight would leave only one to do. I was anxious and ready for a rest. With the exception of Reg, I knew my crew were ready for this rest too. Reg could have gone on indefinitely, thirty-four penetrations into Germany and occupied Europe had affected him no more than would the equivalent number of runs down to the English coast. He loved danger.

The bus that ran us up to the mess was a hubbub of voices: crews exchanging experiences and the terrific pasting they had given the Rhineland town.

I felt dirty and by now my head ached severely as I jumped from the bus and made for the mess cloakroom. A wash and brush-up revived me and I strolled into the small bar. The Wing Commander, in the middle of a crowd, was apologetically referring to the night's trip.

I washed down three Aspro tablets with a small beer then went in search of food. Our ex-hotel chef was a popular fellow and cooked extraordinarily well. Today was no exception: soup, roast beef and Yorkshire pudding, followed by jam tart. We talked of the trip and afterwards took our coffee into the anteroom securing two comfortable armchairs in front of the open log fire. After only a casual glance at one of the daily papers I became drowsy and fell asleep. I must have slept for three hours or so, for when I woke the room was practically empty. The boys would have gone back to their beds to snatch a few hours' rest before they were needed again.

Tea would be ready in half an hour so I decided to stay put in front of the fire. I dozed again but was soon awakened by the crowd – the call of tea had brought them from their beds. Once again the anteroom became alive.

As a night operation was pending, incoming phone calls would be cut; June would not be able to get through. If I didn't call at her home before six o'clock, she would guess I was otherwise engaged.

Three hot cups of tea removed the last traces of my headache and I began to wish away the hours. I slept again until someone tapped me on the shoulder and told me that food was to be had. I didn't feel hungry but struggled through a plate of bacon, eggs and chips, punctuated by sips of hot, milky coffee.

Again we waited for the transport – the early morning procedure would be repeated. The rest of my crew, at this time all NCOs, had been collected separately from the sergeants' mess and at the briefing room I saw them again for the first time since we had parted at lunch time.

Various guesses had been made at the target but it came as a surprise to see the red tapes still forming the same shape as they had earlier: Duisburg. I thought of the chaos that the second air armada within fifteen hours would bring to the German civil defence squads, to say nothing of the misery of the wretched inhabitants of this unfortunate city. But I didn't feel sorry for them and felt that the end of the war was surely close. After all, Germans had bombed our cities and had shown no mercy. Many of my colleagues must have shared similar thoughts, especially the Londoners, for they knew the effect bombing could have on helpless citizens.

The briefing was similar. Again we were to form up with other squadrons to make a bombing force of 1,200 machines. The target was any part of industrial Duisburg that showed lack of attention from the morning's effort. Zero hour 0230. Our bombing time: zero plus five.

At 2314 I waved 'Chocks away!' and swung onto the perimeter track. I kept a safe distance behind the aircraft in front as we taxied round to the west side of the field. His tail light made the outline of his rear gunner visible – a strange, ghost-like sight in his two flying suits and helmet.

The rear turrets would be bitterly cold. Some lucky ones sported electrically heated suits but even with these the cold at heights of four miles high could be most uncomfortable. The rest of the crew were more fortunate: hot air from the engines was circulated throughout the aircraft; except in the case of extremely cold conditions, all but gunners would be reasonably warm.

A green flash from an Aldis lamp was our cue to line up on the runway. I opened up the motors and rolled her into position, a long narrowing avenue of lights made up the flare path which was to guide us on our take-off run into the night. As I opened up the throttles, the four engines roared into action and again took us rapidly down the lighted path lifting our twenty-seven-ton monster into the air.

The lights of the airfield gradually faded into the night. Wilf said we had time to fly on a course to Scarborough and back before setting course proper on the first leg of our run. We could see a faint coastline and distant rings of lights as we climbed. These lights were other airfields and appeared surprisingly close to each other. They were the boundary lights that formed a circle round an entire aerodrome making identification of a landing ground simpler but also assisting pilots in keeping on a close circuit in bad weather. I could now see moving lights all round me: the green and red wing-tip lights of other aircraft contrasted with the ceiling of stars above us – a wonderful sight. I enjoyed flying at night for the air was smoother without the turbulence often experienced during the day.

I thought of the people below who I had envied early that morning – they were now awake in their homes listening to the roar of our stream overhead.

After crossing the English coast, there was only starlight – all wing lights were switched off. How could so many aircraft maintain the same route without some of them colliding? Fortunately this rarely happened, thank God.

As we crossed the Dutch coast we were greeted with familiar starbursts that abruptly trailed into puffs of grey smoke and floated past our wing tips. Again we were fired upon; a couple of searchlight beams added their doubtful beauty to the official welcome. I told Wilf I was altering course temporarily 200 degrees to starboard to evade the beams. To be coned in half a dozen merging streams of lights was blinding and made it extremely difficult to read the instruments on which one relied so desperately at night.

We managed by this slight alteration of course to dodge the beams and subsequently turned back onto course. Far in the distance was a red glow. I checked our position with Wilf who told me that we were 150 miles from Duisburg. It was still burning furiously from the morning's attack. As we flew on, the fire became a carpet of flame against a dim horizon, gradually increasing in area until the winding Rhine showed its shape separating the two sections of the town.

The town was outlined by a ring of searchlights whose beams waved up and down in their feeble efforts to embrace the leading bombers that had already entered the target area. I felt safe enough: gunfire was heavy but inaccurate. As we lined up on our bombing run I looked down into a hell of burning ruins. For the first time I pitied the people below. For the first time I realised the misery and destruction that air bombardment could create.

Wilf giving me our bombing run course interrupted my thoughts. Tonight we were going in on a heading of 065°. I banked and straightened out onto the given course. From the light of the fires below there was little trouble seeing the massed aircraft rolling in towards the inferno that only a little more than half a day ago had been Duisburg, a large, important inland port. Tomorrow it would be a graveyard and the outgoing roads would be crowded with thousands of homeless people. Yes, for a few moments, I did again feel sorry for them. And I thought how the tables had changed from the summer of 1941 when 'The Few' knocked the Hun out of the skies and saved us all by their spirit and unparalleled guts in the air.

Reg asked me to turn on to 070° – he had already picked out his target, a group of factories on the south side of the river. The flak was now a little more accurate but did not compare with the intense barrage of the morning's run. As we bombed, new fires started in previously untouched patches of the town. The inferno grew and as we turned and dived away from the target having collected our photo, a huge curtain of dark grey smoke ballooned over the town.

Still the bombers were going in and still more fires started. Two aircraft went down in the target area which I asked Wilf to log – I was sure they were bombers. I looked away, blazing aircraft falling from the sky were unpleasant sights – and their crews might be our friends.

Again *Friday the 13th* was behaving magnificently. I was now glad we had made this second trip – it left us with one only to do. I felt proud and elated at the thought of completing a tour and shooting a line as an instructor at some training establishment. We flew on fast towards the coast. On either side, a few flak bursts appeared reminding us that we were not alone on our way westward. Here and there searchlights swung across the sky. Somehow, once again we managed to evade them and still diving slightly crossed the Dutch Coast at a little over 10,000 feet. It was easy at times like this to consider the trip complete and disregard the possible menace of fighters. They had a nasty habit of tailing bombers out over the North Sea and then opening up. I'd seen it happen to a Halifax one night. I reminded myself of this and also my gunners, telling them to report anything that looked suspicious. However, we crossed the English coast and still could boast an uneventful trip – an easy one compared with previous night visits to the Ruhr.

A few minutes later, Jock reminded us that it was coffee time and in a few minutes appeared with a cup of greyish brown liquid. Tonight it tasted better than ever. The crew were bantering over the intercom. I reminded them, in a polite way, to shut up. They too felt good, but a fighter attack was still possible and I had no intention of being caught now. If the intercom was used for chatter, it was difficult to hear the gunners should they spot a fighter on our tail. The boys realised this and fell silent. The only noise was the drone of the engines.

At 0440 Brian received a diversionary message over the radio. For reasons unknown, we were not to land at base. Normally this meant bad weather at base, but the weather was so perfect I could not imagine it changing to any great degree over the remaining eighty-odd miles. Wilf deciphered the coded message and informed me that we were to land at Catfoss, a training aerodrome a few miles from our own. So the reason was not the weather.

At 0505 we circled Catfoss and touched down ten minutes later. Within half an hour twenty-five Halifax crews were informed that back at our home base of Lissett Flight Lieutenant MacAdam had had an engine cut on his take-off run, had retracted his undercarriage and slithered to a standstill just short of the boundary fence at the far end. Fortunately the rest of the squadron was already airborne. He and his crew had made a hasty retreat from a partially damaged aircraft containing 10,000 lbs of high explosives. The bombs exploded one and a half hours later causing no damage except a few broken windows on the drome and surrounding farmhouses. The aircraft itself was scattered in little pieces for hundreds of yards around the airfield. The runway was littered with jagged scraps of metal, a danger to the tyres of any aircraft landing – hence our landing at Catfoss.

Dawn was now breaking, but before the sun appeared we were on our way by road to Lissett, our base. I was exhausted when at ten o'clock I pulled back my bedclothes and climbed into their depths. I remembered little more than Fred reluctantly placing his pipe on the chair beside his bed and climbing likewise into his bed.

It was five o'clock when our batman gently woke us and poured boiling water into our respective washbasins for washing and shaving. He'd even cleaned our buttons and polished our shoes. We both showered then proceeded rapidly to Bridlington where we went our separate ways.

My way led me to a pleasant detached house on the outskirts of the town where I arrived in time for tea with June. We listened to the six o'clock news that gave an account of the raids. They could not describe those sights I had witnessed a few hours earlier – that blazing hell! Could people like June, her mother, father and small brother, imagine what it was really like? No they couldn't and I would not want them to.

We didn't go to the pictures after all. Instead we sat around the fire and talked. The war seemed far away and we talked of other things.[57]

---

57 That night, which was fine and cloudless, 1,005 RAF heavies attacked Duisburg for the second time in 24 hours in two waves dropping 4,040 tons of high explosive and 500 tons of incendiaries. Five Lancasters and two Halifaxes were lost. Bomber Support and forces on minor operations had played their part with 141 training aircraft flying a diversionary feint towards Hamburg, turning back before reaching Heligoland. Also 46 Mosquitoes raided Hamburg, Berlin, Mannheim and Düsseldorf while 132 aircraft of 100 Group flew RCM, 'Serrate' and 'Intruder' sorties. One Halifax of the diversionary force was lost. Five Lancasters were lost. Altogether, 1,898 RAF bombers had dropped nearly 9,000 tons of bombs on Duisburg for a loss of 21 aircraft. Despite the enormous effort involved in Operation 'Hurricane', that same night RAF Bomber Command was still able to dispatch 233 Lancasters and seven Mosquitoes of 5 Group to bomb Brunswick.

Chapter 12

Descent into Danger

'Scotty' Young

Foulsham is a typical Norfolk village, situated just off the Norwich to Fakenham road, seventeen miles north west of Norwich. On 25 November 1943, 192 Squadron, a radar countermeasure unit operating Halifaxes, had moved from Feltwell to Foulsham following the formation of 100 Group (Bomber Support). Its task was to identify German radar patterns and wavelengths and during bomber raids the aircraft would provide countermeasures to German radars. Warrant Officer R.F. 'Scotty' Young the cheerful, fresh-faced 25-year-old special operator on the crew of Halifax III NR180 DT-S, skippered by Flight Lieutenant Nathaniel 'Jack' Irvine RCAF *was the author of* Descent Into Danger *(presented by Gordon Thomas and published by Alan Wingate (London, 1954)). On the raid on Chemnitz during Operation 'Thunderclap' on the night of 5/6 March 1945 the crew was as follows: Sergeant L.A. Howard, flight engineer; Flight Lieutenant J.E. 'Canada' Nixon* RCAF, *navigator; Flying Officer D.E. Banks* RCAF, *bomb aimer; Warrant Officer J.A. Martin* RAAF, *wireless operator; Flight Sergeant W.J. McCullough* RCAF, *mid-upper gunner; and Flight Sergeant A.C. Searle* RCAF, *rear gunner.*

The harsh crackling that always preceded a Tannoy message came through the loudspeakers. I rolled over on my back and stared at the cream-and-green speaker perched above the door. The crackling gave way to the magnified, metallic voice of the announcer: 'Attention please! Will all operational crews report to the briefing room at once; I repeat: all operational crews to the briefing room at once. Out.' The chilly, disembodied voice switched off.

'Don't you ever shut up?' The loudspeaker didn't answer my tired, irritable question. But nothing seemed to shut up in this war: life had become a cycle of briefings, take-offs, bombing raids, landings, questions. Then followed the party that was the climax of every raid. Down to the Queen's Head we'd go, a mixture of strained nerves and weariness. Some of us drank to forget those who wouldn't be returning; others to forget that next time it might be their turn. But we all found alcohol a safety valve – it helped us to forget that the war was brutal, senseless killing and nothing else.

Last night's party had been a particularly hectic one; there had been much to forget. Nearly home after a highly successful trip, we'd been surprised by a swarm of Junkers 88s. They had infiltrated our bomber stream and bagged twenty-four Lancaster and Halifaxes before scuttling back across the Channel – scot-free. With our navigational lights on and lulled into false security by the knowledge that the airfield runways were almost below, we were sitting targets. Our remorse was drowned in drink until the early hours of the morning. Then we turned in to get some much-needed sleep.

'But how the hell can you rest when a damned loudspeaker won't give you a moment's peace?' A hangover always made me forget that some of my best friends would be permanently absent from the mess. I slid off the comfortable bunk and buttoned up my serge battledress. Cold water cleared four hours' sleep from my eyes. I was ready for action again.

Outside, a stiff wind sent black nimbus clouds scudding across the Norfolk fens. Lousy looking weather, with the prospect of it getting bad enough to scrub out operations for the night. That cheered me up a bit, because then I could get some rest. Halfway to briefing, I ran into Jack Irvine, my flight lieutenant skipper. Big and hearty, with an irrepressible grin, he'd have looked more at home pulling a pint than at the control column of a Halifax bomber. But there wasn't a finer pilot than Jack in the squadron.

'Jeez, what a night for a trip!' The wind whipped his Canadian voice away from me and blew dust into my eyes.

'Think they'll scrub round it tonight, Jack?'

'What and give Jerry a night off? What do you think this is – a picnic party? There's a war on, boy!' But underneath I could feel his longing for a few hours' uninterrupted relaxation. The strain of nearly six years of war was beginning to show on everybody. But I knew that Jack was right: in spite of snow, rain or fog, we'd still go after the Germans.

'Wonder what tonight's target will be?'

'Well, it won't be Pölitz. After last night's drubbing there can't be much left of the place!'

On that assumption, I thought, Düsseldorf, Hamburg, Frankfurt and Bremen were also out of the running. During the last week, hundreds of bombers had pulverised these cities into a mass of rubble. 'Bet you a whisky it's Essen!'

'I'll take you and a couple of brandies it's Stuttgart's turn. We haven't been there for ten days now; they'll be wondering where we've got to!'

'Done!' We solemnly shook hands outside the briefing room. Facetious betting on our target before a briefing: most aircrew did it. It helped us forget that a lot could happen between briefing and buying a drink in the village bar. We always bought our drinks after a raid – it gave us something to look forward to.

Our briefing room was just like all the others. The walls were lined with maps, plots and charts. A blackboard for sketching in further details stood on a low dais. Red streamers indicated the bombing routes. It was almost like a school classroom. But this was the nerve centre of any raid: it was here that details were worked out which often meant the difference between life and death.

This was my sixty-third briefing and I knew the routine by heart. First came the individual briefings: every member of the crew received his own special instructions. Then followed the general briefing for the raid. First, the squadron commander Wing Commander David Donaldson gave a description of the target: 'As you've just learnt, tonight's target is Chemnitz near Leipzig.' The wing commander jabbed a spot on the large-scale map of Western Europe that completely covered the wall behind him and paused to let his words sink in. I realised that it was a longish trip – about six hundred miles. Anyway, Jack and I had both lost a chance of a free drink.

'Now,' the wing commander went on, 'this is to be another knock-hell-out-of-Jerry effort. We're putting over 700 aircraft into the air. We know we can't hide that many bombers, but we're banking on surprise. Weather conditions are far from good, but that might be to our advantage – the Germans won't be so sharp-eyed as usual. It's the usual rendezvous over Reading. I know you're all tired, but so are the Germans. They're on the run: let's turn it into a chase.'

He turned back to the map and jabbed with his long pointer. 'You can see the bombing route' – his stick followed the red streamers that zigzagged over the surface of Europe and ended up not far from the Polish border.

'Right. This squadron will be one of the first over the target, the Chemnitz railway sidings. Intelligence tells us that a lot of rolling stock and locomotives are stationed there. It's going to be your job to destroy them. The target will be pin-pointed with flares: bomb within them. It's not a bit of use flying six hundred-odd miles then ditching your load off the target. Remember that!

'Two more points. Don't hang about over the target area; once you've bombed, there's nothing more you can do, except offer German ground batteries some useful target practice. And hanging about can jeopardise the safety of those coming in behind you. And let's not have anybody going round for a second run-in. Once he's picked you up on his radar, Jerry will put up a strong defence and you might have to tangle with his night fighters. If any of you are unlucky enough to get hit and can't get home, head east towards the Russian lines. They've been told to look out for any British aircraft that have to come that way. You'll all be issued with special recognition flags later, but remember: don't try any funny stuff with the Russians. Just ask to be put in contact with the nearest British Mission as soon as possible and you'll be back here in a few days. Everything clear?' We all nodded.

The wing commander stepped down from the dais. Now the Meteorological Officer had the floor. In a few sentences he emphasised what the wing commander had said about the weather. Conditions looked like being sticky. His remarks ended our general briefing.

Shortly before take-off we would get our final instructions. But in between there was a lot to be done. Flak positions had to be studied and noted – new ones always seemed to be springing up along a bombing route; equipment had to be checked and parachutes collected. And everybody tried to squeeze in as much rest as possible.

In the last-minute rush after briefing I grabbed one of the recognition flags out of a box holding several hundred and stuffed it into my trousers pocket. The flag wasn't impressive to look at; a small silk square liberally splashed on both sides with the Union Jack. A list of instructions warned me that the Russians might not accept the flag as positive proof of my bona fides. I was advised to learn the expression, *Ya Anglichahnin* – 'I am English.'

'Oh, Young, I'd like to have a word with you.' It was my CO.

Born at Bitterne, Southampton, and educated at Charterhouse, David William Donaldson DSO DFC, 30 years old, a wing commander at 28, had flown Wellingtons on 149 Squadron.

We moved to his office, with its paper-littered desk. Without preamble, the wing commander started. I nodded my head automatically. A quick thrill ran through me, as always when I was given a special job to do.

'Given normal luck, I feel sure that I can pull it off, sir.'

'Good luck, Young.' A quick, firm handshake and I was on my way. Outside, the wind lashed me spitefully. I tried to control a momentary panic: 'Don't be a bloody fool!' I told myself. 'You've done Special Ops before. It's only a routine job!' But the words sounded unconvincing. I thought of the flak position map and saw every one of those innocent-looking pointers as a hail of deadly metal. A premonition of disaster flooded over me. I struggled against the feeling, but inside I knew somehow that this was going to be my last trip. My long run of luck was coming to an end.

The crew coach dumped us under the nose of the Halifax. There were eight of us, swathed in thick flying clothes that didn't quite keep the wind out.

'See you in the morning and have a good trip,' shouted the driver as he swung his coach back towards the camouflaged hangars. He'd be there all right, quiet, efficient, taking our empty thermos flasks, stowing our navigation instruments and treating us like elder brothers. But that was hours away yet. Now we were alone, each with our own thoughts. My panic had gone. Instead I felt a fatalistic numbness. I knew I wouldn't be coming back.

'No point in standing here and shivering,' Jack Irvine broke the silence. Shouldering our parachutes, we moved towards the squat waist of the aircraft. I took a quick look at the crew as they clambered into the fuselage. There was Jack, the skipper, moving easily despite his bulk. Then there was the other Canadian, Jack Nixon, the veteran navigator. The mid-upper gunner, engineer, wireless operator and bomb aimer were all seasoned hands. But the tail gunner was 19 and on his first operation. I felt sorry for him.

'Wonder how long this war will go on?' he said. He didn't seem to be addressing anybody in particular.

'It can't last much longer, otherwise there'll be nothing left of Germany for us to take over !' said the bomb aimer.

'They reckon Hitler's asking for peace!' went on the boy hopefully.

'Don't believe everything you hear!' replied the skipper laconically.

We were in our places now, parachutes and thermos flasks stowed. I looked at my watch: fifteen minutes to take-off. Inside the cold fuselage the air was full of the tang of dope, rubber and bakelite.

'You all right, Scotty?' the skipper's voice came clearly through the intercom.

'Sure.'

'Mid-upper?'

'I'm fine!'

'Tail? You settled in yet?'

'Yes, skipper.' The boy's voice sounded firmer now.

So the check went on. Outside the wind tore at the wings and bounced off the fuselage. At other dispersal points on the airfield, the same process was going on in other aircraft.

Ten minutes to take-off. Suddenly the port, then the starboard, engines coughed out puffs of blue smoke, spun spasmodically, then settled down to their steady rotation. Boosting the engines caused the Halifax to shudder in protest at the restraining chocks under the wheels.

Chocks away, we waddled to the runway, a two-thousand-yard strip of concrete tapering off into the fading distance. Another check: full boost, flaps down, tail trimmed. The Halifax trembled with the soft thunder of the engines; every second the noise got louder and more demanding. It was a demand that could not be resisted; slowly, the throttles were opened and we rumbled down the runway and into the advancing dusk. The time was three minutes past five in the afternoon.

Every moment another bomber joined the widening circle of aircraft revolving above Reading. This was clearly going to be a maximum effort. We linked up with the bomber stream a mile north of the town. On either side there were black-bellied Lancasters for company.

'Looks like being a good show tonight,' I heard myself saying to the skipper.

'Could be,' he replied, nosing the aircraft deeper into the stream. He flew the aircraft automatically, seemingly unconcerned with the twitching, flickering dials on the dashboard. I stood just behind his broad back, supporting myself on a strut. By now it was pitch black outside and only the winking navigation lights and heavy roaring of other aircraft engines showed we were not alone.

Navigation lights doused, we crossed the coast and slid above the blackness of the Channel. A short jarring burst from the mid-upper turret, quickly followed by a longer one from the rear turret, meant that the guns were being tested.

'Don't overdo it, boy,' said the skipper, 'you might need that later!'

It wasn't difficult to imagine the scene in the rear turret. Wedged in, clammy with sweat, teeth tightly clenched, hands hovering over the gun triggers, the boy was no different from anyone else on a first raid. I remembered one raw tail gunner who let rip more than two thousand rounds in a test burst; only repeated cursing by his skipper had loosened his fingers, locked with fear on the triggers. All around was the deep throbbing of well-tuned engines. The inside of the Halifax was silent as we settled down for the long trip.

'Coming up to the Dutch coast,' the navigator's voice came through the intercom. With the skipper holding the Halifax steady at 10,000 feet, we passed high over the dark line of the coast, rumbled over Holland, across the German border and into the Rhineland. I moved back to the waist of the bomber.

There's never any warning with flak. One moment the sky is empty, the next it's full of bursting shells, waving searchlights and dodging aircraft. It was the same this time. Suddenly a bluish finger swayed across the sky. Then two ... five ... ten ... fifteen searchlights joined the master beam.

'Jerry's advance publicity,' said the engineer quietly.

Down on the ground, steel-hatted gunners would be feverishly stoking shells into the slim barrels of their ack-ack guns and waiting for the searchlights to pick out a target for them. They didn't have long to wait.

'They've got one!' jabbered the tail gunner.

'One what?'

'A Lanc, Skipper!'

'Keep your eyes open and your mouth shut!'

'Poor devils!' whispered the mid-upper.

I knew what he meant. The master beam would settle and cling to some luckless aircraft like a silvery leech. The others would follow it, forming a straight-sided cone of light. The aircraft would dive, turn and twist – but still it could not shake off those intelligently handled searchlights. Then the ground batteries got the range and that was that.

'I'm climbing!' said the skipper, interrupting a tense silence. We nosed up through the friendly clouds to safety. The thump of exploding flak and the glare of searchlights faded behind. For the first time that night I was glad of the bad weather conditions; on a clear, starlit night we'd have been lucky to get clear of that murderous barrage. But any hope of surprise had gone. All over Germany the alert would have gone out – radar stations would be plotting our course; night fighters would be climbing to intercept us.

For the moment, the tension was over. So far we hadn't seen anything of enemy night fighters, though the gunners had reported that there seemed to be some tracer flying about down the middle of the stream, about five miles behind.

'Navigator to pilot, forty-five minutes to target.'

'Roger.'

I felt the tension start to mount in the Halifax again. The feet of the mid-upper, swinging almost above my head, wriggled as he settled himself more comfortably on his hard seat. Everybody who could would be scanning the sky with anxious eyes. It was now that the night fighters would make themselves known.

I headed for the cockpit to watch the run-in and bombing of the railway yards.

'Five minutes to target.'

'Roger, navigator,' acknowledged the skipper. 'Everybody quiet from now on and with a stroke of luck we'll be on the way home in less than ten minutes!'

A couple of miles in front, a dull red glow reflected off the clouds. Exploding flak shells flashed in the blackness. Away to our port, a flickering tongue of light showed that night fighters had sneaked into the stream. Another flash of tracer and a bomber burst into a ball of fire, keeled over on its back and rolled down through the layer of clouds.

'Three minutes to target.'

'Roger, navigator.'

The sky in front was a turbulent mass of shells, searchlights, aircraft – all reflected in the ever-widening glow of the fires that raged on the ground. By the time we were over Chemnitz, German defences would be slinging everything they had at us. I hated to think what it would be like for the last aircraft in the stream.

'Target sighted,' said the bomb aimer calmly. 'It's clearly pinpointed, thank God.' He was flat on his stomach, eyes peering through the bombing window, bombsights adjusted, a finger ready to press the button that would release our load of high-explosive. From now on he would be in control of the Halifax's path.

'Right a shade now, Skipper ... a shade more.' Painfully slowly the bomb aimer brought the target in line with his sights. The flak was thick now, stretching across the flaming sky: an almost solid wall of death that we had to cross.

'Steady now, Skipper, steady ... left a shade.'

'Why in the hell don't you hurry up?' It was the tail gunner.

'Shut up!' snarled the skipper.

'A shade left again.' The bomb aimer seemed not to hear the interruption. 'Left ... left ... perfect. Bombs gone!'

His shout was lost as the Halifax, its load gone, jumped higher in the air. We'd have to wait for the photo-flash picture to know if the nerve-racking bombing run-in had been worthwhile. The wireless operator signalled base that we'd done our share. Nose down with the airspeed indicator hovering at the 160 mph mark, we sheered away from the target, now a blotchy mess of reddish-brown mushrooms. It didn't look as if there'd be many locomotives fit to be used tomorrow. The bomb aimer reappeared from his lonely perch up front, his sweat-stained face smiling broadly. His main part in the raid was also finished.

Suddenly a tremendous explosion rocked our port wing. A probing searchlight groped, fixed its unblinking eye on the aircraft, wavered and then held us in a remorseless stare. Another finger of light zigzagged across the sky, settling on us and then another.

C-R-U-M-P-H! The impact of a soft-nosed shell striking the belly of the Halifax shook me in my seat. Another bluish finger zigzagged across the inky sky ... and another, settling on us, breaking the darkness into patterns of black and white.

Suddenly over the intercom came a shout from the tail gunner. 'Night fighter!' the rear gunner said in a strangled voice which was then lost in the chattering of his guns.

'Me 262 closing on starboard quarter. Corkscrew starboard!' came the steadier voice of the mid-upper, as he too opened up.

As the Halifax plunged over on its side the fighter got in a quick burst, raking us from nose to tail. A jagged line of punctures appeared above my head. In the cruel spotlights that clung to us like silvery leeches I saw the tensed figure of Jack Irvine struggling to hold the bomber in its corkscrew. First we plunged onto our starboard side, then onto our port, then we climbed onto our starboard side. It was a breathtaking switchback round the sky. There was another blinding flash and the Halifax was once more peppered with white-hot steel. The stench of cordite filled the aircraft. In all my sixty-three operations I'd never seen such a barrage as this.

'Look out. ... Hell!' bellowed the bomb aimer. Too late! The nose of the Halifax vanished in a flurry of Perspex and metal particles. We had collided with the tail assembly of a Lancaster! It dropped like a stone. The Halifax heeled over, out of control. I was pitched against a bulkhead with a sickening smack on the head. Ice-cold air rushed in through the severed nose.

The aircraft Irvine had collided with was a Lancaster on 434 'Bluenose' Squadron RCAF skippered by Pilot Officer J. Kitchen who had also just bombed the target from 16,500 feet when the Halifax rose up beneath his tail. The night-fighter crew then attacked Kitchen's bomber, damaging the hydraulic system and starboard wing, but Kitchen's gunners drove them off and he began the struggle to bring his damaged aircraft home.

Then, above the deep-throated roar of overtaxed engines, came a high-pitched scream. Cannon shells had jammed the 19-year-old rear gunner in his lonely turret! This was his first op – you couldn't blame him screaming: 'I can't move,' blubbered the tail gunner, 'I'm stuck!'

'Shut your mouth – we'll have you out in a minute,' croaked the wireless operator.

'Everybody else all right?' said the skipper, wrestling to check this nerve-shattering plunge. 13,000 feet ... 12,000 feet ... we dropped to 10,000 feet before the dive was controlled. At 8,000 feet the bomber started to respond to the cursing of the skipper. But everybody was alive. Perspex had grazed the bomb aimer's face, hysterics had reduced the tail gunner to a raving fool and a warm sticky trickle down my neck told me that my scalp was cut. I plastered my handkerchief over the wound to stop the blood running and held the makeshift bandage in place with my helmet.

But at least we had lost the night fighter and the searchlights. A long way above us, the rest of the stream droned over and away from the target that was spreading in a red glow a few miles behind. The cut on my head was swelling and throbbing painfully. Everything seemed hazy. The bomb aimer had managed to stop his face bleeding and the skipper was still crouched over the control column.

'Where's the engineer?' he muttered. 'I can't fly this thing myself!'

I remembered that I'd seen him heading for the escape hatch at the rear of the fuselage clutching his parachute. I didn't blame him for that; in a smash it's every man for himself.

'Get him back here!'

But there wasn't any need for me to fetch him back. He came himself, still grasping his chute, slithering back into his seat without a word and started to check the gauges. The skipper gave him a long, hard look but said nothing. There was nothing to say.

'Scotty, get the kid out of that damned turret before he goes mad!' shouted the skipper. 'Take Nixon to help you!'

Nixon was lucky: he'd escaped with only a shaking. In silence we crawled to the jammed rear turret, Nixon grasping the emergency axe. The night fighter's cannon shells had broken the rollers on the twin doors that led back into the aircraft fuselage. A few swipes of the axe and we yanked the boy out. For some reason he'd taken his flying boots off. He tried a feeble joke about not wanting to die with them on, but a curt 'Don't be a bloody fool!' from Nixon damped any further attempt at humour. With his boots zipped up again, we guided him back to the pilot's cockpit.

Chemnitz was only a couple of minutes away and we saw the first of their bombs blasting the area. But we were finished.

'Now listen, everybody'. The skipper forced any trace of panic out of his voice, shouting to be heard above the wind howling through the nose.

'We can't get home. So we're going east towards the Russian lines. You all have identification flags. Just do as you're told to do on the flags and everything will be all right.

'There's nothing to worry about yet, but we're in a pretty bad way. I want everybody to check their parachutes and stand by to jump if I say so.'

Dead silence greeted this: none of us had ever bailed out before. The tail gunner's lips started to move, but no words came through. Turning to Nixon, the skipper asked, 'I suppose you haven't any idea where we are?'

He hadn't. The gale had swept his instruments to the floor, shattering them into useless pieces; his maps and charts had been blown deeper into the aircraft and were ripped beyond recognition. Nobody said anything, but we all realised that things were bad: steadily losing height and with no means of navigation, we were a perfect target for a night fighter.

Battered and crippled, the Halifax crawled towards what we hoped were the Russian lines. Fortunately, no prowling night fighter appeared.

'I suppose none of you speak Russian?' the skipper's tight voice broke the silence. 'What the hell did you learn at school, then? Didn't they tell you that Russian is a useful language to know in Russia?'

We raised a few weak smiles at this brave attempt at humour.

Snow and hail drove against us, piling up on the floor and soaking everybody with an icy numbness.

'I want to puke,' gasped the tail gunner.

'Well, don't do it over me,' snapped Nixon, pushing the boy away from him. I watched the boy be sick, coughing his last meal up on the floor.

'Give him some coffee,' shouted the skipper. 'And the rest of you get a hot drink down. It'll do you the world of good.'

Without speaking, I turned to get my thermos. But my frozen hands couldn't hold it; it slipped to the floor and smashed to bits. When I got back to the cockpit, the others had swigged their drinks. By now the snow was inches deep. Worst hit was the skipper. Huddled over the controls, he was coated with a film of ice. It thawed and trickled down his face, only to freeze again when it reached his flying suit collar. Soon he had a thickening girdle of ice under his chin, chafing his skin raw. Clumsily, Nixon and I poured his flask of lukewarm coffee down his throat. He gulped it greedily. Then, leaving Nixon and the mid-upper supporting the pilot, I grabbed the axe. The blood had stopped dripping from my scalp, but the sweat of panic made both my hands sticky. There was one last thing I had to do.

'Scotty! Get the escape hatch open.' The wind slung the skipper's words back at me. 'I can't keep her up much longer!' Blindly I headed for the hatch, followed by the rest of the crew.

Frantically, my hands pushed at the hatch. It was stuck. In desperation we took turns to hack it open with the blunt hatchet. I rechecked my parachute – it seemed all right.

'Stand by for jumping. I'm holding her steady at 2,000.' The skipper's voice had taken on an odd, high-pitched tone. 'Start jumping!'

Nobody moved. A few seconds slipped by. We clustered round the yawning hatch, staring at the pitch-black void outside. But nobody moved. Panic had gripped us. It's one thing to jump without thinking, but now we'd had time to think; it was at least ten minutes since the skipper first warned us to stand by to bail out.

'For Christ's sake what are you waiting for? I can't hold this bloody kite steady forever!' I thought I could detect a sob in the skipper's voice.

We formed a semi-circle round the gaping hatch. Seven frightened men, each waiting for somebody else to make the first move, each unwilling to admit that fear had turned him into a coward.

'Who's going first? How about you, kid?'

The tail gunner shook his head. 'Scotty, you go first!' Nixon half-screamed.

'Jump! The plane's breaking up!' shrieked the skipper from the cockpit.

I braced myself in the open hatch, tucking my emergency rations deeper into the uppers of my flying boots. Helmet and goggles off, I jumped. The wind clutched at me, spinning me into and then clear of the slipstream. Then, parachute open, I was falling. I forced myself to concentrate, to forget about everything that had just happened. I struggled to marshal the thoughts shooting through my brain into some sort of order.

Irvine told RAF intelligence officers later: 'The target was well ablaze at this time and made a very bright patch on the undercast. Our bombs were dropped as ordered and at that moment the tail gunner spotted a Ju 88 on the port quarter. There was no flak. A few seconds later the tail gunner gave me a corkscrew to port. This I did on instruments. At the bottom of the dive to port and just after the start of the climb to starboard I instinctively looked up to see the belly and tail of what I think was another Halifax directly above me and about thirty feet away. There was no time to avoid a collision and the nose of my aircraft struck the tail turret of the other aircraft. The impact took about five feet of the nose of my aircraft completely off. The other aircraft did not appear to be seriously damaged. The Ju 88 had followed us into the corkscrew and at this point opened fire, scoring hits on the port wing. The Ju 88 again attacked, but this time we lost it for good by a corkscrew to starboard given by the mid-upper gunner.

'We proceeded south of the target to our first turning point. It was there I decided to make for the Russian lines... I had lost all of the instruments on my blind flying panel and I would never be able to stand the intense cold of the four or five hour trip to England. My feet and hands were already quite numb. It was impossible to stand in the nose of the aircraft, so I ordered all of the crew except the two gunners to the rest position in order to keep as warm as possible. I flew east for an hour and a half until we figured we were well behind the lines of the Russian Front. At the same time I descended to try to lessen the cold. By this time both my legs were numb from the hips down. My left hand was also completely numb. My right hand I kept warm by sitting on it. At this point we ran into a snowstorm and had to turn back to the west. Soon afterwards I spotted the lights of a small town which I began to circle. It was then that both escape hatches were found to be jammed. Two of the crew used the aircraft's axes to chop open the fuselage door. This operation took about twenty minutes. When the door was finally opened I gave the order to bail out.'

Warrant Officer Young later related what a terrible ordeal the pilot had gone through as snow blowing in from the shattered nose had built up until it lay inches deep in the cockpit. 'Huddled over the controls, he was coated with a thin film of ice,' he said. 'It thawed and trickled down his face, only to freeze again when it reached his flying suit collar. Soon he had a thickening girdle of ice under his chin.

'Our crippled Halifax crawled towards the Polish border, losing height all the time. We couldn't stay in the air much longer... A few hours back - it seemed a century now - we'd all stood chatting on the perimeter track at Foulsham. We had agreed that the war couldn't last much longer. We in the Halifax had played our small part in hammering Jerry into the ground. Our lethal visiting cards were dotted all over the Rhine.

'It was galling having to finish like this, with the end of the war so near... But with no nose, a gale force wind whipping snow into the aircraft and our height decreasing every minute there was only one thing to do: get out - quick!

'Panic sweat made my gauntlet-covered hands sticky as they forced the emergency axe to demolish the special radio equipment we were carrying. I clubbed it into a shambles; Jerry would never learn its secrets. Frantically, my hands turned to the escape hatch. It was stuck! I used the axe again.

A wall of icy air hit me as I dived through; the slipstream swirling me around. I pulled the release. The 'chute pulled me up with a jerk and I floated there in the semi-darkness; a couple of thousand feet above... What? Maybe Germany, maybe Poland - I had no idea. I struggled to control the flow of thoughts shooting through my dazed brain.

'Nearing the ground I could see in the half-light that I would come down in open country. The wind was drifting me quite a bit, but I managed to land without mishap and quickly got rid of the chute.'

'Where were the rest of the crew? I would have given anything to see one of them. I started searching the nearby fields and small woods... but nothing disturbed the silence except the rustling of the trees.'

I was the first to bail out, coming down in a frozen landscape forty miles west of Kraków and at intervals as the Halifax continued to drone further west, back towards the German front line, the other six crew members followed, beginning with Flight Lieutenant Jack 'Canada' Nixon.

Flight Sergeant W.J. McCullough the mid-upper gunner was shot by a Russian sentry and spent weeks in a Polish hospital before being repatriated. Irvine knew he would not be able to bail out himself because of his frozen legs and hands. He said: 'I had to attempt a crash landing. It was still quite dark, but luckily I spotted a road with vehicles' headlamps moving along it. I descended over this to about fifty feet with landing light on. By use of the light I found what seemed to be a decent field. I circled it twice, then dropped the flaps and came in for a belly landing. In doing so the aircraft took a chimney off a house and cut down two telephone poles which I did not see. The landing was OK, but I was knocked out by the impact. When I came to the aircraft was sitting in the field and had not caught fire. It took me some time to get my straps undone and as I couldn't stand up I fell from my seat and crawled to the front of the aircraft and out through the hole.'

'Scotty' Young sat down and considered his plight. 'If I was in Germany the chances were that I would soon be captured. If across the Russian lines, I would presumably be among friends; or, at any rate, Allies. Until I was certain of my whereabouts – just knowing which country would help – I would travel eastwards. That night, after remaining hidden all day, I started the trek in the darkness; following my button-sized compass. Through woods and across open country I stumbled; seeing no sign of life and hourly becoming hungrier and hungrier. I cursed the fact that my emergency rations had been lost during the bail-out. Flying boots, I soon discovered, were not intended for cross-country treks. The temperature was well below zero and the driving snow seeped through my flying suit.

'After the second day, sleep became a perpetual nightmare. I dreamed of huge steaks, only to wake and find there was nothing in sight but desolate frozen wastes. I tried eating a mixture of moss and snow and vomited.

'On the fourth day – after being chased from a remote farmhouse by a snarling Alsatian – I came across a road heavily criss-crossed with tyre impressions. I could go no further; I would wait for the next vehicle to pass. If it turned out to be German – well, that was just too bad. I was past caring. I lay in the ditch beside the road. An hour or so later a groaning, mud-spattered truck appeared in the distance. As it got nearer I could see a large red star on the bonnet. It was Russian! I scrambled out of the ditch, shouting and waving a small Union Jack which I carried. But the lorry roared past. Either they hadn't seen me, or they couldn't be bothered to stop. I crawled back to my hideout at the side of the road, not caring whether I lived or died. A few minutes later I heard footsteps. The truck driver and his mate had decided to come back and investigate. They stood a few yards from me: thick-set, faces muffled in coarse scarves, bodies well-wrapped in quilted uniforms. Under their arms they carried sub-machine guns. Once again I scrambled out of the ditch, hands held high and fluttering my Union Jack. As I did so I heard the ominous click of safety catches.

'*Ya Anglichahnin! Ya Anglichahnin!*' My swollen tongue forced the words out.

'The taller of the two men spat on the ground. He seemed in favour of shooting me there and then and kept jabbing his gun in my direction. His mate pointed down the road and said something I didn't understand. To my relief, the tall man nodded sullen agreement. They searched me, took my cigarette lighter, watch and Union Jack and then indicated that they wanted me to get into the back of the truck. One of them kept his machine gun pointing in my direction during the drive, which lasted about an hour. We arrived at a small military post [a war-torn former mansion] and then came my first interrogation. I gave my name, rank and number – the rest I filled in by pantomime gestures. But my questioner, who appeared to be some sort of army NCO, didn't seem to understand or believe me.

'A drive in the truck to a small town and the same process was repeated. This time my interrogator was an old crone, who punctuated her shrill questions with "I haf bin to America thirty years back!" Still my captors were not satisfied. But they gave me a little bread to eat; they had to or I'd have passed out. Once again I was bundled into the truck and driven to the small town of Bielitz [now Bielsko-Biala] near Kraków. Another woman interrogator. This time the questions came in short bursts of

French and Russian. I replied as best I could. My answers didn't convince them. For, after one long last tirade from the female interrogator, they reached their decision: I was a German spy! I was in a hell of a spot.

'As a spy I could only expect a rifle bullet. I had heard tales of the 'jokes' Russians had with condemned prisoners. A prisoner would be taken out to the execution yard and tied to a stake. Then the firing squad would load, aim and pull their triggers. But there were no bullets in the rifles! Repeat the process a few times and the condemned man realised it was done to test his nerves. Then one day there would be bullets in the guns... the 'joke' was over. A glorified version of the famous Russian roulette.

'For a week I sweated in my cell waiting for the final summons. An armed guard paced the corridor outside the cell door. Escape was impossible. My continual demands to be taken to the British Military Mission in Moscow were met with sneers and cries of German Schwein!

'Even my daily exercise period became dangerous. Only vehement protests by my guard stopped Red Servicemen from pumping bullets into me as I shuffled through the town's main street. Then the questions started all over again: What was I doing in Russian territory? Wasn't I a spy? Wasn't I a German bombing Russian women and children? How could I be an Englishman; the British never flew over Germany! Only the Red Air Force was bombing the Germans into submission! Wasn't I a spy? Over and over again the same questions were hurled at me. It was a form of psychological warfare. I was determined not to crack. More truck journeys, more questions and more threats about a firing squad. I wondered how long it would go on. But one thing gave me hope: the Russians had some doubts. If they hadn't, I reasoned, I'd be dead by now.'

Meanwhile Jack Irvine had arrived back in Britain and given his report of his last flight. It was then supposed that Young and Nixon had not survived. On 21 April Wing Commander David Donaldson wrote letters of sympathy to relatives of the two missing men. His letter to 'Scotty' Young's father in Glasgow read:

One member of your son's crew is back in this country now and has given us an account of what happened to the aircraft... They were all seen to leave the aircraft, but unfortunately nothing was afterwards heard from your son. The remainder landed more or less safely. By the time they bailed out the aircraft had been forced very low and it is possible that when your son jumped they were passing over some very high ground and his parachute would not have had time to open. It is, of course, impossible to say absolutely definitely that there is no hope, but I feel that if he was alive we should almost certainly have heard from him by now.

'Scotty' Young was sent to a political prison at Pless (now Pszczyna), not far from the Nazi extermination camp of Auschwitz discovered by Soviet forces in January, but eventually after more questions and denials he was transferred to a Soviet army prison camp where he had one of the happiest surprises of his life:

'I saw Flight Lieutenant Jack 'Canada' Nixon, the navigator of my crew! It was some days before we could talk together, but eventually we were able to compare notes. He told me that he too had jumped and, like me, had been picked up for questioning. But apparently his answers – or perhaps merely his accent – had convinced the Russians that he wasn't a German. After that, life became worth living again. We were allowed to remain together and we talked endlessly of escape. The Russians treated us a little better now, feeding us on weak raisin tea, even weaker stew and chunks of hard black bread. There came a last final interrogation and then Nixon and I were handed over to the Red Air Force.

'Our Air Force captors had a different approach. They were friendly. A mistake had been made about branding me as a spy. But of course I would agree that the Russians are the most security minded in the world? The Russian Air Force was the best in the world; their pilots the most brave? Day after day this propaganda was pumped into us by smooth-tongued, well-mannered English-speaking officers. Russian newspapers never mentioned Allied gains and Radio Moscow never broadcast our successes. All the time it was what Russia was doing. But we were interested in only one thing: when would we be sent home? And always the answer was the same – "tomorrow".

'Then one morning we were we were told that Nixon and I were to go to Moscow. Maybe they were still doubtful about us! We decided to make a break for it... It was easy; we just strolled out of the camp gates past a dozing sentry. So much for Red security! We contacted a local British Mission, but before they could help us the Russians arrived and we were back inside the camp. They warned us curtly that any further escapades would mean a rifle bullet; and that, I learnt later, was the fate of the dozing sentry!

'On to Kiev in the Ukraine. We never seemed to stop travelling. Frustrated and long past caring, Nixon and I decided to make a further attempt to get away – rifle bullet or not.'

They were imprisoned in a hut with sixty USAAF flyers, some of whom had flown B-29s and had been shot down 'by mistake'.

'We talked over our idea with them of trying to get to Odessa, the Black Sea port. Allied ships often put in there. The Americans were enthusiastic and together we worked out our plans. Escapees would leave in pairs while the rest of us kicked up a shindy at the furthest point from the exit. Once clear of the two-storey prison, nothing stood between them and a nearby wood. Nixon and I were to be the fifth pair away. It worked for the first three pairs. Then the Russians tumbled to the trick and that was that. Apparently our lack of consideration upset our captors and they sent a bemedalled officer to talk to us. In good English he asked us why we were unhappy as Russian guests. We pointed out that 'guests' were not normally kept chained like dogs. A few days later the six Americans were recaptured and brought back; to face solitary confinement.

'Then, one morning, came the great news that 'Canada' Nixon and I were to leave for Odessa on the following day. We had suffered a lot. Nixon was haggard, his clothing hung on him like a shroud. I looked little better. If this trip turned out to be another Russian "tomorrow" we might not last much longer.

'I hardly slept that night. I thought of home, of Glasgow, of my parents, of a pint in the local, of peace. In the morning word came: we were definitely going! The Americans crammed personal messages into our pockets – to be posted when we got back home. There was a last visit to the prison guard-room. A major confiscated the letters we were carrying, explaining that they might contain top-secret Russian information! I gave up trying to explain that we'd been cooped up day and night and never saw anything of military value. We were then asked to write a letter saying we had received humane treatment at the hands of the Russians. It was adding insult to injury – but we wrote the letters. We would have written anything to get back to Blighty!

'A drive to the station and we started the 36-hour train journey to Odessa. We were given a reserved compartment, though the train corridor was crowded with servicemen. Glowering looks came our way and more than one tired-looking soldier tried to force his way into the compartment. Our escorting officer gave them a threatening look and they retreated back to the corridor.

'Slowly we chugged and puffed into Odessa, where we were herded off to a reception centre. The place was full of French, Czech and Polish workers. A lot vanished overnight – possibly to die in front of an execution squad or linger in a salt mine. After a week, during which time the local British Mission worked wonders in getting us back into shape – Nixon and I embarked on a Norwegian ship.

'Four months of nightmare were over. We were going home.

'I was back from the dead.'

Index